WITHDRAWN

Antonio Gramsci

Routledge Education Books

Advisory editor: John Eggleston
Professor of Education
University of Keele

Antonio Gramsci
Conservative schooling for radical politics

Harold Entwistle
*Professor of Education
Concordia University, Montreal*

Routledge & Kegan Paul
London, Boston and Henley

*First published in 1979
by Routledge & Kegan Paul Ltd
39 Store Street, London WC1E 7DD,
Broadway House, Newtown Road,
Henley-on-Thames, Oxon RG9 1EN and
9 Park Street, Boston, Mass. 02108, USA
Set in IBM 11 on 12pt Press Roman
and printed in Great Britain by
Lowe and Brydone Ltd,
Thetford, Norfolk
© Harold Entwistle 1979
No part of this book may be reproduced in
any form without permission from the
publisher, except for the quotation of brief
passages in criticism*

British Library Cataloguing in Publication Data

Entwistle, Harold

*Antonio Gramsci. – (Routledge education books).
1. Gramsci, Antonio 2. Communism and
education
370.1   HX288.G7   79-40118*

*ISBN 0 7100 0333 1
ISBN 0 7100 0334 X Pbk*

Contents

	Acknowledgments	vii
	Introduction	1
	Gramsci's relevance	1
	Gramsci's life	6
	Education and the concept of hegemony	10
1	The schooling of children	18
	Introduction	18
	The curriculum of the school	18
	Curriculum and the sociology of knowledge	28
	Curriculum as 'the entire thought of the past'	40
	School assessment and examinations	49
	Educational method: school as work	53
	Instruction or education?	64
	Authority, teachers and teaching	68
	Education and Fascism	78
	Politics and schooling: correspondence or contradiction?	87
	The structure and organisation of the school system	92
	Educational theory as counter-cyclical	104
	Schooling: towards the education of adults	107

2	The education of adults	111
	Political education as adult education	111
	Education and the problem of the intellectuals	113
	Technical and vocational education	129
3	Theory and practice in education	149
	The philosophy of praxis	149
	Polytechnical education and the relationship between theory and practice	151
	Education and Gramsci's conception of praxis	160
	Theory, practice and the education of teachers	165
	Theory, practice and the problem of relevance	168
	Conclusion	176
	Notes	180
	A note on sources	191
	Bibliography	193
	Index	201

Acknowledgments

My interest in Gramsci's theory of education was stimulated several years ago through a paper on his concept of hegemony presented by James Robinson to the seminar on 'Proletarian Ideologies' at the Interuniversity Centre for European Studies in Montreal. At about the same time, references to Gramsci's work began to appear in the literature of education. It struck me that the inferences which were being drawn from his writings with reference to education varied widely and I subsequently attempted to explore the paradoxes implicit in his own work in two papers presented to the seminar in Montreal. Since that time I have benefited greatly from critical comments offered by members of that group, by my own colleagues in the Department of Education, especially Arpi Hamalian, Joyce Brand, Bill Knitter, and Geof Fidler, and by Norman Klein in the Department of Anthropology at Concordia.

During a sabbatical leave spent at the Institute of Education in the University of Bristol in 1975-6, I discovered a growing interest in the implications of Gramsci's work for modern educational theory and practice, and lengthy discussions there, especially with Ray Bolam, Chris Sinha, Eric Hoyle and Gordon Reddyford, prompted me to write the first draft of this text.

My thanks are due to my own university which made funds available from its Canada Council General Research Fund to visit the *Istituto Gramsci* in Rome in 1977. The staff of the Institute, especially its librarians, gave me invaluable

Acknowledgments

assistance in the collection of materials relevant to my research. The Interuniversity European Centre in Montreal also made funds available for the purchase of books and materials.

Fred Bassett, Geof Fidler, David Godwin, Dieter Halbwidl, Arpi Hamalian and Eric Hoyle read a complete draft of the text and I am indebted to them for the time they devoted to this and to subsequent discussion of the comments they made. I am also grateful to Ronnie Braendel, Mary Jean, and Beverley Cobb for their services in typing different drafts of the text.

Finally, my thanks are due especially to my wife who, on this occasion, has made more than the usual contribution to my work. Her assistance has been invaluable in discussing with me the Italian sources, checking my translations and helping with the secretarial chores which are inseparable from a work of this kind.

Introduction

Gramsci's relevance

The name of the late Italian Marxist, Antonio Gramsci, appears increasingly in the cultural media of the English-speaking world. Not unexpectedly, it occurs especially in the literature of politics, but his work has also been an inspiration for the novel (e.g., John Fowles's *David Martin*) and in the theatre (Trevor Griffiths's *Occupations*). Since Gramsci took a theory of education to be integral to political theory, reference to his work has also begun to appear in the literature of education. In this latter context, the invocation of Gramsci is usually little more than academic name-dropping with the occasional promise, as in Karabel and Halsey, for example, that for educationists 'Gramsci's concept of ideological hegemony would seem to open up a particularly promising avenue of thought' (1977, p. 369, note 9; see also ibid., p. vi). Indeed, linked with the name of Gramsci, the notion that the school is hegemonic threatens to become one of those slogans which frequently serve as substitutes for detailed consideration of our educational arrangements. But it is by no means clear that a close examination of Gramsci's work would confirm him as authority for the radical rhetoric of much contemporary neo-Marxist educational theory and, especially, for that of those 'new' sociologists of education who invoke his name.[1] To be sure, Gramsci's relevance lies precisely in his treatment, within the context of his radical political theory, of exactly those themes which exercise

Introduction

modern radical educationists: the sociology of the curriculum, the apparent discontinuity between the culture of the school and that of daily life, problems of language and literacy in education, the role of the state in the provision of education, the cultivation of elites and the role of intellectuals, the relative functions of authority and spontaneity in education and the ambiguous relationship of these to differing political ideologies (especially to Fascism), problems of vocational education, the place of theory in the curriculum and its relationship to action in the world outside the school; and, in particular, the consideration of these themes in relation to the education of the working class. Unfortunately for most of those who call upon his name but who evidently know little of his work, Gramsci's conclusions on these matters point in quite different directions from those of current neo-Marxist educational theory.

However, the relevance of Gramsci's writing for today lies not merely in its substantive contribution towards clarification of these problems but, equally, in its illustration of their apparent intractability, once one escapes from rhetorical sloganmongering into an examination of the complex relationships between politics and education. There is no doubt that Gramsci was primarily concerned with radical socio-political change and his work ought to be especially relevant for radicals committed to counter-hegemonic educational activity. It is also true that the notion of hegemony is central to Gramsci's social theory, and that he recognised the school, amongst other institutions of civil society, as an instrument of political hegemony. From this it tends to be inferred that Gramsci saw the substitution of working-class for middle-class hegemony resulting from a social revolution based upon a radical reform of schools, especially their curriculum and pedagogical processes. But, paradoxically, Gramsci's prescriptions for curriculum and teaching method are essentially conservative. My task in this book is to attempt to resolve this apparent contradiction between his revolutionary political and social theory and his emphasis upon the value of traditional educational practice with reference to the content and processes of schooling.

When read in isolation from the rest of his work, there is no doubt that Gramsci's explicitly educational writing reads

Introduction

like a Black Paper[2] forty years before its time. His *Notebooks* and *Letters* could appropriately serve as authoritative texts for the current 'back to basics' movement in education, and one Gramscian scholar has claimed that his 'opinions and prejudices' on education would even 'bring students out in a boiling rash in St. Davids College Lampeter' (a small religious foundation in mid-Wales not noted for student activism — Gwyn A. Williams, 1975, p.336). The paradox is only underlined by the fact that Gramsci's fascist adversaries seemed to be speaking the language of progressive education. Hence, one implication in his educational writings is that progressive education has intimations of political authoritarianism, whilst a 'back to basics' educational emphasis, contrary to assumptions that this is a reactionary movement which ought to be resisted by liberal educationists, is an essential requirement for development of that temper of mind on which radical social criticism depends. In the light of Gramsci's analysis, it is arguable that we need to reconsider the conventional equation of traditional, didactic schooling with political authoritarianism, and of progressive education with democracy; it should give us pause before we dismiss as reactionary and fascist the current criticisms of the excesses of progressive education. Indeed, with reference to the debate about the kind of educational practices which are integral to radical social change, it is odd that such interest in Gramsci's work should be displayed by neo-Marxist educational theorists who take him to be an exponent of critical sociology and cultural Marxism, but who themselves espouse educational ideologies of an idealist complexion which have more in common with those of Gramsci's persecutors than with Gramsci himself. One of the themes to be taken up presently will be the question of what constitutes an education for Fascism, in view of Gramsci's conservative educational theory having been articulated, in part, in criticism of the apparently progressive educational reforms undertaken by Mussolini's Minister of Public Instruction in 1923 (see pp.78-86 below).

The argument developed here will be that, far from the paradox of Gramsci's political radicalism and educational conservativism being one of his 'creditable inconsistencies', his writing in fact reveals a coherent socio-pedagogic theory

Introduction

of relevance to anyone interested in radical social change. From this point of view Gramsci's work has to be taken seriously as a model for socialist education. Currently, the most explicit attempts to explore the relationship between socialism and education are occurring in the United States. But Gramsci's work lends support neither to Jencks, who implies that there is no connection between socialism and education, nor to Bowles and Gintis who assume that in a socialist society traditional disciplinary constraints would be removed from children in school, much as the constraints imposed by the institutions of corporate capitalism would be lifted from adult workers. To the contrary, Gramsci was especially interested in the cultural potential of a disciplined approach to work which he called 'Americanism' and his prescriptions for technical education are quite the reverse of those required by neo-Marxists for the life of work in a socialist society (see pp. 87-92 below).

However, to claim consistency for Gramsci's socio-educational theory, in that the paradox of a conservative educational theory in service of a radical political ideology is capable of resolution, is not to ignore the contradictions which do appear in his work. Inconsistencies are evident, for example, between his early writings, which display a good deal of dogmatic radical rhetoric with reference to schools, and the much more tentative and open conclusions of his mature work. Manacorda reminds us that Gramsci's position at any time prior to his imprisonment has to be read in the context of the rapidly changing circumstances in which he found himself, especially his experience of the Russian Revolution and his belief that its spread throughout Europe was imminent (1976, pp.39-40). Given these (for him) optimistic expectations, the uncompromising rhetoric of his early writings is understandable. But from the time of his imprisonment, he was writing in the face of the disappointment of these hopes; hence his conclusion that the replacement of the existing hegemony required painstaking and protracted political education. Thus, following the ephemeral and now defunct radical educational rhetoric of the late 1960s, the evolution of Gramsci's educational thought is of peculiar relevance for any examination of the relationship between education and social change. It is

Gramsci's intensely committed, but abortive, practical political experience, the watershed between the earlier and later periods in both of which he functioned primarily as a theoretician, that sets his work apart from most accounts of what constitutes a radical political education.

The second, mature thoughts of the *Notebooks* and *Letters* were not simply the result of an enforced incarceration which gave him the 'leisure' to revise and systematise his thought, but also a consequence of having participated in the leadership of a failed revolution and of suffering from a successful fascist counter-revolution. As Clark concludes, 'much of Gramsci's lasting contribution to European social thought emerged from a critical rethinking of his own past' (1977, p.225). His experience of failure, no doubt, contributed to the tentativeness of his early prison writing. Of this period, Manacorda notes that 'everything is presented as problematic and uncertain' with the recurrence of phrases like 'I have not yet decided what to think' and 'In general, I think . . .' (1976, p.85). He concludes (ibid., p.89),

> the hard apprenticeship of his scholarly career, his essentially idealistic education, the educative experience of his political militancy and, lastly, his recent experience as a father frustrated by imprisonment and the growing disagreement with his family about educational matters, constitute a tangle of experiences, often discrete and contradictory, from which Gramsci had not yet matured a coherent, motivated and profound conclusion.

It is not surprising that, as Gramsci himself implied, his head was a battleground for quite contrary educational theories. These contradictions — what McInnes (1971, p.15) called 'his creditable inconsistencies' — are the product of an intelligence struggling candidly with apparently intractable problems and of a refusal ultimately to be dogmatic. Indeed, in his own life and work there is immanent the dialectic of theory and practice and a constant attempt to fuse them into praxis. In both the *Notebooks* and the *Letters*, 'personal experience was always the point of departure for theoretical generalisations' (Manacorda, 1976, pp.155-6). The point about Gramsci is not simply, as Frith and Corrigan (1977, p.255) would have it, that he was (like Althusser) a member of the

Communist Party; rather that, as Anderson shows, he was probably the last of the Western Marxists whose writings derived from involvement in an attempt to engineer a socialist revolution (1976, p.54):

> The *Prison Notebooks*, the greatest work in this whole tradition, were written by a revolutionary leader of the working class, not by a professional philosopher, from a social background much poorer and lower than that of any Marxist intellectual in Europe, whether Western or Eastern, before or after the first World War.

By contrast, after Gramsci, Marxist theorists became secluded 'in universities, far from the life of the proletariat in their own countries', whilst there was 'a contraction of theory from economics and politics into philosophy' (ibid., pp.92-3).

But if imprisonment effectively removed Gramsci from the practice of politics, a tenuous link with educational practice was provided through correspondence with his sister about the education of her children and, subsequently, with his wife about the upbringing of his own sons. Gramsci himself warned against using a writer's correspondence as critical material without due precaution: 'a confident assertion made in a letter would not perhaps be repeated in a book . . . in letters, as in speeches or in conversations, logical errors occur more frequently' (*Notebooks*, p.385). And especially in the later letters to his sons, allowance has to be made for the increasing frustration, even desperation, which came from his not being present to give their upbringing the redirection which he clearly felt was necessary. Yet, as Manacorda's parallel and sequential analysis of the educational content of the *Letters* and the *Notebooks* shows, the 'continuous contact with reality' afforded by the former was part of the dialectic from which the general principles of the *Notebooks* were derived (1976, p.108).

Gramsci's life

It is evident that much more than is the case with most other educational theorists (and, not least, theorists of political

Introduction

education), Gramsci's biography is crucial to an understanding of his work. As Hoare and Nowell Smith observe, 'The relation between autobiography and sociological reflection in Gramsci's thought is . . . intimate and complex' (1971, p.25, cf also Cammett, 1967, vol. 4, p.192). Indeed, since his explicit notes on education are relatively brief, these gather significance not only from being read in the wider context of his early writings and the prison notes and letters, but also from the facts of his personal life and political activity.[3]

Born in Sardinia in 1891, Gramsci was the child of a minor government servant who was imprisoned for six years in 1900, convicted of embezzlement of electoral funds. There is some doubt about his guilt and an assumption that the conviction was motivated by his opposition to the successful candidate. However, the significance of this for the young Antonio was that he was removed from school at the end of the fifth grade and forced to work ten hours a day in the local land office carrying about register books which weighed more than he did, an occupation which severely taxed his strength (*Lettere*, p.299). Of this period he later complained that he habitually cried himself to sleep and rarely experienced a day without pain. In fact, Gramsci spent most of his life in ill-health. Hunchbacked from the age of six, the result of being dropped down a flight of high stairs by a girl left to look after him, he suffered the indignity as a child of being hung from the ceiling by the arms in an effort to straighten his spine.

By 1908, he was able to return to secondary school (gymnasium) in the nearby town of Santu Lussurgiu. He had continued to study hard during his enforced absence and was so successful in gymnasium that he was able to win scholarships, first to the *liceo*, then to the university in Turin where his studies were constantly interrupted by illness. Eventually he left the university before graduating and became a journalist, contributing to a number of radical newspapers before founding in 1919 (along with three others) and editing *L'Ordine Nuovo* (*The New Order*), a weekly newspaper (which in 1921 became a daily) aimed at the political education of workers in the automobile factories of Turin, where he spent most of his adult life before his imprisonment.

Introduction

In 1921, Gramsci broke with the Italian Socialist Party and became a founder member of the Italian Communist Party. He was its General Secretary from 1924 and became a Communist Deputy in the elections of the same year. However, these events coincided with the rise to power of the Fascist Party, and in 1926 Gramsci was imprisoned by his former socialist colleague, Mussolini, who gave instructions that his brain must be stopped from functioning for at least twenty years.[4] (In 1921 Mussolini had commented that Gramsci had 'an unquestionably powerful brain', Cammett, 1967, p.138.) Paradoxically, it was during the next decade of this imprisonment that Gramsci wrote the works for which he is best known outside Italy, the *Letters* and the *Notebooks* which constitute his systematic contribution to political and social theory. Refusing to ask for the clemency to which his steadily deteriorating health would have entitled him, he was eventually released into 'hospital arrest' only months before his death, in 1937, from a combination of chronic insomnia and indigestion, tuberculosis, hyper-tension and, finally, a stroke. Rather than from overt persecution in prison, his physical decline stemmed from neglect (despite most of his imprisonment being spent at the Turi special prison for prisoners in ill-health); a want of proper medical attention, of diet appropriate to his complaints, and from being located at the noisiest point in the cell block which prevented him from having more than two or three hours' sleep nightly over a period of several years.

In 1923, in Moscow, Gramsci had married Giulia Schutz, an Austrian refugee. By her he had two sons, the younger of whom he never saw; the elder he knew for only a few months. Not the least poignant feature of his letters from prison is their growing desperation as he attempted to maintain contact with his two sons, who evidently found difficulty in regarding him as more than a remote stranger; in particular, the way in which he advises upon their education and his evident frustration at what he regards as the mismanagement of their schooling.

Reading Gramsci and his biographers is a moving as well as an intellectually stimulating experience. Obviously, at a personal and domestic level, his life is the stuff of which classical tragedy is made. Indeed, Trevor Griffiths has seized

Introduction

upon the dramatic possibilities of Gramsci's biography in his play *Occupations*. However, in this work, Gramsci's tragedy is political rather than personal. He figures as the central actor in the drama of the Turin workers' strike, its denouement hinging on whether the workers would establish the revolution by a complete takeover of the factories — thus establishing Communism — or would settle for benefits within the existing industrial system. In the event, they settled for the latter (cf. Cammett, 1967, pp.120-1).

In terms of Gramsci's overriding commitment to revolution through Factory Councils, this outcome has to be judged the failure of his work as a practical politician. One student of his life and work has concluded that he was a failure then and now — the former a reference to the collapse of the Turin revolt, the latter to the fact that he has become the patron saint of the modern Communist Party in Italy, a party which has engineered the so-called 'historic compromise' with the democratic parliamentary parties in Italy, and is confronted with the possibility of attaining power through the democratic machinery of the ballot box with the inevitable compromises which this implies (cf. Boggs, 1976, p.80).

However, Gramsci was himself no stranger to compromise, a fact which contributes a further element to his tragedy as a politician. For, as we have seen, Gramsci is the political radical committed to action, and tragic consequences are implicit in the willingness to compromise which this entails. For example, he was advocate of an alliance against Fascism of all workers and peasants irrespective of their party allegiance, a stance attracting criticism from the intransigents in the Party. Perhaps the most poignant of his letters from prison records his abortive attempt, towards the end of his life, to organise a seminar aimed at convincing his fellow political prisoners that he had not ceased to be a Communist (cf. Cammett, 1969, p.182; Pozzolini, 1970, pp.xviii-xix). This sensitivity to the need for compromise and alliance with non-Marxists has earned for Gramsci the titles 'Open Marxist', 'Liberal Marxist', 'Western Marxist', 'Cultural Marxist', 'Creative Marxist' and, from both Marxists and non-Marxists alike, the judgment that he was not a Marxist at all[5] (Gwyn Williams, 1975, p.306; Kiernan, 1972, p.11;

Introduction

Boggs, 1976, pp.16, 19; Cammett, 1967, p.123).

A recent reviewer of a new edition of the *Letters from Prison* has wondered 'how long would his humane and open Marxism have survived the corrosive atmosphere of Stalin's harsh and closed system'. Having 'died at the height of the great purge in Russia, he had emphasised the duty of being prepared to die but had ignored the danger of being prepared to kill' (Walter, 1975). Gramsci was obviously saved from this tragic dilemma (as Hobsbawm puts it 1974, p.43, 'by a pleasing irony of history' he was 'saved from Stalin because Mussolini had him put behind bars'), but his biographers and editors commonly employ the notion of tragedy to epitomise the outcomes of his political experience. MacIntyre has referred to 'Trotsky's view that the gap between aspiration and achievement will be a permanent feature of human life, so that tragedy will be permanently relevant to the human experience' (1970, pp.36-7) and, in a different context, to the fact that 'the tragic is a category which . . . remains a possibility wherever the attempt is made to live within and transcend a society' (1971, p.86). And it is essentially in these terms that Kiernan has underlined the tragedy of Gramsci's political life: 'Mankind's sense of the tragic lies close to this disparity between intention and consequence. What makes tragedy is not failure in action, but the impossibility of seeing its results, so that every tragedy is a tragedy of errors . . .' (1972, p.27). For an understanding of his work, the point of this reference to its tragic dimensions is that it alerts us to the paradoxes, if not contradictions, which it manifests. Broccoli reminds us that the *Notebooks* are 'disinterested' in the sense of being reflections upon his political experiences with a view to accounting for 'the reasons for the failures as well as the victories' (1972, p.91).

Education and the concept of hegemony

A number of students of Gramsci have judged his development of the notion of hegemony to be his unique contribution to political theory. Raymond Williams has traced a renewed interest in, and a wider application of, the concept particularly to Gramsci's influence, and has concluded that his understanding of hegemony was 'at a depth which is . . . rare' (1973). Williams also observes that the notion of hegemony is complex (ibid.):

> We have to give a very complex account of hegemony if we are talking about any real social formation. Above all we have to give an account which allows for its elements of real and constant change. We have to emphasise that hegemony is not singular; indeed that its own internal structures are highly complex and have continually to be renewed and defended; and by the same token, that they can be continually challenged and in certain respects modified.

Clearly, there are dangers in attempting to characterise hegemony briefly, but this must be attempted since the notion is essential to an understanding of Gramsci's conception of the function of education.

The notion of hegemony is most familiar in political history and international affairs where it refers to situations in which one nation exercises political, cultural or economic influence over others. But, following Lenin, Gramsci extended its reference to apply to relationships between groups, especially social classes. Hence, one social class can be thought of as exercising hegemony over other 'subaltern' classes. In capitalist society the bourgeoisie is hegemonic in relation to the industrial working class. In its turn, the point of socialist revolution is that it is counter-hegemonic, aimed at replacing bourgeois by proletarian hegemony.

Gramscian scholars have debated how far this use of hegemony is simply an alternative formulation of the familiar notion of class dictatorship and, hence, how far it is applicable to a democratic society. In one of the earlier English-language analyses of Gramsci's use of the concept, Gwyn Williams saw hegemony as corresponding 'to a state power conceived in stock Marxist terms as the dictatorship of a class' (1951, p.587). Similarly, Hughes considers it to be 'a totalitarian thought clothed in liberal guise' (1958, pp.101-2). On this view, use of the word hegemony does seem to be a tactic for emptying the notion of class rule of the pejorative implications of dictatorship. Given that assumption, however, the substitution of proletarian for bourgeois hegemony would only be exchanging one dictatorship for another: that is, if hegemony is merely a euphemism for dictatorship, and since every society has its hegemonic class, we already have class dictatorship exercised by a 'respectable' class, the bourgeoisie. Indeed, Gwyn Williams took it that by hegemony Gramsci probably had in mind what we now call an Establishment. Others, however, have argued an essential difference between hegemony and dictatorship: 'Hegemony is a key word in Gramsci implying opposition to "dictatorship" in the sense that cultural predominance can be distinguished from political power' (McInnis, 1971, p.11, note 4; cf. also Cammett, 1967, p.204; Joll, 1977, p.9).

It does seem essential to Gramsci's notion of hegemony that the implication of rule by physical coercion, which the notion of dictatorship commonly entails, is absent. Boggs sees Gramsci's conception as a point of departure from 'the classical Marxist approach to power (which) was onesided in the exclusive attention paid to the role of force and coercion as the basis of ruling class domination' (1976, p.38). Joll argues that neither the exercise of economic nor physical power is central to Gramsci's conception of hegemony (1977, p.8) and that even political power is unnecessary to the establishment of the moral and cultural influence on which it depends (ibid., p.11). In Gramsci's formulation, hegemonic direction is by moral and intellectual persuasion rather than control by the police, the military, or the coercive power of the law: 'rule by intellectual and moral hegemony is the form of power which gives stability and founds power on wide-ranging consent and acquiescence'. For this to be so, 'every relationship of "hegemony" is necessarily a pedagogical relationship' (*Quaderni*, vol. II, p.1331). Control of the subaltern classes is much more subtly exercised than is often supposed; it operates persuasively rather than coercively through cultural institutions — churches, labour unions and other workers' associations, schools and the press.

In the stock Marxist phrase, bourgeois hegemony depends upon the 'false consciousness' of the working class: or, as Raymond Williams puts it, so totally do the complex forces of hegemony saturate the whole process of living 'that the pressures and limits of what can ultimately be seen as a specific economic, political and cultural system seem to most of us the pressures and limits of simple experience and common sense' (1977, p.110). That is, we are persuaded that maintenance of the *status quo* could not but be in our own best interests. Moreover, it is possible for the existing hegemony to accommodate alternative and counter-hegemonic cultural forces, 'neutralising, changing or actually incorporating them' (ibid., p.114). As a concrete example of this, Klein has analysed the radical, active, student counter-culture of the 1960s, to demonstrate how a hegemony 'can operate to absorb, assimilate and integrate a variety of forms of protest into its own ideological network'. In the modern, complex, industrial society resort to force is redundant (1969, p.313). Indeed, erosion of active consent to the existing socio-cultural order, to a degree that the ruling class is driven to resort to force, would already be an indication of collapse of its hegemony. Cammett notes intimations of this consensual requirement of hegemony in Machiavelli, who influenced Gramsci's intellectual development: 'the best fortress (of the Prince) is love of the people; for although you may have fortresses, they will not save you if you are hated by the people' (1967, p.211, quoting Chapter XX of *The Prince*; cf. *Notebooks*, p.126).

It follows that resort to violence by a subaltern class is not a sufficient condition for establishing its own hegemony; this requires a profound change in mass consciousness (Joll, 1977, p.79; *Notebooks*, pp.57-8):

> A social group can, and indeed must, already exercise 'leadership' before winning governmental power (this indeed is one of the principal conditions for the winning of such power); it subsequently becomes dominant when it exercises power, but even if it holds it firmly in its grasp, it must continue to 'lead' as well.

Gramsci went on to assert that 'there can, and must be hegemonic activity even before the rise to power, and that one should not count only on the material force which power gives in order to exercise effective leadership' (ibid., p.59). This suggests that the description of a counter-hegemonic revolution would not be the history of a successful armed

Introduction

coup by a revolutionary group and of the way it confirmed and sustained itself in power by resort to force. It would necessarily be a cultural history, a description of those educational relationships which sustain its own moral and intellectual hegemony (*Political Writings*, p.12):

> every revolution has been preceded by an intense labour of criticism, by the diffusion of culture and the spread of ideas amongst masses of men who are at first resistant, and think only of solving their own immediate economic and political problems for themselves.

As McInnis puts it, it is only when cultural predominance and political power coincide that there is revolution (1971). Clark, who insists that Gramsci believed working-class militancy to be 'useless in constructing socialism' and, hence, devoted 'life-long efforts to "educate" the workers away from "militancy" ', also concludes that 'revolution, for Gramsci, was not a specific event, but a "dialectical process of historical development" ' (1977, 6, p.59). And Cammett concluded (1967, pp.205-6):

> The fundamental assumption behind Gramsci's view of hegemony is that the working class, before it seizes State power, must establish its claim to be a ruling class in the political, cultural and ethical sense . . . . Hegemony — rule by consent, the legitimation of revolution by a higher and more comprehensive culture — is the unifying idea of Gramsci's life.

This amounts to the claim that workers must learn to think and act 'like a ruling class', and the continuous controversy in which Gramsci was involved with colleagues in the Italian Socialist and Communist Parties was substantially about the place of education in the making of a socialist counter-hegemony. That he himself saw education as integral to this task is indicated by the rubric which the first issue of *L'Ordine Nuovo* carried on its masthead: 'Instruct yourselves because we shall need all our intelligence. Agitate because we shall need all our enthusiasm. Organise yourselves because we shall need all our power.'

His assumption that workers must come to think 'like a ruling class' makes clear that he saw the counter-hegemonic task as one of education. This is implicit in Gwyn William's summary of Gramsci's distinctive contribution to political theory (1975, p.183):

> Gramsci's most creative and distinctive development of Marxism, was his exploration of the *essential* problem of breaking the bourgeois hegemony over workers' minds, the need for workers and the workers' party to *think* themselves into *historical autonomy*, without which no permanent revolution is possible.

However, as Williams shows, emphasis upon the educational task involved in bringing the working class to the point where it thinks like a ruling class, also raises the question, 'How do Gramscians *take* power?' (ibid., p.184). The conclusion of his adversaries was that 'the revolution could never be the product of education, culture or the technical capacity of the working class' (ibid., p.180). His chief rival, the intransigent abstentionist Armadeo Bordiga, had taunted those socialists who, like Gramsci, stressed education: 'The need for study is something proclaimed by a congress of school teachers and not of socialists. You don't become a socialist through instruction but through experiencing the real needs of the class to which you belong' (quoted by Joll, 1977, p.41). For Gramsci this was, of course, a false dichotomy; as in his own life, nothing could be more of a political education than experience of class interests and needs. Nevertheless, he also believed the formal instruction associated with schooling to be a necessary basis for understanding one's personal and class predicaments (through knowledge of history, for example) and for articulating one's needs and interests (through mastery of the skills of literacy, for example). Hence, as Gwyn Williams shows, Gramsci's response to crisis was apt to be in the form of an educational initiative (1975, p.219; cf. also Davidson, 1977, pp.124, 151, 215, 223-4). Patronising critics tended to dismiss him, maliciously, in judgments like, 'Gramsci leans towards exposition, teaching, the school' by contrast with others who prefer 'to command armed battalions' (Ruggero Grieco quoted by Gwyn Williams, 1975, p.302). Even a sympathetic critic has suggested that he 'may be open to the charge of supposing that the hand that fills the inkpot rules

Introduction

the world' (Kiernan, 1972, p.29). He was a born (if not always a successful) teacher and it could validly be claimed that, where two or three were gathered together, there Gramsci would organise a class.[6] In his view, this educational task was inescapable, and in the *Notebooks* he defined the purpose of Marxism in distinctively educational terms. One of its fundamental tasks was 'to educate the popular masses, whose culture was medieval ... and to create a group of intellectuals specific to the new social group whose conception of the world it was' (*Notebooks*, pp.392-3).

As we saw, it was in the various institutions of 'civil society' that Gramsci found concrete expression of the hegemonic educational relationships, particularly in the school. It is at this point that we encounter the paradox which we have already noted: the pursuit of a radical political education through a traditional curriculum and pedagogy. If schools are a major hegemonic instrument of existing class rule, how can counter-hegemonic change occur except through radical curricular reform and a liberal pedagogy? Do not the schools which already serve the capitalist hegemony succeed in developing a false working-class consciousness through manipulation of the curriculum in order to transmit falsehood, half- or irrelevant truths and values, and by adopting a pedagogy whose 'hidden' curriculum serves to perpetuate work habits and values which are functional only for the maintenance of corporate capitalism? Part 1 of this study is an attempt to discover how Gramsci understood the school to be hegemonic and how the traditional organisation of schooling served the existing hegemony, but also in what respects its traditional pedagogy might have revolutionary potential. Part 2 considers how and why, in Gramsci's view, schooling can only fructify in the education of adults. No doubt, as students of Gramsci's conception of hegemony are at pains to insist, the processes and relationships of hegemony are subtle and complex. This is true of the way in which the school functions within the hegemony and neither Gramsci's observations on schooling, nor an analysis of them, can be an exhaustive description of the school's place in the complex of hegemonic traditions, institutions and values. Nevertheless, his account of the matter focuses issues which remain at the centre of educational theory and is of interest, not least, because from his perspective a good deal of current radical educational theory is clearly heresy and, as such, more likely to serve the existing hegemony than the educational needs and interests of the working class.

Part one

The schooling of children

Introduction

An ambiguity attaches to the word 'school' following from different usage in Europe and North America. In North America, school tends to refer to the total complex of institutions of formal education, including colleges and universities. When young adults speak of 'being in school' or of 'going back to school', it is higher education to which they are referring. But in Europe school usually refers to the institution devoted to the education of the child and the young adolescent: school covers the period of compulsory education and upper secondary schooling, and it is in this sense that Gramsci habitually uses the Italian equivalent, *scuola*. As will become evident, it is of importance to understanding Gramsci's concept of education as hegemonic that this distinction be drawn between school as concerned with the education of children and school as referring to formal education at any level, including institutions for the education of adults.

The curriculum of the school

A striking feature of Gramsci's writing is its positive valuation of traditional, mainstream, humanistic culture. Throughout his own work his debt to this is immense; his erudition, especially in the fields of history and literature (including foreign literature), is impressive. There is no dismissal of this mainstream culture, its source in Graeco-Roman civilisation, as 'bourgeois' in any pejorative sense. McInnes has remarked upon 'that substantial part of Gramsci's work that consists in the defence and illustration of formal logic, classic culture, liberal education and disinterested enquiry' (1971, p.15; cf. also *Quaderni*, III, pp. 2346-7). In a letter dated March, 1918, Gramsci explained the objectives of his club for young adolescents (*La Club di Vita Morale*) as 'the disinterested discussion of ethical and moral problems, the formation of a habit of research, of disciplined and methodical reading, of the simple and clear expression of one's convictions' (quoted Manacorda, 1976, pp.24-5). Similarly, when calling upon the Italian Socialist Party to create 'cultural associations' aimed at educating the working class, he urged that these should develop in the Italian people those qualities which he felt they lacked, 'the love of free discussion, the desire to search for truth rationally and intelligently' (*Formazione*, p.95): 'to the proletariat is necessary a disinterested school, a humanistic school, in short, as was intended by the ancients and more recently by the men of the Renaissance' (*Scritti Giovanile*, p.57). One Italian Gramscian scholar concludes with reference especially to his early writings, that 'it does not seem possible to deny, above all in examining the content of education, that Gramsci shows himself for the most part to be anchored to the model of the traditional bourgeois school' (Broccoli, 1972, p.35). Moreover, when he insisted that Marxism 'maintains a dynamic contact with the masses and aims continually to raise new strata of the masses to a higher cultural life' (*Notebooks*, p. 397), he did, indeed, see the higher cultural life as a product of the dialectical engagement of popular culture with high culture: 'the philosophy of praxis (i.e., Marxism) was born on the terrain of the highest development of culture in the first half of the nineteenth century' (*Notebooks*, p.399). For Gramsci there is no so-called proletarian or working-class culture to be idealised, absolutely discontinuous with the historical cultural mainstream. In this respect he is at one with the traditional Marxist-Leninist postion (see below, pp.43-6). He was, of course, aware of the anachronism of a humanistic culture which remained dominated by the classical languages (*Notebooks*, pp.37-40). Intrinsically valuable as he believed these to be as instruments of personal discipline, he recognised the need for schools to teach a 'new humanism' focused upon those modern forms of knowledge which were intrinsic to an industrial civilisation.

In the educational essays there is no attempt to outline, systematically, a programme of subjects for the curriculum. What Gramsci does, again paradoxically, is to praise the traditional Italian elementary school, which he believed to have been the object of mistaken reform by the fascist government in 1923. This positive evaluation of the existing elementary school has proved puzzling to some Gramscian scholars. The editors of the *Notebooks* feel it necessary to warn their readers that many references in the *Notebooks* and the *Letters* had to be euphemistic in order to circumvent censorship by the prison authorities (*Notebooks*, p.xiii). In their view, the eulogy of traditional educational institutions is 'a device which allowed Gramsci to circumvent the prison censor, by disguising the future (ideal system) as the past in order to criticise the present' (ibid., p.24). Hoare and Smith's point is taken with reference to Marxist concepts and to the founding fathers of Marxism. But when education is under discussion it is not clear that Gramsci's defence of historical institutions was a disguise for advocacy of new, radical educational content and practices which he preferred in substance, but thought it prudent not to describe. We shall see that his prescriptions for the upbringing of children are, indeed, conservative and it would be odd if the entire thrust and substance of his discussion of educational principles had been completely misleading and unreliable hints of his own preferences. In the event, when he took the initiative in organising a school for his fellow political prisoners on the island of Ustica, this was modelled on the pattern of the traditional elementary school (Manacorda, 1976, p.70; Lawner, Letters, no. 2). Though some references to his own schooling are disparaging, this seems less a disenchantment with schools, as such, than a criticism of the shortcomings of a small backward country school in Sardinia where half of his fellow-pupils could only speak Italian haltingly, and of his small gymnasium where three overworked 'self-styled professors' relied 'more on brazen cheek than competence' (*Lettere*, no. 6, 387; 295; Edinburgh Letters, no. CLXXX; cf. also Davidson, 1977, p.37). These criticisms cannot be read as criticism of the *principles* underlying the traditional school: 'It was right to struggle against the old school, but reforming it was not so simple as it seemed. The problem was not one of model curricula but of men, and not just the men who are actually teachers themselves but of the entire social complex which they express' (*Notebooks*, p.36). Earlier in the same note he had also distinguished the educational principles embodied in the old school law (the Casati Act of 1859), of which he approved, (see Manacorda, 1976, p.325) from their actual implementation, about which he remained agnostic. After outlining its aims, he concluded: 'That was the real basis of the elementary school. Whether it yielded all its fruits, and whether the actual teachers were aware of the nature and philosophical content of their task, is another question' (*Notebooks*, p.35). In this connection it is interesting that a modern English historian of the Labour Movement, E.P. Thompson (1968b), has concluded that elementary education, especially, has 'resisted and thrown back ... the meaner manifestations of cultural domination and social control' which were characteristic of much nineteenth-century educational and cultural priggishness with reference to the working class.

Gramsci's positive evaluation of the elementary school as it existed under the old school law referred especially to its contribution towards the conquest of ignorance and superstition. Though he recognised in everyone the capacity to be a 'philosopher', 'artist', 'man of taste', participating in 'a particular conception of the world' (*Notebooks*, p.9), it is also evident that he believed that philosophy, artistry, taste and conceptions of the world could be mistaken or cognitively and aesthetically barren (ibid., p.323):

> It must first be shown that all men are 'philosophers', by defining the limits and characteristics of the 'spontaneous philosophy' which is proper to everybody. This philosophy is contained in: 1. language itself which is a totality of determined notions and concepts and not just words grammatically devoid of content; 2. 'common sense' and 'good sense'; 3. popular religion and, therefore, also in the

entire system of beliefs, superstitions, opinion, ways of seeing things and acting which are collectively bundled together under the name of folklore.

Put in the language of Piagetian psychology, this amounts to saying that the untutored intelligence frequently manifests itself in conceptions which are pre-operational with reference to natural scientific and social modes of thought. 'Common sense' is a blend of 'good sense' and folkloristic superstition, and Gramsci saw education as an enterprise for enlarging the component of good sense within common sense (see below, pp.33-5. for elaboration of this distinction between common sense and good sense). The merit of the traditional Italian school had been in its pursuit of this objective:

> The School combatted folklore, indeed every residue of traditional conceptions of the world. It taught a more modern outlook based essentially on an awareness of the simple and fundamental fact that there exist objective intractible natural laws to which man must adapt himself if he is to master them in his turn – and that there exist social and state laws which are the product of human activity, which are established by men and can be altered by men in the interests of their collective development. (*Notebooks*, p.34; cf. also Manacorda, 1976, p.226-7)

A contemporary of Gramsci confirms that the Italian elementary school before the 1923 reforms had become involved in combating folklore, though the critical tone in which this confirmation is offered suggests that he (Codignola) did not approve of this development (1930, p.390):

> Little by little, teachers became convinced that they should devote themselves to a sort of secular priesthood, that it was their function to liberate minds from family, social and religious idols by means of an initiation to rational examination and unprejudiced observation of facts, and that it was for them to liberate the thought of children from the fables of the mother and priest, the national language from dialect, reason from sentiment, and even consciousness of humanity from the narrowness of love of country.

The schooling of children

This characterisation of the old Italian elementary school by an observer who was not unsympathetic to the Fascist government's school reform provides further support for the view that Gramsci's belief in the radical potential of the old elementary school was well founded. As we shall presently see, his view of examinations and of the importance of teaching facts, his own proposals for the teaching of language and his insistence that the local culture of family and neighbourhood must be superseded through transmission, by the school, of a universal humanistic culture, are in line with Codignola's description of the aims of elementary school teachers before 1923.

The distinction which Gramsci drew between natural laws which are intractable and social laws which are normative, given only by men, recalls Popper's (1966) conception of 'critical dualism'. Based on this distinction a curriculum aimed at replacing folklore with a more modern outlook would necessarily include the teaching of natural science and social studies. According to Gramsci, that aspect of the latter which is concerned with 'rights and duties' had been neglected in the past, and teaching of these civic values must be added to the 'first, "instrumental" notions of schooling — reading, writing, science, geography, history' (*Notebooks*, p.30). It is in his insistence upon rigorous, formal study of these intellectual instruments, especially language, that Gramsci reinforces the claims of the elementary tradition.

From the *Letters* and *Notebooks* there is no warrant for inferring that anything less than a rigorous standard of literacy will serve the working class. A reading of these offers no support to those modern educationists who question the value of a print culture and, hence, of literacy for the working class (see e.g., Young; Postman). From this point of view, Gramsci's work is of special interest in the context of the current debate about differential, class-based language codes and the question of 'bilinguality' in relation to restricted language codes (working-class speech, or Black English) and the so-called elaborated code of the middle class and the school (Labov; B. Bernstein). It is true that Gramsci made two points which might appear authoritative for anyone wishing to encourage 'lower-class' speech or dialect

The schooling of children

in schools. In a letter to his sister he advised her to let his nephew speak Sardinian 'dialect' if he wished (*Lettere*, no. 23):

> I hope you'll let him speak Sardinian and not pester him about this. It was a mistake it seems to me not to let Edmea (his niece) speak Sardinian freely when she was small. This was detrimental to her intellectual development and put her imagination in a straitjacket . . . I entreat you not to make the same mistake, and to let your children pick up all the 'sardisms' they wish and to develop spontaneously in the natural surroundings where they were born.

But it is clear that Gramsci regarded the acquisition of 'sardisms' only as part of a 'romance' stage in the development of language skill. Manacorda reminds us that this advice was given to the mother of a two-year-old (1976, p.80), and Gramsci himself had in mind that the local Italian was itself a poor and deficient slang (*Lettere*, no. 23). His considered conclusion in the *Notebooks* was an assertion of the need to master the standard form of a language (p.325):

> If it is true that every language contains the elements of a conception of the world and of a culture, it could also be true that from anyone's language one can assess the greater or lesser complexity of his conception of the world. Someone who only speaks dialect, or understands the standard language incompletely, necessarily has an intuition of the world which is more or less limited and provincial, which is fossilised and anachronistic in relation to the major currents of thought which dominate world history. His interests will be limited, not universal . . . it is at least necessary to learn the national language properly. A great culture can be translated into the language of another great culture, that is to say a great national language with historic richness and complexity, and it can translate any other great culture and can be a world-wide means of expression. But a dialect cannot do this.

Indeed, part of Gramsci's reason for entreating his sister to allow the children to speak Sardinian was that this is itself a language, not a dialect, despite its having no great literature (*Lettere*, no. 23).

It is evident that so far as Gramsci does offer insight into the current debate about education and social class, he gives no underpinning for those who see in Black English or 'lower-class' English a vehicle for rational thought as cogent as (and, indeed, with advantages over) Standard English. In a passage in the *Notebooks* he writes of the importance of teachers understanding peasant speech (*Notebooks*, pp.35-6). But he is also clear that the object of schooling is the complete mastery of the standard form of the language and a high standard of literacy. The current questioning of the value of literacy follows from the assumption that the teaching of reading is itself a means of social control and, hence, is necessary for maintenance of the existing socio-cultural hegemony (Postman). Gramsci seemed committed to the opposite view of the politics of literacy.[1] Without mastery of the common, standard version of a national language, one is inevitably destined to function only at the periphery of national life and, especially, outside its political mainstream. Teaching of the standard written and spoken forms of a language is, therefore, a democratic necessity. And if he did not explicitly commend literacy as a tool of the revolution, Gramsci did recognise that absolute mastery of written communication was necessary for anyone engaged in the communication of ideas. Describing how the specialised editors on *Ordine Nuovo* worked with him in committee to improve their individual and collective performances, he wrote (*Notebooks*, p.29):

> Such activity requires an unyielding struggle against habits of dilettantism, of improvisation, of 'rhetorical' solutions or those proposed for effect. The work has to be done particularly in written form, just as it is in written form that criticisms have to be made – in the form of terse succinct notes . . . the writing down of notes and criticisms is a didactic principle rendered necessary by the need to combat the habits formed in public speaking – prolixity, demagogy and paralogism.

And he concluded by underlining the importance of the discipline of writing, especially for the working class intellectual attempting to educate himself: 'This type of intellectual work is necessary to impart to autodidacts the discipline in study which an orthodox scholastic career provides in order to Taylorise intellectual work' (ibid., p.29; and cf. Fiori, 1970, p.151; *Quaderni*, I, pp.135-6 and Manacorda, 1976, pp.59-60; see *Notebooks*, pp.302 ff. for significance of the reference to Taylorism). Pozzolini refers to Gramsci's disinclination to make concessions to those who argued that his language was too difficult for most of his readers on the grounds 'that to impoverish his language would often have meant to impoverish the debate' (1970, pp.108-9). And, as Broccoli reminds us, since Gramsci was concerned with the problem of bringing the 'popular classes' into their heritage of the national culture, it is not surprising that he was unable to conceive of this achievement without mastery of the national language (1972, p.196).

Gramsci's assessment of the educational possibilities latent in the cultural environment of the child's own family and neighbourhood was much the same as his judgment about the limitations of dialect. He recognised that local culture is often starkly at odds with the culture which the schools attempt to transmit:

> the individual consciousness of the overwhelming majority of children reflects social and cultural relations which are different from and antagonistic to those which are represented in the school curricula . . . There is no unity between school and life, and so there is no automatic unity between instruction and education.

From this conclusion, however, Gramsci did not dismiss school as irrelevant to life. To the contrary, he saw it as the teacher's function:

> to be aware of the contrast between the type of culture and society which he represents and the type of culture and society represented by his pupils, and conscious of his obligation to accelerate and regulate the child's conformity with the former and in conflict with the latter (*Notebooks*, pp.35-6).

In discussing the dangers involved in popularising scientific knowledge (which he took to be a necessary function of intellectuals — see below, pp.144-7) he wrote critically of situations in which 'the rough and uneducated environment has dominated the educator, the vulgar common sense has imposed itself upon science and not vice versa' (*Quaderni*, II, p.877).

It is clear that Gramsci subscribed to the notion of the child as (in modern educational jargon) 'a deficit system', and a critique of deficit theory (as, for example, in Esland, 1971, p.89) would be tantamount to a dismissal of Gramsci's position on curriculum, pedagogy and examinations. Again, he can be no authority for those sociologists of education who dismiss cultural deprivation as a myth whilst asserting the adequacy of all sub-cultures as valid ways of life (see, eg., Keddie, 1973). Far from being adequate or valid, he concluded, the 'popular average' level of culture was 'very low' (*Notebooks*, p.392). He did not fall into the conservative trap with reference to popular culture which the cultural adequacy thesis leads to.[2] One difficulty with this position is that, logically, it offers no possibility of the kind of creative, progressive outcomes (especially the fusing of theory and practice) which Gramsci believed could follow from a dialectical engagement of different conceptions of the world, i.e. of different sub-cultures (see pp.119-21 and pp.160-5 below).

However, Gramsci acknowledged the fact that life in different sub-cultures would evoke differing perceptions of school and academic learning (*Notebooks*, pp.42-3):

> Undoubtedly the child of a traditional intellectual family acquires this psycho-physical adaptation (i.e., to the work of the schools) more easily. Before he ever enters the classroom he has numerous advantages over his comrades, and is already in possession of attitudes learnt from his family environment . . . . This is why people think that the difficulty of study conceals some 'trick' which handicaps them — that is, when they do not simply believe that they are stupid by nature.

But Gramsci's solution to the problem of the difficulties in schooling encountered by children of the 'lower' or 'subaltern' classes was not to convince them that they are victims of an academic confidence trick. They are not encouraged to find 'adequacy' in their own cultures, nor to search for alternatives to the content and pedagogy of the traditional school. The only 'trick' lies in hard work, 'tears and blood': 'If our aim is to produce a new stratum of intellectuals, including those capable of the highest degree of specialisation, from a social group which has not traditionally developed the appropriate attitudes, then we have unprecedented difficulties to overcome' (*Notebooks*, p.43). No doubt, part of overcoming these difficulties will lie in teachers' awareness of the spontaneous culture with which the culture of the school is 'in conflict'. But the former cannot be normative for the school. At most, Gramsci saw the child's own sub-culture as a bridge, or point of departure. In itself, it could not constitute the data of an education as, indeed, we have seen that dialect could not. It is clear that Gramsci believed in an *active* teacher, transmitting the mainstream humanistic culture, enforcing linguistic discipline and accuracy.

Curriculum and the sociology of knowledge

This conclusion that teachers should address themselves to the question of how the 'alien' culture of the school can be brought to bear upon the child's cultural development makes it difficult to use Gramsci as authority for the view that the school's hegemonic function derives from its imposition of a curriculum and the view that the learner, from the perspective of his own sub-culture, should define what counts as educational knowledge. Yet this seems exactly the intention of Young, a leading exponent of the so-called 'new' sociology of education.

In an essay from the volume which has become authoritative for the view that a new sociology of education should be derived from the sociology of knowledge, Young summarises what he takes to be Gramsci's contribution to an educationally relevant sociology of knowledge. He refers to Gramsci's 'distinction between "common sense" and "philosophy" in which he sees that some people's common sense becomes formally recognised as philosophy, and other people's does not, *depending on their access to certain institutional contexts*' (1971, p.28, emphasis added). This is exactly what Gramsci does *not* do. However, Young continues with the claim that 'this suggests that sociologists should raise the wider question of the relationship between school knowledge and commonsense knowledge, of how, as Gramsci suggests, knowledge available to certain groups becomes "school knowledge" or "educational" and that available to others does not." The context of this reference to Gramsci (Young's polemic on behalf of the view that no one's knowledge is superior to anyone else's) imputes to Gramsci the same view, implying that, like himself, Gramsci saw no intrinsic epistemological or cultural reasons why some people's common sense should be recognised as philosophy, the only reason being political, i.e. that one social group controls educational institutions whilst other social groups are under its control.

There are two explanations of why knowledge might become school knowledge:

1 Such knowledge could be judged valid or worthwhile as the data of an educational experience either by reference to intrinsic criteria (i.e. standards of truth, coherence, objectivity, aesthetic or moral values) or, instrumentally, by reference to its generalisability as a resource for daily living.
2 Because those who control schools have the authority or power to determine what counts as school knowledge by reference either
  (i) to the possession of skill and knowledge through which criteria under (1) are applied; that is because they are authorities or experts; or
  (ii) because they control schools 'ideologically' or hegemonically in permitting the transmission of only such knowledge (and in such a manner) as serves the interests of the ruling class.

The distinction between (i) and (ii) is crucial. Young's assumption is that the last of these, (ii), constitutes the reason why school knowledge comes to be what it is. The clause, 'depending on their access to certain institutional contexts', takes it for granted that some people's common sense is dignified as philosophy for exclusively political reasons. The principles on which academic curricula are based can be seen as social definitions of educational value, and thus become problematic in the sense that if they persist it is not because knowledge is in any meaningful way best made available according to the criteria they represent, but because they are conscious or unconscious cultural choices which accord with the policies and beliefs of dominant groups at a particular time (Young, 1971, p.38).

Thus, from Young's relativist point of view there is nothing philosophically or scientifically superior, or educationally valuable, about what comes to be defined as school knowledge instead of other conceivable alternatives. Those who define the curriculum depend simply upon political power, not on scholarly authority. Implicitly, there is no reason, other than the political, why any world view or 'philosophy' should not be the substance of the curriculum. On Young's account of it, philosophy is simply that species of common sense which has the sanction of political power; it is not that common sense which has the characteristic of being 'good sense'.

Young's intention is to question 'the assumption that thought systems organised in curricula are in some sense "superior" to the thought systems of those who are to be (or have not been) educated' (1971, p.13). Hence, for him, the new sociology of education begins by 'rejecting the assumption of any superiority of educational or "academic" knowledge over the everyday commonsense knowledge available to people as being in the world' (1973a, p.214). However, Gramsci provides no support for this questioning of the conventional wisdom about the superiority of the thought systems of the educated. His answer to Young's research problem — 'to discover how some categories and not others gain institutional legitimacy' (1971, p.13) — would have amounted to the response that it is precisely because some thought systems *are* cognitively and logically superior to others that they become the curriculum content of formal educational institutions. Despite his understanding of folklore and his empathy with those whose world view it permeates, it represents a culture which is 'fossilised and anachronistic' (*Notebooks*, p.35): he simply did not see it as an adequate philosophical basis for revolutionary praxis.

The schooling of children

Quite the contrary, if the subaltern classes are under the control of the hegemonic class, it is their own often superstitious, folkloristic conception of the world which is favourable to maintenance of the *status quo*.[3] As we have already seen, this is exactly how (for Gramsci) hegemony works: when the subaltern classes' spontaneous cultural perceptions are that the social order could not be other than it is. As Young concedes, certain categories of knowledge and thought *are* favourable to the exercise of political control, and he claims that the paper in which he employs Gramsci as authority examines 'the processes by which the availability of such categories to some groups enables them to assert power and control over others' (1971, p.8). But he never examines the possibility that these knowledge categories are politically powerful because they offer more logical, coherent, systematic and complete accounts of the socio-political universe and, hence, that having access to these categories would be beneficial for anyone from any class wanting to understand the mechanisms of social control. Gramsci's position is that some forms of knowledge are in this sense superior. He insisted that the elementary school should teach about 'rights and duties' precisely because the perceptions of State and society that are acquired in 'the various traditional social environments' often amount to nothing more than folklore (*Notebooks*, p.30). If this is the case, why would any subaltern class in pursuit of hegemony not want to accept the definition of what counts as superior political knowledge by those exercising political control over others? Indeed, the young Gramsci had insisted on the need for initiatives to educate converts to socialism by raising 'their culture to that of professors'. The focus of this education was to be on 'the great works of European culture' (Davidson, 1977, pp.178-80). As we shall see, it is one of Gramsci's persistent themes that one must learn from one's adversary whom one should be careful not to belittle. How, he asked, if you are superior to him 'did he succeed in dominating you?' (quoted by Davidson, 1977, p.200).

With reference to the question of whether there are superior and inferior conceptions of reality, it is a fact that Gramsci does discuss the relationship between philosophy and common sense and that he employs common sense as 'a collective noun', indicating that 'there is not just one common sense ... every social stratum has its own "common sense"' (*Notebooks*, p.326, including note 5). Implicitly, there is also a middle-class 'folklore', having its own peculiar admixture of good sense and superstition, the latter often exemplified, for example, in what could be called 'the coal in the bath syndrome' — a perception of the working class as defiling everything civilised that it touches. But, although there is this sociological differentiation of common sense, for Gramsci the question of the relationship between common sense and philosophy is epistemological, not sociological. Moreover, the different notion of 'good sense' is essential to understanding his formulation of this relationship and his position on what ought to count as school knowledge.

In Gramsci, philosophy is identical with a world view or ideology (in what he calls 'its highest sense of a conception of the world that is implicitly manifest in art, in law, in economic activity and in all manifestations of individual and collective life' — *Notebooks*, p.328). However, he insists that philosophy exists at all cultural levels from 'common' or 'popular' philosophy (the spontaneous, unconscious world view which all men have) to 'scientific' philosophy (the systematic world view of the specialist when 'philosophy is intellectual order'). This last is philosopher's philosophy (*Notebooks*, p.344):

> The history of philosophy as it is generally understood, that is, the history of philosophers' philosophies, is the history of attempts made and ideological initiatives undertaken by a specific class of people to change, correct or perfect the conceptions of the world that exist in any particular age and thus to change the norms of conduct that go with them; in other words, to change practical activity as a whole.

But it is also the case that 'the majority of mankind are philosophers in so far as they engage in practical activity and in their practical activity (or in their guiding lines of conduct) there is implicitly contained a conception of the world, a philosophy' (ibid.). Gramsci insists that the difference between the professional or 'technical' philosopher and the rest of mankind is in terms of the 'greater or lesser

The schooling of children

degrees of "homogeneity", "coherence", "logicality", etc. at the different levels' (ibid., p.347). At different cultural levels, philosophy will be characterised by the peculiar admixture of religion, superstition, folklore, daily empirical experience and 'science' which compounds the world view of an individual or group. To be in school is to be moving from the level of the spontaneous, unconscious philosophy towards philosophers' philosophy, towards ordering 'in a systematic, coherent and critical fashion one's own intuitions of life and the world' (ibid., p.327). Spontaneous or unconscious philosophy means thinking 'without having critical awareness, in a disjointed and episodic way'. It is 'a conception of the world mechanically imposed by the external environment, i.e., by one of the many social groups in which everyone is automatically involved from the moment of entry into the conscious world'. It is the passive and supine acceptance 'from outside (of) the moulding of one's own personality' (ibid., pp.323-4). This contrasts with philosophy as intellectual order, a conception of the world which is 'a coherent unity' raised 'to the level reached by the most advanced thought in the world' (ibid., p.324). At this level of intellectual coherence one has the capacity 'to work out critically and consciously one's own conception of the world and thus, in connection with the labours of one's own brain, choose one's sphere of activity, take an active part in the creation of the history of the world, be one's own guide . . .' (ibid., p.323). This is a description of the autonomous, rational man traditionally conceived as the outcome of a liberal education. Elsewhere, Gramsci referred to the difference made by acquisition of traditional academic skills as that between 'complete men' and 'men at random' (*Formazione*, pp.97-9).

However, since most men are not destined to be professional or technical philosophers, requiring specialised professional training, the common, universal schooling of childhood is concerned with the development of 'good sense' (what Prestipino (1976) calls 'the positive potential of common sense'), a state of mind in which common sense is purged of its superstition and folklore and given a 'coherent unity' through exposure to philosophers' philosophy and, one can add, to scientists' science ('Just as every man is a philosopher, every man is a man of science' – *Notebooks*, p.354): 'Philosophy is the criticism and superarching of common sense. In this sense it coincides with 'good' as opposed to common sense' (ibid., p.326).

Nevertheless, despite the inability of spontaneous philosophy to sustain a coherent, systematic world view, 'it is not possible to separate what is known as 'scientific' philosophy from the common and popular philosophy' (ibid., p.328). These are the extremes of a spectrum rather than discontinuous or contradictory. When Gramsci writes of every man's being a philosopher, he has in mind that common, non-specialised conceptions of philosophy capture the essence of the philosophical stance. Everyday expressions containing the words 'philosophy', 'philosophical', etc., are usually 'an invitation to people to reflect and realise fully that whatever happens is basically rational and must be confronted as such, and that one should apply one's power of rational concentration and not let oneself be carried away by instinctive and violent impulses' (ibid.). Spontaneous philosophy is inadequate, not because it does not contain the seeds of 'good sense', but because of its incoherence as a mixture of folklore and good sense, 'a fragmentary collection of ideas and opinions'. Much the same point could be made about the relationship between commonsense science and scientists' science. For example, the superstition in removing cutlery from the table during thunderstorms is based upon the knowledge (however inappropriately applied in this instance) that steel is an efficient conductor of electricity. In the same way, folkloristic history may contain the essence of historical truth. The story of Alfred and the Cakes is merely a legend but, arguably, it contains a historical truth about Alfred — that he was magnanimous in the use of power.[4] It is simply sound pedagogy to derive philosophy, science, history, etc., in the classroom from popular folklore and commonsense.

Gramsci writes of the 'primitive philosophy of common sense' from which it is necessary to lead the 'simple' to 'a higher conception of life' (*Notebooks*, p.332). Common sense is a philosophy or world view which partakes, indiscriminately, of both superstition and good sense, of parochial discrimination as well as universal moral norms (ibid., p.324):

When one's conception of the world is not critical and coherent but disjointed and episodic, one belongs simultaneously to a multiplicity of mass human groups. The personality is strangely composite: it contains Stone Age elements and principles of a more advanced science, prejudices from all past phases of history at the local level and intuitions of a future philosophy which will be that of a human race united the world over.

Common sense, then, is rooted in folklore but enriched 'with scientific ideas and with philosophical opinions which have entered ordinary life' (ibid., p.326, note 5). Good sense is this 'healthy nucleus which exists in "common sense" ... and which deserves to be made more unitary and coherent' (ibid., p.328). But, common sense 'cannot constitute an intellectual order, because [it] cannot be reduced to unity and coherence even within an individual consciousness, let alone collective consciousness'. If this is so, it is not clear how common sense could ever count as educational knowledge. For, with reference to the quotation from Young with which this discussion began, it is evident that, for Gramsci, nobody's common sense could ever become formally recognised as philosophy. The question then becomes that of whether what comes to count as school knowledge is merely the common sense or spontaneous philosophy of a particular social class (the hegemonic class) which is as incoherent and riddled with superstition as that of any other class. Or, on the other hand, given the distinction between common sense and good sense, whether the school curriculum has traditionally consisted merely of the incoherent common sense of the hegemonic class to the exclusion of what might be shown to be the good sense of the subaltern classes; or whether the school has simply seen its function as the cultivation of good sense. So far as Gramsci is helpful in approaching this kind of question about traditional schooling and the sort of school reform which might foster working class hegemony, we cannot ignore his belief that, when uncorrected, unsystematised and unrefined, the popular world view of common sense, folklore, is fatally flawed with superstition, incoherence and fragmentation, especially as a cultural resource for replacing the existing hegemony.

The schooling of children

Yet, oddly, in a footnote, Young (1971, p.43, note 39) calls on the authority of Gramsci when elaborating his claim that the traditional model of 'high status knowledge' is linked to 'what I have called the unrelatedness of academic curricula, which refers to the extent to which they are 'at odds' with daily life and common experience' (ibid., p.38).[5] However, it is strange that Gramsci should be thought relevant to substantiating this complaint that academic curricula are at odds with daily life. For him, academic curricula could not be other than 'at odds' with daily life and common experience as it manifests itself in much of common sense: 'Education is a struggle against folklore' (*Quaderni*, I, p.498). And if the cognitive raw material which the child brings to school consists of 'magical conceptions of the world and nature which the child absorbs from an environment impregnated with folklore' (ibid.), it is impossible to avoid the conclusion that its transformation into good sense requires the active intervention of specialists who function as authorities with reference to human knowledge, having a special claim, on epistemological grounds, to define what ought to count as educational knowledge.

As we have already noted, with reference to social class Gramsci does hint that no social stratum is especially privileged in having a monopoly of good sense. On the contrary, 'every social stratum has its own "common sense" and its own "good sense" ' (*Notebooks*, p.326, n. 5); that is, its own world view, an admixture of 'scientific knowledge' and its own particular lore or superstition. But it clearly is not Gramsci's point that it is the common sense of one social class which becomes formally recognised as philosophy for no other reason than that this class is hegemonic, in political control of educational institutions like the school. His appeal is rather to a theory of knowledge that distinguishes what is educationally fruitful from what is not in terms of epistemological rather than social criteria. Formal philosophy is not the legitimised common sense of any social class but the systematic world view of specialised workers – professional philosophers – whose authority derives from intellectual, not social criteria (*Notebooks*, p.347):

The professional or technical philosopher does not only

'think' with greater logical rigour, with greater coherence, with more systematic sense than do other men, but he knows the entire history of thought. In other words, he is capable of accounting for the development of thought up to his own day and he is in a position where he can take up a problem from the point which it has reached after having undergone every previous attempt at a solution. He has the same function in the field of thought that the specialists have in their various scientific fields.

And, as we shall presently see, Gramsci was quite happy to enlist in the service of the working class, those traditional intellectuals who had served the existing hegemony because, nevertheless, their services had been technical, not ideological; that is, their concern had been with the disinterested development of philosophy and science as logically rigorous, more coherent and systematic modes of thought.

It is these same specialists from the various fields of philosophy and the sciences, deriving their authority from training in the history and the logic of their specialisms, who are competent to define what counts as educational knowledge (ibid., p.341):

> Who is to fix the 'rights of knowledge' and the limits of the pursuit of knowledge? It seems necessary to leave the task of searching after new truths and better, more coherent, clearer formulations of the truths themselves to the free initiative of individual specialists, even though they may continually question the very principles that seem most essential. And it will in any case not be difficult to expose the fact whenever such proposals for discussion arise because of interested and not scientific motives. Nor is it inconceivable that individual initiatives should be disciplined and subject to an ordered procedure, so that they have to pass through the sieve of academies or cultural institutions of various kinds and only become public after a process of selection.

As this last sentence indicates, the conception that knowledge is produced by specially trained authorities does not rule out the notion (emphasised by some new sociologists of education) that all knowledge should be seen as the outcome of social interaction. Indeed, Gramsci himself reminded us that in those institutions concerned with the development of knowledge (e.g. university faculties, scholarly and intellectual journals and reviews, etc.) there are frequently conflicting theories and accounts of the phenomena under consideration: 'authority does not belong to one side ... the State as such does not have a unitary, coherent and homogeneous conception' (ibid., pp.338-9, 342). Nor does the fact that knowledge is the product of critical interaction between specialists (therefore always provisional, open to falsification) logically commit us to the view that any social interaction where knowledge is at issue (i.e. any particular manifestation of what Whitty calls 'doing knowledge') is as good as any other; that is, that no form of knowledge is superior to any other. Gramsci wrote, without reservation, of 'an educated class' whose 'historical function is to lead the popular masses and develop their progressive elements' (*Notebooks*, p.90).

However, if academic authorities are to decide, as for Gramsci, what counts as knowledge, the educational task is also one of connecting with common sense. Gramsci's traditional, academic curricular emphasis — his insistence upon the *precision* of learning — must be located within the context of a phase of *romance* where emphasis is on the need to connect with commonsense conceptions of the world as a condition of the fusion of theory with practice (ibid., pp.344-5; see also pp.160-5 below):

> From our point of view, studying the history and the logic
> of the various philosophers' philosophies is not enough.
> At least as a methodological guideline, attention should be
> drawn to the other parts of the history of philosophy;
> to the conceptions of the world held by the great masses,
> to those of the most restricted ruling (or intellectual)
> groups, and finally to the links between these various
> cultural complexes and the philosophy of the philosophers.

This amounts to saying that the curriculum should include the history of common sense as well as the history of philosophy. But the difficulty with this assumption, as Gramsci himself recognised, is the absence of a history of common sense, a history which he believed it is impossible to construct for want of documentary material. Inevitably this means that 'it is the history of philosophy which must remain the main source of reference' (ibid., p.331). Nevertheless, it is of the utmost importance for schooling to demonstrate that the philosophical outlook is not the intrusion into everyday life of an alien, esoteric, otiose knowledge, but is an essential dimension of universal human experience (ibid., pp.330-1):

> [it is] a criticism of 'common sense', basing itself initially, however, on common sense in order to demonstrate that 'everyone' is a philosopher and that it is not a question of introducing from scratch a scientific form of thought into everyone's individual life, but of renovating and making critical an already existing activity.

Thus, Gramsci insists upon the need for keeping in touch with the 'simple' as a necessary condition for 'elaborating a form of thought superior to 'common sense' and coherent on a scientific plane' (*Notebooks*, p.330). This mundane reference should be the source of philosophical problems: 'It is a matter of starting with a philosophy which already enjoys, or could enjoy, a certain diffusion, because it is connected to and implicit in practical life, and elaborating it so that it becomes the renewed common sense possessing the coherence and the sinew of individual philosophies' (ibid.). But there is no doubt that Gramsci regarded the task of elaborating a superior form of thought, necessary to raise common sense to the status of good sense, as the work of intellectual elites 'which cannot be formed or developed without a hierarchy of authority and intellectual competence growing up within them' (ibid., p.340; cf. also *L'Ordine Nuovo*, p.326).

Human knowledge, that is, is necessarily stratified. Gramsci's position is the opposite of that of Young, who asks us to believe that the revolutionary educational alternative is one where 'a curriculum is based on knowledge which is differentiated but not stratified' and leading one to consider 'whether the terms teacher, pupil and examination in the sense normally used would have any meaning at all' (1971, p.36). Consideration of this 'revolutionary' alternative curriculum 'suggests that assumptions about the stratification of knowledge are implicit in our ideas of what education "is" and what teachers "are" (ibid.). But it is precisely this 'false' (i.e. in Young's view) assumption which Gramsci himself makes. As we shall presently see, he *is* committed to the notion of an active teacher, a didactic pedagogy, a hard-working desk-bound pupil and a traditional view of academic standards and the function of examinations. In a different context, Young claims that these are themes beloved by the political Right and conservative Black Paper educationists: 'The arguments are presented, plausibly enough, not as the protecting of the interests of the few (which they are), but as the only basis for a just society for all' (Young and Whitty, 1977, p.4). But for Gramsci it was, indeed, the universalisation of these traditional, 'conservative' themes, and not some 'revolutionary' alternative education for the working class, which was potentially counter-hegemonic in fostering 'a just society for all'. It is precisely the initiation of working-class children into the traditional mainstream culture which, for Gramsci, is most likely to lead to 'a redistribution of rewards in terms of wealth, prestige, and power', Young's ostensible aim (Young, 1971, p.39). So far as the curriculum sustains the existing hegemony, it would be Young's and others' 'revolutionary' alternative that would be hegemonic, not Gramsci's emphasis upon tradition. Indeed, it is difficult to envisage what kind of social theory is at work for educationists who ask us to contemplate that ' "low" social class' might be 'treated as a source of desirable cultural identity' (Young and Whitty, 1977, p.3); hardly socialism in any of its forms and certainly not Gramscian socialism. It is Gramsci's persistent theme that a lower or subaltern class cultural identity — a sub-culture rooted in folklore — is an inadequate basis for the replacement of bourgeois by proletarian hegemony. Young's and Whitty's 'low' social class is inconceivable as a hegemonic class.

Curriculum as 'the entire thought of the past'

Gramsci was clearly committed to the notion that there is a historical culture which is the basis for the development of good sense and the point of reference for radical political activity. Responding to those of his socialist colleagues who argued that it was sufficient that the proletariat be prepared for the future merely through practical involvement in the class struggle (see pp.14-16 above), the young Gramsci retorted, to the contrary, that a knowledge of history was essential (*Political Writings*, p.13):

> If it is true that universal history is a chain made up of the efforts man has exerted to free himself from privilege, prejudice and idolatry, then it is hard to understand why the proletariat, which seeks to add another link to that chain, should not know how and why and by whom it was preceded, or what advantage it might derive from this knowledge.

In order to know oneself and to acquire self-discipline in pursuit of an ideal one must also 'know others, their history, the successive efforts they have made to be what they are, to create the civilisation they have created and which we seek to replace with our own' (ibid.). His mature conclusion in the *Notebooks* was that (*Notebooks*, pp.395, 400):

> The philosophy of praxis presupposes all this cultural past: Renaissance and Reformation, German philosophy and the French Revolution, Calvinism and English classical economics, secular liberalism and historicism which is at the root of the whole modern conception of life. The philosophy of praxis is the crowning point of this entire movement of intellectual and moral reformation . . .: the philosophy of praxis has synthesised the entire culture of the age.

However, Gramsci was not a historicist in the sense of believing in inevitable outcomes of the historical process. His attitude was that of 'voluntarism' the 'conviction that men could influence events, that historical developments were not pre-ordained, that in history you could not necessarily predict that the oak tree would grow out of the acorn' (Joll, 1977, pp.78-9; cf. Cammett, 1967, pp.60, 90). A knowledge of history contributed towards the development of self-knowledge, not to the assurance that one's liberation is inevitable. And what is true of the race in this macro sense is also true for the individual who 'is a précis of all the past'. Hence (*Notebooks*, p.353),

> it is not enough to know the *ensemble* of relations as they exist at any given time as a given system. They must be known genetically, in the movement of their formation. For each individual is the synthesis not only of existing relations, but of the history of these relations.

Gramsci also notes that the democratic ideology of progress — 'the widespread consciousness that a certain relationship has been reached between society and nature such that as a result mankind as a whole is more sure of its future and can conceive "rationally" of plans through which to govern its entire life' — only has meaning in reference to history (ibid., p.387):

> In the idea of progress is implied a possibility of quantitative and qualitative measuring, of 'more' and 'better'. A 'fixed' or fixable, yardstick must therefore be supposed, but this yardstick is given by the past, by a certain phase of the past or by certain measurable aspects.

Interestingly, Gramsci's last letter to his son, Delio, was an affirmation of the cogency of a study of history in illustrating this notion of progress as a product of human endeavour (*Lettere*, no. 415):

> I think you will like history, as I liked it when I was your age, because it deals with living men and all human problems. Contemplating all the men of the world, who come together in the society to work, struggle, and better themselves, cannot but please you more than any other thing.

Thus, the study of history in school is not merely an experience to be enjoyed for its own sake; it is, indeed, the essence of an education (*Notebooks*, pp.34-5):

> It provides a basis for the subsequent development of an historical, dialectical conception of the world, which understands movement and change, which appreciates the sum of effort and sacrifice which the present has cost the past and which the future is costing the present, and which conceives the contemporary world as a synthesis of the past, of all past generations, which projects itself into the future.

For Gramsci, then, the history and philosophy of this cultural past does not constitute an abstract, literate culture which, in Young's words, is 'at "odds" with daily life and common experience' (Young, 1971, p.38). In fact, as we have seen, it is Gramsci's persistent theme that 'academic' philosophy *is* appropriate to everyday life and, especially, to the interests and aspirations of the proletariat. And in his sense of 'philosophy' in which everyone can be 'a philosopher', having 'a critical and coherent conception of the world', he insists that nothing is more 'immediate and relevant' than having a historical perspective, a consciousness of 'the phase of development which it (one's philosophy) represents and of the fact that it contradicts other conceptions or elements of other conceptions' (*Notebooks*, p.324).

It is, of course, a commonplace of Marxist-Leninism that the founding fathers themselves took the view that the only adequate cultural resource for the development of revolutionary practice was what had served as the substance of the traditional humanistic curriculum: in Lenin's words, 'all that mankind has accumulated for the benefit of men' – 'the knowledge of all the wealth created by mankind'. Addressing the Congress of the Youth Communist League in 1920 on 'The Tasks of the Young Leagues', Lenin was clearly at pains to frustrate any initiatives in search of an alternative proletarian culture. Whilst insisting that the tasks of youth could be summed up in one word – *learn* – he also allowed that the 'important and material questions' were 'to learn what; and how to learn?' But his answer was unequivocal (1943d, pp.467-8):

> The tuition, training and education of the youth must be based on the material that was bequeathed to us by the old society. We can build Communism only on the sum of knowledge, organisations and institutions, only on the stock of human forces and means left to us by the old society.

He warned his listeners, 'you would be committing a great mistake if you attempted to draw the conclusion that one can become a Communist without acquiring what human knowledge has accumulated' (ibid.). Trotsky commended this cultural perspective of Lenin (he saw Leninism as 'the resultant and the highest achievement of the whole preceding culture') and himself concluded: 'Culture is the sum total of knowledge and skill — the whole knowledge and skill accumulated by mankind in its whole preceding history' (quoted by Shore, 1947, p.295, note 269). Lilge concludes that, although he would have resented the comparison, Lenin's concept of culture — 'that store of human knowledge' — was not essentially different from Mathew Arnold's 'the best that has been thought and said in the world' (1976, pp.566-7).

When he spoke of making 'educated people' of young people in schools, Lenin was, indeed, making quite conventional assumptions about what it means to be educated through initiation into the existing mainstream culture. There was no alternative proletarian culture available as a curricular resource. Proletarian culture could only be created by 'reworking' the traditional culture (1943e, p.485):

> Proletarian culture is not something that has sprung from nowhere, it is not an invention of those who call themselves experts in proletarian culture. That is all nonsense. Proletarian culture must be the result of the natural development of the stores of knowledge which mankind has accumulated under the yoke of capitalist society, landlord society and bureaucratic society.

And the same year, in a different context, Lenin insisted on the need to reject 'as theoretically wrong and practically harmful all attempts to invent a special culture' (ibid.; and cf. p.486). Croce noted that in *Anti-Dühring*, Engels had come 'close to postulating a proletarian ethics, and even a proletarian logic, dialectic, theory of knowledge'. He concluded, however, 'that this view of proletarian philosophy, religion, morality, science and art were empty desires and not reality, words and not concepts' (1946, p.114). And, obviously, Marxists like Lenin and Gramsci could not have called for an alliance of intellectuals and workers (see below, pp. 113-29) if they had dismissed traditional culture as bourgeois, in the sense of being 'false' or irrelevant to the needs of the working class.

In Lenin's view, Marx's doctrines themselves had only captured 'the hearts of millions and tens of millions ... because Marx took his stand on the firm foundation of human knowledge which had been gained under capitalism' (1943d, p.470). Marx admired the prodigious accumulation of data on behalf of Royal Commissions of Enquiry into social conditions in England and used this 'bourgeois social science' liberally in his own work. In his own words (quoted by Bernstein, 1971, p.51):

> We wish to find the new world through criticism of the old. Even though the construction of the future and its completion for all times is not our task, what we have to accomplish at this time is all the more clear: *relentless criticism of all existing conditions*.

Richard Bernstein comments on this (1971, pp.51-2):

> Marx's remarks help us to appreciate his life-long preoccupation with understanding *present* institutions rather than speculating about the future. Projecting future possibilities, speculating about the nature of utopian future societies, is idle and irrelevant. One must understand the tendencies inherent in present institutions .... Criticism is not a matter of arbitrarily *condemning* an institution or belief, but of understanding it.

But to understand something one must know it. Even, as Gramsci suggests, to supersede an existing mode of thinking — whether it be common sense or philosopher's philosophy — one must engage with it critically (*Notebooks*, pp.330-1). Thus he insisted that criticism of a culture, as a condition of cultural revolution, involved its mastery:

> In scientific discussion, since it is assumed that the purpose of discussion is the pursuit of truth and the progress of science, the person who shows himself most 'advanced' is the one who takes up the point of view that his adversary may well be expressing a need which should be incorporated, if only as a subordinate aspect, in his own construction. To understand and evaluate realistically one's adversary's position and his reasons (and sometimes one's adversary is the whole of past thought) means precisely to be liberated from the prison of ideologies in the bad sense of the word — that of blind ideological fanaticism (*Notebooks*, p.344 — here 'science is obviously

being used in a special, but historically familiar sense, referring to any organised body of knowledge).

But if there are occasions when one's adversary is the whole of past thought, better familiarise oneself as comprehensively as possible with 'truths already discovered'.

It is a fact that the younger Gramsci had, indeed, written of 'a proletarian culture (a civility), totally diverse from that of the bourgeoisie' and that 'there will exist a poetry, a novel, an art, a music characteristic of proletarian civility' (*Duemila*, I, p.553). But this promise of proletarian culture was in the future tense. It was not offered as a present point of reference for the schools but as a hope, an outcome of radical social change dependent, in part, upon those educational initiatives on behalf of the working class which Gramsci conceived as the transmission of the cultural heritage. In macro historical terms there are two phases with regard to culture: 'a phase in which it is still instrumental to the struggle and a second phase dedicated to creation, pure and simple' (Broccoli, 1972, p.51). The educational correlate of this is 'the strictly scholastic relationship by means of which the new generation comes into contact with the old and absorbs its experiences and its historically necessary values and "matures" and develops a personality of its own which is historically and culturally superior' (*Notebooks*, p.350). For Gramsci, cultural creativity (as Dewey also insisted) requires that the would-be innovator take a tradition into himself. History, philosophy, the arts and science, as well as being human activities, are also cultural capital, the product of earlier activity on the part of historians, philosophers, artists and scientists. Gramsci evidently subscribed to a view of human knowledge as objective – 'out there' – in Popper's sense of a 'third world' of knowledge 'totally independent of anybody's claim to know': 'the world of objective theories, objective problems, and objective arguments' and including 'the contents of journals, books and libraries' (Popper, 1972, pp.107-9). In the same way, 'culture is (for Gramsci) not only the subjective organisation of one's own internal ego, but is also objective, external . . .' (Manacorda, 1976, p.25). We have already noted that in its struggle against folklore the school must point to 'the simple and fundamental fact

The schooling of children

that there exist objective intractable laws to which man must adapt if he is to master them in his turn' (see pp.22-3 above). It was both 'a practical necessity' and 'an ideal requirement' that the socialist school should 'reach out to embrace all branches of human knowledge' (*L'Ordine Nuovo*, pp.451-3).

In his insistence upon the need for learning of truths already discovered, Gramsci emphasised learning not only as a process, but also as a *product*, a store of knowledge available to the learner as an outcome of his schooling. Part of his criticism of the 1923 fascist educational reform was of the 'progressive', idealist notions on which it was based. In particular, the reform was to replace a system where 'in an attempt to be objective, teachers stressed dates, names, figures and facts' (Marraro, 1936, p.8). The new emphasis upon opinion, belief, judgment, etc., Gramsci dismissed as reactionary. Displaying a nostalgia for the old secondary school, he spoke of its 'degeneration' being related to the rhetoric which was implicit in the new verbalism without a basis in concrete information. By contrast (*Notebooks*, p.36):

> previously, the pupils at least acquired a certain 'baggage' or 'equipment' (according to taste) of concrete facts. Now that the teacher must be specifically a philosopher and aesthete, the pupil does not bother with concrete facts and fills his head with formulae and words which usually mean nothing to him, and which are forgotten at once.

It is evident that Gramsci held a view of learning which is not inconsistent with the notion, now used pejoratively, of education as banking (in a different metaphor he emphasised the need for personal culture to be 'broad and well-grounded', *L'Ordine Nuovo*, p.493). And his notion that there is a cognitive 'baggage', which necessarily facilitates one's travels through the ongoing experiences of life, is echoed in Bourdieu's conception of 'pre-knowledge that individuals owe to the school' which is especially important for the proper understanding and appreciation of cultural artefacts (Bourdieu, 1973, pp.195-6; and cf. my own elaboration of this point, 1978, pp.153-7). Just as Bourdieu's French workingmen regretted that the school had denied them 'pre-knowledge' of the arts, some of Gramsci's working-class colleagues confessed to 'a new feeling of dignity and freedom when they read poetry or heard references to artists and philosophers, and they asked, regretfully, "Why didn't the school teach these things to us as well?" ' (*L'Ordine Nuovo*, pp.451-3).

However, it is also true that the young Gramsci had written critically of the 'habit of seeing culture as encyclopaedic knowledge, and men as mere receptacles to be stuffed full of empirical data and a mass of unconnected raw facts, which have to be filed in the brain as in the columns of a dictionary, enabling their owner to respond to the various stimuli from the outside world' (*Political Writings*, pp.10-11). But the problem which Gramsci was raising in this essay, titled 'Socialism and Culture', was that of how schooling could bring people to use knowledge in praxis (see pp.160-5 below) rather than in a mere display of erudition or as a status symbol. His mature conclusions indicate that this dismissal of encyclopaedic knowledge is not to be taken as a scorn for concrete facts. For as the essay just quoted goes on to insist, and as Gramsci's own educational history and erudition underlines, the danger of encyclopaedism lies not in having mastery of a vast array of facts, but in pedantry, in ostentatious intellectual display and the assumption that this confers social superiority (cf. Broccoli, 1972, pp.39, 43). Culture, Gramsci insists, consists not in erudition but in the 'organisation, discipline of one's inner self' (*Political Writings*, pp.10-11). Part of being educated consists of learning how to 'give an order' of one's own to the 'baggage' one accumulates (*Notebooks*, p.36). But, he concluded in the *Notebooks* (ibid.), 'With the new curricula ... there will no longer be any baggage to put in order.' Indeed, the very conception of an active learner requires that there is objective data to be structured. But 'the more the new curricula (i.e., those denying that there is information, facts, descriptions, formulas, etc. to be learned) nominally affirm and theorise the pupil's activity and working collaboration, the more they are actually designed as if the pupil were purely passive' (*Notebooks*, p.37). Here Gramsci has in mind that without the baggage of 'concrete notions' which the effective teacher

The schooling of children

transmits, 'education gets reduced to words without sense', especially at the secondary level where the new emphasis was upon student creativity, judgment, opinion. Without a concrete reference to what is often pejoratively dismissed as 'mere information', judgment and opinion is mere abstract rhetoric (see pp.173-5 below.) From the occasional glimpses he had of his own children's education, he sensed his elder son's had gone astray precisely because it had developed in him what he called an 'abstract imagination' instead of a 'concrete imagination', and he stressed the importance of initiation into 'a solid and realistic culture devoid of every element of rancid and stupid ideology' (*Lettere*, no. 402). In this letter to his wife, even allowing the possibility (which he himself did go on to acknowledge from want of proper information) that he was mistaken about his child's schooling, Gramsci is underlining that the danger is not so much that the school emphasises abstract learning, but that it fails to attend to the relationship which the abstract has to the concrete. An unacceptable education is not one which deals in abstractions but one which leaves the learner having 'words without sense', incapable of turning the abstract back upon the concrete, unable to cash abstractions in terms of the concrete environment in which life has to be lived and to which action necessarily relates: the school 'has to prepare young people who will have a complete intellect, ready to gather every aspect of reality . . . habituated to ascend from facts to general ideas, and with these general ideas to assess every other fact' (*Formazione*, p.92). This would stand as a description of Gramsci's own intellectual style: 'His intellectual method is one which involves replacing the false abstractions of so much Marxist theory by concrete case studies — not for him the "rise of the bourgeoisie", but the variety of rises and falls of a variety of bourgeoisies' (MacIntyre, 1975).

School assessment and examinations

However, not only is there this concrete intellectual baggage or equipment to be acquired; the extent and accuracy of its acquisition can also be evaluated. Gramsci's conviction that the thought of the past had to be mastered, even as an adversary, also led him to take an objective view of assessment and examination in school. There is a 'correct' view of the world — good sense — which it is the task of the school to transmit and which it was also its responsibility to transmit effectively. Hence, evaluation and examination is intrinsic to the functions of the school. There is no warrant in Gramsci for the sort of criticism of schools as 'answerlands' which one finds, for example, in the work of Holt. Indeed, far from anticipating one of the currently popular assumptions that there cannot be an examinable product of learning, Gramsci emphasised the importance of received knowledge and the capacity for reproducing this in an examination. In a letter to his mother commenting on his nephew's marks, he raised the school examination to the status of an initiation rite (Edinburgh Letters, no. CXXXIII):

> The first exam is a very important thing in life; Franco can say now that he has made his entry into manly society and has become a citizen because he has made an effort to let other people see what he has to show for his age, and these others have sat in judgment and their verdict has been favourable. It's a much more important thing than the first communion in my opinion.

And later, writing to his elder son shortly before his death, he underlined the importance of marks and grades: 'Now you have marks given to you every month, it'll be easier to see how you are getting on in general' (ibid., no. CXC). This last phrase, of course, indicated his belief that there is an intrinsically educational justification for marks and grades, as assessment, not least to enable the student to monitor his own progress. Notwithstanding superficial appearances to the contrary, examinations do not turn the learner into 'a passive and mechanical recipient, a gramophone record'. Gramsci's position was exactly that of Flew who, in the course of a recent attack upon those educationists who would abandon examinations on the grounds that they are anti-educational, concluded: 'assessment and examination in some form are essential to systematic education as such'. Part of Flew's reason for this assumption echoes Gramsci's letter to his son (Flew, 1976, pp.89, 91):

If, therefore, anyone is a genuine learner trying to master some piece of possible knowledge, or an authentic teacher trying to bring it about that someone else masters such an item of possible knowledge; then, necessarily, they must be concerned whether, how far, and how well they are succeeding. But they can scarcely claim to be this concerned if they take no steps to discover the answers to those questions. And the most general word for all such attempts is . . . 'assessment'.

However, Gramsci's advocacy of assessment and the awarding of marks was also instrumental. They served a social purpose in establishing the case for equitable arrangements for schooling. Hextal and Sarup have recently drawn on the concept of alienation in developing a critique of traditional evaluation procedures: 'A concrete example of the relation between evaluation and alienation resides in the process by which evaluation procedures separate man from man' (1977, p.157). Their objection to evaluation is to 'the particular form it takes, the way it is used to create and sustain hierarchies' (ibid., p.156). But Gramsci was insistent on the need to create such hierarchies in order to establish the claim to secondary schooling of socially disadvantaged children. His appeal to examination results was to emphasise that educationally relevant academic hierarchies traditionally often bore little relationship to socio-economic stratification. For him, alienation was already there in the class system; it was not a product of marks and examinations. On the contrary, the point of academic grading was to underline the educational inequities deriving from the social system. He wrote of the 'instinct of rebellion awakened by the fact that I, who had got ten out of ten in everything, could not go on studying, while the butcher's boy, the chemist's boy, the draper's boy, all rich men's sons were able to' (quoted by Fiori, 1970, p.26). For Gramsci, the separation which examinations achieved was the educationally relevant separation of the able poor from the less able rich (see below, pp.99-100). His appeal to the value of academic evaluation was on behalf of the gifted but disadvantaged child threatened with exclusion from academic institutions by educationally irrelevant economic criteria. And this is the very ground on which

The schooling of children

public examination systems were devised in the nineteenth century; as an instrument of fair and equitable competition in place of nepotism, patronage and privilege (cf. *Sotto La Mole*, pp.238-9). If this is an accurate perception of the origins of the examination system, then the politics of examinations relates to the substitution of relevant academic criteria for irrelevant social criteria in the allocation of social roles.

But Gramsci was also conscious of the limitations of examinations, especially when misused by being 'liberalised' in order to assess things other (e.g. creativity, aesthetic response, character development, etc.) than mastery of facts. Part of his polemic against the fascist educational reform of 1923 followed from the fact that it had, paradoxically, legislated to liberalise the examination system (Marraro, 1936, p.5):

> The reform had radically altered the underlying principle of examinations, and provided that the student should be judged not according to criteria of the past, but rather by those of the future; not for what he had done, but for what he was capable of doing; not by the quantity of information he was able to lay before the commission, but in the light of the maturity of mind and character that he displayed.

Gramsci believed this trend was dangerous because open to quite arbitrary decisions by examiners. If the school is concerned at all with the transmission of values it should, logically, abolish examinations entirely: 'to take an examination now [i.e. under the reforms of 1923] must be fearfully more chancy than before. A date is always a date, whoever the examiner is, and a definition is always a definition. But an aesthetic judgment or a philosophical analysis?' (*Notebooks*, p.36). In other words, Gramsci's conception of the proper function of examinations as assessing the student's mastery of 'concrete facts' hangs logically together with his insistence upon teaching as instructing and his conception of schooling as necessarily concerned with the acquisition of cognitive baggage or equipment which becomes the resource for subsequent self education and cultural innovation.

Educational method: school as work

Gramsci's insistence upon work as the key to social organisation and human culture is central to an understanding of his views upon pedagogical method:

> Civil and state laws govern men in the manner which is historically best suited to their dominating the laws of nature, that is to facilitate their work which is the specific way in which man participates actively in natural life in order to transform it and socialise it ever more deeply and extensively. One can say, therefore, that the educative principle on which the elementary school was founded is the idea of work, whose power cannot be fully realised expansively and productively without an exact and realistic knowledge of natural laws and without a legal order which regulates organically men's life in society ... The concept and the fact of work (of theoretical and practical activity) is the principle immanent in the elementary school,[7] since it is through work that social and State order (rights and duties) is introduced and identified within the natural order. (*Quaderni*, III, p.154; see also *Notebooks*, p.34)[6]

It follows that all education is vocational education (see below, pp.129-48). But, for Gramsci, the point was not only that school should introduce the child to work as man's fundamental cultural activity; for him, work is also intrinsic to the activity of learning. The emphasis which he placed upon instruction, and his rejection of the notion that school learning can be spontaneous or natural, inevitably commits him to a conception of schooling *as* work. It was in this sense of *being work*, that schooling had obvious vocational relevance for Gramsci. There could be no learning without effort, drill, even drudgery. In particular, discipline (probably externally enforced, albeit as a condition of self-discipline) is the key to learning (*Notebooks*, pp.37, 42):

> In education one is dealing with children in whom one has to inculcate certain habits of diligence, precision, poise (even physical poise), ability to concentrate upon specific subjects, which cannot be acquired without the mechanical

repetition of disciplined and methodical acts . . . it is also true that it will always be an effort to learn physical self-discipline and self-control; the pupil has, in effect, to undergo a psycho-physical training. Many people have to be persuaded that studying too is a job, and a very tiring one, with its own particular apprenticeship — involving muscles and nerves as well as intellect. It is a process of adaptation, a habit acquired with effort, tedium and even suffering.

In common with Whitehead who was writing at much the same time, Gramsci was in no doubt about the need for a stage of *precision* in the learning cycle. But he also saw discipline, drill and method in learning as preparatory, a training for the future demands of adult life: 'Would a scholar at the age of forty be able to sit for sixteen hours on end at his work-table if he had not, as a child, compulsorily, through mechanical coercion, acquired the appropriate psycho-physical habits?' (*Notebooks*, p.37). This view seems curiously outdated (the notion of sixteen hours at the table no doubt reflects his own habits of study under conditions of imprisonment) that in school one should train for the element of drudgery which is a necessary component of even the most interesting tasks; as is the notion that the entire child population should be rigorously disciplined because of the intellectual needs of a small minority. However, Gramsci seemed committed to the traditional conception of equality of opportunity, where the objective is the cultivation of meritocracy from amongst all the available talent. From that point of view there was logic in Gramsci's insistence that every child should be confronted with something of the rigorous demands which intellectual occupations impose (ibid., emphasis added):

> If one wishes to produce great scholars, one has to start at this point and apply pressure *throughout the educational system* in order to succeed in creating those thousands or hundreds or only dozens of scholars of the highest quality which are necessary to every great civilisation.

Of course, as we saw when discussing his attitude towards

literacy, Gramsci's insistence upon the need to produce an intellectual elite is also related to his belief that counter-hegemonic, working-class activity must be led by intellectuals who are organic to the working class itself (see also below, pp.113-29).

In the letters to his wife and sister, Gramsci returned repeatedly to the theme that their children's schooling should be disciplined, especially with reference to academic standards in the use of language. This response was apt to be triggered by receipt of letters from the children as, for example, one from his niece which evoked the comment: 'at Mea's age I should have died of shame if I had made so many spelling mistakes' (*Lettere*, no. 159). On a different occasion, he commended her ability "to express her feelings in spontaneous and lively phrases,' but he also complained that 'she commits a number of spelling blunders too great even for a scholar who is scarcely in the third year' (ibid., no. 113). We have already noted the importance which Gramsci attached to a stringent standard of literacy in the preparation of working-class intellectuals. But it was clear that he believed the basis of this had to be laid in the early schooling of the child. Spelling is repeatedly referred to as a '*pons asinorum*', ' "the ass's bridge" of a non-disciplined intelligence' (Manacorda, 1976, p.102). Thus it was not only a matter of children's needing habituation to the discipline of hard work: discipline was also implicit in the curriculum itself. School subjects (often themselves referred to as disciplines) impose 'didactive necessity': they 'have to be acquired through work and reflection' (*Notebooks*, p.42).

However, these austere conclusions about the strict disciplinary function of the school were Gramsci's mature reflections upon the education of the young. In 1924 he had written to his wife expressing a preference for the educational ideas of Rousseau over those of Lenin (Manacorda, 1976, pp.89-90). But in the early years of his imprisonment he began to entertain doubts about the Genevan conception of 'education according to nature'. In a series of letters in 1928 and 1929, his ambivalence was revealed in reflections upon the cultural implications of the newly invented Meccano, a set of which he had had sent to his son, Delio, as a birthday present. At first it seemed a good idea: 'The principle of Meccano is certainly excellent for modern children' (Edinburgh Letters, no. XXXII). But in a letter to his wife some months later he was not so sure (ibid., no. XXXIX):

> you ought to tell me how Delio is getting on with the Meccano. This is of real interest to me, because I have never been able to decide whether Meccano is the best modern toy for children or not, seeing that to a certain extent it seems to rob boys of their own inventive spirit . . . In general my feeling is that modern culture (American pattern) of which Meccano is an expression, has the tendency to make men rather dry, machine-like and bureaucratic, and to create an abstract mentality . . . .

Nevertheless, he was soon to conclude that the imperatives of the technological culture, of which Meccano was a symbol, were such that the claims of an education according to nature[8] were substantially diminished (ibid., no. XLVII):

> I'm rather afraid that a childhood like my own of thirty years ago is no longer possible today: . . . the radio and the aeroplane have destroyed forever Robinson Crusoe-ism which was the food for the daydreams of so many generations. The invention of Meccano in itself shows how the child of today is rapidly becoming more intellectual.

Gramsci's uncertainty about the educational implications of Meccano was but a particular example of the ambivalence he felt towards the doctrines of Rousseau which, he believed, were basic to the 'new' or 'active' school created by the fascist legislation of 1923.

In April 1929 he wrote of two ideologies which were 'fighting it out' in his head (ibid., no. XLII):

> whether to be Rousseauesque and leave matters to Nature which never makes a mistake and is fundamentally good — or on the other hand to be 'authoritarian' and to force Nature, introducing into evolution the expert hand of man, and asserting the principle of authority.

But in a letter to his wife of that same year, concluding that she had obviously been 'greatly influenced by Geneva and by the environment saturated with Rousseau,' he observed that he himself had 'wandered rather far' (ibid., no. XLVIII). In a note written at that same time, he characterised Rousseau's theory as 'a confused philosophy strung together on a series of empirical rules' (*Quaderni* I, p.114). It is evident that he had begun to attribute the deficiencies in the children's education (what he regarded as their extreme backwardness and childishness for their ages) to their suffering from the application of Rousseau's concept of negative education 'which does not stimulate development', 'a corrupted education because deprived of any element of didacticism or disciplinary constraint' (Manacorda, 1976, pp.93, 101).[9] As evidence of this backwardness he instanced the poor spelling and barren prose in the children's letters, the lack of spatial perception in his son Delio and his having gone uncorrected when learning to write from right to left (Manacorda, 1976, p.101). By now, his uncertainty about the educational claims of spontaneity as against authority was clearly resolved in favour of the latter. In a note written in the period 1929-1930 he concluded:

> It is imagined that the child's mind is like a ball of string which the teacher helps to unwind. In reality each generation educates the new generation, that is, forms it, and education is a struggle against the instincts linked to the elementary biological functions, a struggle against nature, to dominate it and create the 'contemporary' man of the times. If analysed, 'spontaneity' becomes ever more problematic (*Quaderni*, I, p.114; see also *Lettere*, no. 162).

He had come to believe that to emphasise spontaneity implies not only the abandoning of children to the casual, fortuitous influence of the environment, but also an abdication of the older generation's responsibility for education (Manacorda, 1976, pp.97, 213):

> Any attitude of respect for spontaneity, although apparently showing respect for the nature of the child, is in reality to renounce education, to bring up men according to human standards; it is the complete abandoning of the child to authoritarianism, or the objective pressures of the environment.

The schooling of children

Gramsci attributed the failure of older generations to accept their dominant role and their responsibility for preparing the young to succeed them to a manifestation of the spirit of 'après moi le deluge' (*Quaderni*, I, p.116). In this connection it is interesting that in response to what he took to be his sister's misunderstanding of his comments on his niece's poor academic attainment he wrote: 'It is obvious that my observations were not directed at Mea, but at those who educate and guide her' (*Lettere*, no. 189).

As we have noted, Gramsci rejected schooling based upon the negativism of Rousseauan naturalism, partly because of the evidence he believed he had of its effects in retarding the development of children in his own family. However, he believed that from a psychological point of view, emphasis upon the child's spontaneous learning was bound to be mistaken because, in terms of the unwinding metaphor just quoted, he concluded that there is no ball of string to unwind. He rejected the notion of innate human potential waiting to be realised and, instead, emphasised the existence of a determining environment in which, when he is abandoned to spontaneity, the child's development cannot but be fortuitous and chaotic. Writing to his wife he observed (Lawner Letters, no. 42):

> the conception you and others in the family have is far too metaphysical. You imagine that a baby contains the whole man potentially and that he must be helped to develop an already latent content, or the like. I believe, on the contrary, that man is an entirely historical formation obtained through coercion (not just in the brutal sense of extreme violence).

This belief necessarily also entailed the notion of an active parent or teacher, since 'the refusal to teach a child amounts to allowing his personality to develop haphazardly by incorporating principles and values chaotically from his general surroundings' (*Lettere*, no. 140; cf. also *Lettere*, nos. 162 and 202).

Gramsci's ultimate preference for authority and discipline has been dismissed pejoratively by some critics as Leninist (see, e.g., Hughes). However, summary dismissal of Gramsci's educational theory in this way does less than justice to the

The schooling of children

intrinsically pedagogical merits of his position. Recognition of the claims of authority in schools is shared by educationists to whom application of the 'Leninist' epithet would be absurd, despite some parallels between their own epistemology and conceptions of cultural transmission and those of Lenin. For example, one recent contributor to the 'conservative' Black Papers, Anthony Flew (whom we have already noted articulating a view of examinations consistent with Gramsci's position), has acknowledged parallels between his own critique of the idealism in the new sociology of education and Lenin's polemic against 'empiro-criticism' (1976, p.10). But, as a further comment in the same essay indicates, Flew is far from claiming to be 'a true Leninist' (ibid., p.27). That students of education as diverse as Lenin and Black Paper authors, as well as Gramsci and some modern liberal educationists, should emphasise the need in schools for authority, discipline and conventional academic standards need not divert us from a consideration of the intrinsic educational merits of this position.

Gramsci's notion of education as a struggle against instincts recalls R.S. Peters's notion of 'education as initiation' and his characterisation of the initiation process as akin to one of bringing the barbarians inside the gates of civilisation. But not only is untutored human nature unfriendly to civilisation; so also is Nature itself. It is central to Gramsci's educational theory that Nature is fortuitous in its coerciveness. Manacorda notes that he emphasised 'the coincidence of causality, mechanism, naturalness, chaos, in opposition to what is known and willed by man ... nature, that is to say environment, means fortuitousness and chaos' (1976, pp.113, 104). In a letter to his brother Carlo, Gramsci wrote: 'the environment does not justify anything. It seems to me that all our life is a struggle to adapt ourselves to the environment but also, and above all, to dominate it and not be overwhelmed by it' (*Lettere*, no. 162). With reference to the notion of the environment as teacher, and the claims of 'natural' learning, he had evidently reached a conclusion similar to that of T.H. Huxley, who condemned Nature as a brutal, stern, uncompromising and undiscriminating teacher (1893, p.85):

> Nature's discipline is not even a word and a blow, and
> the blow first: but the blow without the word. It is left
> to you to find out why your ears were boxed. The
> object of artificial education is to make good these
> defects in Nature's methods.

This is to call into question the much vaunted values of learning by experience and by trial and error: such learning can be nothing better than trial by ordeal, and the prescription never allows the possibility that the error may be irreversible, if not fatal. In educational theory, Naturalism has been a philosophical basis for free, spontaneous pedagogy. But both Gramsci and Huxley were implying that being free comes from breaking free of Nature's arbitrary constraints and from knowing those human artifices — natural and social science — which contribute towards understanding the environment as a necessary condition of escaping from its bondage.

This notion that education is an artificial function which serves to transform the given, natural environment — that the environment has itself to be 'educated' in order for it to educate others — is implied in Marx's well-known phrase that 'the educator must be educated'. Although this is often popularly assumed to refer to the need for a reciprocal relationship between pupil and teacher (such that the teacher approaches his work also as a learner), its context in the Third Thesis on Feuerbach suggests otherwise (see Appendix to Engels, 1941):

> The materialist doctrine that men are products of
> circumstances and upbringing and that, therefore,
> changed men are products of other circumstances and
> changed upbringing forgets that circumstances are
> changed precisely by men and that the educator must
> himself be educated.

Though gnomic, this thesis was a thrust against the fatalism of what now tends to be dismissed as vulgar Marxism, and was an emphasis upon the idea that although the environment shapes human life, this mould can itself be radically altered by human action. When applied to schooling, the Third Thesis implies not so much that the teacher must be

The schooling of children

'put right' (though he will, indeed, be wise to learn from his students, their parents, the local community, etc.), as that it is the teacher's function to 'educate' the environment. This means that he must select from the environment and appropriately organise those experiences which he believes will be educationally fruitful (having in mind factors like the learner's actual state of development), whilst also screening out whatever environmental manifestations would, in his view, be mis-educational in frustrating learning or promoting only learning which is intellectually, morally and aesthetically crippling. That, in an open society, there will be differences of opinion about what is educationally valuable does not relieve the teacher of this task of organising the child's environment in ways which he believes to be fruitful for learning. In part, the accommodation within the learning process of conflicting values will take place through application of the Third Thesis in the popular sense already noted, i.e. as implying a reciprocal educational relationship between teacher and student. Gramsci did, indeed, employ the Third Thesis in this way (*Notebooks*, pp.349-50).

It is in line with his conclusions about the indifference of the natural environment towards human life that Gramsci should urge upon his family the importance of concerned adults standing between the child and the environment (*Lettere*, no. 162):

> If you abstain from intervening and guiding her, by using
> the authority which comes from affection and family
> life, applying pressure on her in affectionate and loving
> fashion but nevertheless rigidly and inflexibly firm, it will
> happen without any doubt that the spiritual growth of
> Mea will be the mechanical result of the casual influx of
> all the stimuli of her surroundings.

This point of view is the reverse of that canvassed insistently by Holt — that children have a natural and powerful way of thinking and learning out of which they are trained by adults who 'teach them to think badly'. Implicitly, children would be better off if they never went to school but relied upon their own natural, untutored instinct for learning. Holt does not pretend to have empirical evidence for this claim and is candid that his assertion is an act of faith. However, he attempts to demonstrate the reasonableness of his faith by resorting to a natural metaphor. By nature, he argues, fish swim and birds fly; by analogy, he implies that learning is as natural in humans as is swimming or flying in other creatures. But swimming and flying presuppose, naturally, only the objective existence of water and air. These, unambiguously and alone, are the elements which have to be mastered in learning to swim or fly. But what is the correspondingly simple and uncomplicated environmental element which is the context for human learning and which would render Holt's naturalistic metaphor apposite? In fact, the environmental elements which challenge human learning are legion and complex as they combine to confront the learning human. Moreover, much of men's environment presents itself as non-natural symbols and signs (especially mathematical and linguistic) and little of human learning relates, nakedly, to the immediate physical environment which is water to the fish or air to the bird. This is to say (a factor which Holt neglects but which Gramsci underlines), that the environment to which children must adapt and learn to control is largely an artificial human construct, a culture. Culturally, the fish makes little out of water, nor the bird from air. It was with this sort of thing in mind, no doubt, that Gramsci took the view that 'one cannot speak of the nature of man, but only of a historically determined environment' (Manacorda, 1976, p.104). Manacorda links Gramsci's rejection of the pedagogical insistence upon spontaneity with his belief that man is 'a historical not a natural creation' (ibid., p.93). And, especially, the struggle against nature in which man is involved includes the struggle against human nature: 'it would seem to be a cruel fate for humans, this instinct that drives them to devour one another in place of bringing their united strength to bear on the struggle against nature' (*Political Writings*, pp.3-5). Hence, civilised or cultured human nature is a 'second nature' relative to the skills, knowledge, artefacts and institutions developed by a particular civilisation: otherwise, why would any century prior to the nineteenth not have given birth to soccer or baseball players of genius, to skilled computer programmers, to atomic scientists or, indeed, to Marxist revolutionaries? And it is because there are not such modes of activity which are natural to man, independent of the cultural environments of particular times and places, that the child's development cannot be abandoned to his own spontaneous reponse to his surroundings. In this respect, 'Gramsci insisted upon the opposition between natural gifts and those which can be acquired and therefore one ought to be made to acquire' (Manacorda, 1976, pp.116-17). Wondering why his son had been left to learn to write, spontaneously, from right to left like the Arabs, the Persians and the Turks, Gramsci asked, ironically, why the logic of this laissez-faire pedagogy had not been universally applied (Edinburgh Letters, no. LXXVII):

> Why was he forced, when he was smaller, to dress like other people? Wouldn't it have been more correct to leave his personality free not only as far as learning to write is concerned but in such matters as clothing as well: what right did anyone have to bring him up to follow convention so mechanically? Wouldn't it have been better to leave the articles of clothing dotted about the room and then wait for him to choose spontaneously: socks on his head, shoes on his hands, gloves on his feet etc.? Or better still, why weren't a little boy's clothes and a little girl's clothes both laid out near him, so that he could have freedom of choice in that as well?

Of course, it was Gramsci's position that these social norms and conventions were arbitrary, capable of change by human choice. But if the artificial human culture is open to modification by men (on the principle of the Third Thesis), to the very young it is as necessary, i.e. *given*, as the natural environment in being a constraint upon free, spontaneous development. For Gramsci the fundamental fact about human learning is that it relates to a cultural as much as to a natural environment, to an environment which is the product of human work and creativity. We have already noted Gramsci's distinction between natural and social law, the latter pertaining to an environment which man can adjust to his own purposes. And even as (in Huxley's metaphor) our knowledge of the laws of nature — our science — is less painfully acquired through artificial teaching than through a process of 'having one's ear boxed' by Nature herself, so is the social universe only properly and efficiently internalised by socialisation through others. As Berger and Luckman imply, when accounting for how and why adults contrive deliberate socialisation, the reason for the shape of this social, institutional world are opaque to all except the generation which initially devised the institution for its own purposes (Berger and Luckman, 1966, pp.56-63). This is why the older generation cannot 'renounce its responsibility to educate'.

A new generation may come to reject what it considers obsolete or tyrannous in the conventions and institutions it inherits, but the reason why things are as they are must be a necessary input into any consideration of social change. As we have seen, this need to know exactly what it is with which the revolutionary has to contend is the reason why Gramsci argued for a curriculum based upon 'truths already discovered'. And coming to grips with this human heritage in such a way that it becomes practically useful is something which demands discipline, work and attention to what Whitehead called the 'grammar of a subject'.

Instruction or education?

According to Gramsci, the rhetoric of the 1923 Italian educational reform had distinguished between the notions of education and instruction in a way which excluded the latter from the former, as though instruction were necessarily counter-educational, something 'narrow, formal and sterile' (*Notebooks*, p.24).[10] Gramsci's perception of the debate which the Gentillian reform engendered in Italy was that it diminished the importance of instruction in the teacher-pupil encounter, and his purpose was to stress its importance as a function of schooling (ibid., pp.35-6):

> It is not entirely true that 'instruction' is something quite different from 'education'. An excessive emphasis upon this distinction has been a serious error of idealist educationalists and its effects can already be seen in the school system as they have reorganised it . . . . There is no unity between school and life, and so there is no automatic

unity between instruction and education. In the school, the nexus between instruction and education can only be realised by the living work of the teacher . . . . If the teaching body is not adequate and the nexus between education and instruction is dissolved, while the problem of teaching is conjured away by cardboard schemata exalting educativity, the teacher's work will as a result become yet more inadequate.

Here Gramsci seemed to be taking a stance similar to that of Jacques Barzun who has argued, that there cannot be 'education without instruction' (1959, ch. 4) nor 'instruction without authority' (ibid., ch. 5). Indeed, the conservative Barzun repeatedly echoes Gramsci's theme of schooling as work, concluding that for a majority of students, who want an education 'free of work', 'the drudgery of fundamental discipline seems unbearable'. Affirming that schooling requires 'the exercises of serious work', he regrets that 'people forget that learning requires attention and assiduity'. In writing of the need for 'sobriety' in school work, he employs a word which recent Italian scholars of Gramsci have used to characterise his own attitude towards learning. Like Gramsci who complained of 'cardboard schemata exalting educativity', Barzun also saw the degeneration of schooling in the tendency to displace the notion of instruction by that of education (a word notoriously elusive of definition), believing it 'an evil day' when education replaced schooling and instruction, making the latter seem 'dry and mean, finally making unpalatable the ancient discipline of work'. And, as Gramsci saw in the romantic attachment to progressivism a failure of responsibility in the older generation to initiate the young into the existing culture, Barzun concluded that the attempt to achieve education without instruction involves 'the abdication of the teaching power'.

In the literature of education the concept of education itself is much less amenable to definition than is that of instruction and, in the passage from the *Notebooks* just quoted, the meaning which Gramsci wishes to attach to the word is not clear. In part, it seems, he wishes to stress that in becoming educated the pupil must actively structure what he learns in order to make it his own. But he is also insisting that instructing him, giving him the cognitive 'baggage' to put in order, does not turn him into a passive recipient. The rhetoric of Italian idealist educational theorists (as of some modern progressive educational rhetoric) did seem to assume that instruction is only appropriate to the pedagogy of the 'bucket and pump', of the notion that children's minds are empty receptacles waiting to be filled by teachers. But, whilst stressing the active role of the teacher in forging the instruction-education nexus, Gramsci was emphasising that there cannot be a passive pupil (whatever the assumptions of the teacher) and that instruction is not inconsistent with the notion that the pupil is actively assimilating and structuring the instruction he is receiving: 'For instruction to be wholly distinct from education the pupil would have to be pure passivity, a "mechanical receiver" of abstract notions — which is absurd' (*Notebooks*, p.35). Thus, if an instructor thinks he is transmitting information for storage in exactly the way in which he transmits it, he is deceiving himself. Despite his own intentions, the pupil's active intelligence will structure or use the knowledge in ways which suit his own purposes and dispositions, much as the worker uses inert tools to serve his own particular purposes: 'The "certain" becomes "true" in the child's consciousness' (ibid.). Here Gramsci had resort to a distinction made by Vico in his *Scienza Nuova* between *certum* and *verum*. Isaiah Berlin (1976, pp.99-123) finds that Vico failed to clarify the distinction thoroughly but, as employed by Gramsci, 'certain' appears to refer to the 'objective' knowledge created by others which is transmitted through instruction and assimilated, made 'true' for himself, by the learner. Thus, the 'certain' is the necessary raw material of the 'true', as is instruction for education. Gramsci underlined this point with reference to the study of grammar and logic (*Notebooks*, p.42):

> Formal logic is like grammar: it is assimilated in a 'living' way even if the actual learning process is necessarily schematic and abstract. For the learner is not a passive and mechanical recipient, a gramophone record — even if the liturgical conformities of examinations sometimes make him appear so. The relation between these

educational forms and the child's psychology is always active and creative, just as the relation of the worker and his tools is active and creative.

This is to argue that an activity pedagogy which stresses pupil intellectual activity (and not mere physical movement) must have recourse to instruction. Because teachers are didactic, pupils need not be passive.

The sense of education which is implicit in this insistence that instruction must not be separated from education is that of a learner making into his own the accumulated wisdom of the race. But a somewhat different sense is implied in Gramsci's notion that education, when bereft of instruction, is mere educativity. He was also drawing a distinction between education which (provided it encompasses instruction) is a proper outcome of schooling and 'educativity' which is something different and suspect. In his debate with the Italian idealist philosophers and educationists, educativity carries the sense of a moral enterprise, entailing that the learner internalises 'spiritual' values, those of religion and nationalism, for example (cf. Gentile, 1922, pp.239-40). It is this notion of education which Italian idealists wished to distinguish from instruction, the transmission of knowledge and skills, against which their polemic was directed (M.M. Thompson, 1934, p.12; and see below, pp.80-1). Education in this sense is not disinterested and it seems to be Gramsci's position (as it was Marx's and Lenin's —see below pp.176-7) that, as such, it is a function of adult life when the individual can choose his religious, ethical and political commitment in the context of a maturing life experience, especially as a worker. By contrast, the instruction of children in school should be disinterested with reference to this kind of moral dimension. As Broccoli puts it, Gramsci's intention was 'to disengage morals from pedagogy' (1972, p.93). Bereiter is a recent exponent of the view that the school should concern itself with instruction, education being a matter of adult choice (1973, pp.8-9):

> Education, therefore, insofar as it deals with these characteristics (i.e., beliefs, values, personal traits, etc.) of a person, should be provided only in the form of options for people who are old enough to choose how

they want to change themselves. Thus it would appear that education should not be offered as a public service to children but only for adolescents and adults.

This conclusion seems to fly in the face of the received wisdom that raising children (whether we call it schooling or education) is a moral enterprise. Peters, for example, insists that education as initiation is value impregnated in at least two ways. First, it is initiation into 'worthwhile' activities, involving ethical judgments about what knowledge and which skills have superior cultural values. Second, the processes of initiation ought to be conducted through pedagogic procedures which are morally unobjectionable. There is no evidence to suggest that Gramsci would have wished to disengage morals from pedagogy in either of these respects. Indeed, to the contrary, we have already argued that he did see some forms of knowledge as superior to others (pp.28-40). The disengagement implied by Broccoli is Gramsci's insistence that the school should be disinterested (itself a moral concept) with reference to the teaching of particular religious or political ideologies. There is no reason to believe that those who, like Peters, insist upon a relationship between morals and education, require education to be morally biassed in this second sense. Of course, it is evident that Gramsci believed that maintaining an open, disinterested stance with reference to knowledge (especially historical knowledge) would eventually point one unerringly in the direction of socialism. But, as we shall presently see, the deliberate organisation of learning in pursuit of revolutionary ends is a function of adult education. Meanwhile, for children, if upbringing is not to be a mere product of gratuitous encounters with the environment (especially a cultural environment saturated with folklore), then the 'living work of the teacher', as instructor, is essential to providing that systematic initiation into knowledge and skill which Gramsci took to be the distinctive function of the school.

Authority, teachers and teaching

Most of Gramsci's concrete references to particular teachers and to the teaching profession are critical (see, for example, his essay on 'The Pedagogic Ox', *Scritti Giovanile*, pp.26-7). This is especially true of his early writing where the polemic against professors was often bitter and derisory. We saw that he spoke of the professors in his own high school as incompetents who survived as teachers on 'brazen cheek' (pp.20-1 above). Elsewhere he referred to unskillful teachers who threaten the working class by dispensing to them 'attractive rubbish' (*Duemila*, I, p.741); 'or the scoundrelly professors, crammed with attractive junk, vendors of trifles, distributors of baskets of victuals which stuff the stomach but give no nourishment' (Manacorda, 1976, p.26). The young Gramsci concluded that he preferred peasants to professors. His mature conclusion in the *Notebooks* was that teachers were 'a rather poor expression – certainly not an *avantgarde*' of the ' "civic consciousness" of the nation' (*Notebooks*, p.35). One of his difficulties with Gentile's school reform was that the introduction of the new curriculum coincided with 'a general lowering of the level of the teaching profession' (ibid., p.36), an especially pessimistic conclusion in view of the expansion of the teaching profession which, he recognised, his own proposals for school reform would require and his conclusion that what was wrong with the traditional school was not its curriculum but its 'men'.

But Gramsci's critical evaluation of the quality of the teaching profession in Italy has to be separated from his positive view of the function of teaching in the educational process. From his criticism of teachers as he knew them, neither the young nor the mature Gramsci went on to pose a solution to the problem by concluding that students would be better left alone to teach themselves; nor did this criticism lead to any weakening of his view that the older generation has an active role to play in cultural transmission. Because the teaching function was often badly performed, this did not absolve adults from their responsibility to defend the immature against the fortuitous impact of the environment by initiating them into the existing culture, what Gramsci called 'the enriched patrimony of the past' (*Quaderni*, III, p.1730). Indeed, because so much of the child's time is spent 'abroad' in the world of people and the world of things, from which 'extra-scholastic' sources he tends to acquire his values, this makes that fraction of his time spent in school subject to deliberate adult didactic intervention 'much more important than is commonly supposed'. It is important that, contemporaneously with his brushing against the natural and social environments, he should be put 'in contact with human history and the history of 'things' under the control of the teacher' (ibid., I, p.114). This conception of an active, didactic teacher, committed to schooling as cultural initiation, is entailed by Gramsci's repudiation of spontaneity and autodidacticism with its denial of the solid virtues of 'order, discipline, coherence, intellectual sobriety' and its encouragement of 'sensual libertinism and fantasising' (Manacorda, 1976, p.171); and by his insistence upon the need for instruction and upon adult responsibility to nourish the younger generation towards 'maximum possible enlargement of its cultural horizons' in the face of an environment whose impact is casual, fortuitous, chaotic and capricious (cf. Manacorda, 1976, p.125).

If it is 'men', i.e. teachers, who are the weak link of the educational system, then insistence upon the importance of teaching also entails an improvement of the teaching profession. This, in turn, could be approached in two ways: by an improvement in teacher education and/or the recruitment to the profession of a different type of person. With reference to this last possibility, Gramsci had nothing explicit to say but, implicitly, his insistence on the need for developing a corps of organic intellectuals has relevance to the problem of improving the teaching profession (see below pp.113-29, 165-8). No doubt some organic intellectuals would be recruited to the teaching service. And his proposals for developing a system of comprehensive secondary education for all would make available a new source of teacher supply from amongst the 'subaltern' classes.

With reference to improving teacher education, that is, to the question of what constitutes effective teaching, Gramsci did not have much to say which is not entailed by his emphasis upon the teacher as instructor. However, in the teacher he expressed a preference for persistence and patience rather than charisma and histrionics, reflecting, perhaps, his own teaching style (see note 6). In the context of his insistence that the student needs to acquire cognitive baggage or equipment, he pays tribute to what he calls the 'mediocre' teacher who 'can devote a scrupulous and bureaucratic conscientiousness to the mechanical part of teaching', managing 'to see to it that his pupils become more informed', even if he does 'not succeed in making them better educated' (*Notebooks*, p.36). Indeed, it seems that Gramsci did not look for an improvement in teaching in terms of a science of teaching (though he did list 'research' as one of the economic costs of his educational reforms), but rather through acquaintanceship with what I have called 'contextual educational theory', especially philosophy, sociology and history of education (see Entwistle, 1971, p.101). In complaining that what was wrong with the traditional school was not its curriculum but 'men', he had in mind not so much the personal inadequacies of teachers as classroom practitioners, as the fact that they were the expression of 'an entire social complex' (*Notebooks*, p.36). The remedy was to make teachers more aware of 'the nature and philosophical content of their task' (ibid., p.35).

The notion that the problem with teachers is their being representative of an existing hegemony — 'an entire social complex' — is reminiscent of present-day rhetoric that schools are middle-class institutions, if not because they transmit bourgeois knowledge, at least because they emphasise middle-class values.[11] The remedy sometimes proposed for this is that schools should regard all sub-cultures as adequate and valid ways of life and, indeed, that teachers should learn to speak the language of the lower classes. However, the point of this insistence that teachers should become 'bi-cultural' is not always clear; whether, that is, it is intended as a means towards teachers' connecting with children from other cultures in order to transform their cultural perceptions and valuations, or whether the intention is more effectively to reinforce children's assumptions that their own culture is as adequate and valid as anyone else's. We have shown that Gramsci would have had no sympathy with the second of these intentions, the teacher's task being to emphasise the value of the culture of the school — the historical mainstream culture — against that of the home and the neighbourhood. With the first intention he would have had every sympathy.

The schooling of children

Part of a teacher's education, in pursuit of better understanding of the 'nature and philosophical content' of his work and as a means towards 'understanding the world of the child and the diverse worlds of individual children' (Broccoli, 1972, p.164), would consist in a study of folklore. However, in an essay commenting on a proposal that folklore should be part of the curriculum of the teacher's college, he insisted upon a number of important distinctions.

First, folklore was not to be identified simply with myth and legend, 'not, that is, as bizarre, an oddity, or something picturesque, but as something which is very serious and to be taken seriously' (*Quaderni*, III, p.2314). And folklore is to be taken seriously precisely because it is pervasive of daily life (not, as a picturesque oddity, something peripheral), being 'a conception of the world belonging to the subaltern social strata' (Manacorda, 1972, p.235; see also above, pp.28-40). In modern sociological jargon, folklore is the sub-culture of the lower classes. As such it has to be challenged and superseded.

The study of folklore by future teachers could only be justified on the assumption that the task of the school was to combat folklore, to eliminate 'the gap between modern culture and popular culture or folklore'. On the efficiency with which the teacher accomplishes this task depends 'the birth of a new culture amongst the masses'. Teachers must confront folklore, not disinterestedly as the object of aesthetic contemplation and a means towards their own personal cultural enrichment, nor as something to be revered 'which they ought not to destroy', but as an adversary to be fought and crushed. The school is in competition and conflict with other explicit and implicit conceptions of which not the least important and tenacious is folklore, which therefore ought to be 'overcome' (*Quaderni*, III, pp.2313-14):

> For the teacher, therefore, knowing folklore means knowing that other conceptions of the world and of life are influencing the moral and intellectual development of the younger generation, in order that he may uproot them and replace them with conceptions which are deemed superior.

In fact, as we have already noted, Gramsci believed that this task of systematically defeating folklore had already been undertaken in existing educational institutions. In the old elementary school (*Notebooks*, pp.33-4),

> [children] were taught the rudiments of natural science, and the idea of civil rights and duties. Scientific ideas were intended to insert the child into the *societas rerum*, the world of things, while lessons in rights and duties were intended to insert him into the State and into civil society. The scientific ideas the children learnt conflicted with the magical conception of the world and nature which they absorbed from an environment steeped in folklore; while the idea of civic rights and duties conflicted with tendencies towards individualistic and localistic barbarism — another dimension of folklore.

Teaching folklore to future teachers should merely serve to reinforce what had already been achieved in schools and colleges at every level in the educational system (*Quaderni*, III, pp.2313-14).

If teachers were to succeed in combating folklore, it was important that the nature of folklore, as something more than a picturesque oddity, had to be understood. Understanding it, however, depended upon a distinction being drawn between folklore itself (that is, 'the existence of folklore'), knowledge of folklore, and what Gramsci called the 'science of folklore' (ibid.). This last would seem to stand in a similar relationship to folklore itself as that between literature and literary criticism, for example. Without this critical apparatus (science of folklore), Gramsci implied that the teacher is ill-equipped to enter into the necessary adversary relationship with those cultural assumptions and socialised dispositions which the child acquires fortuitously through spontaneous interaction with the environment and which hinder the development of common sense into good sense. Earlier we noted his conclusion that for want of a history of common sense, the history of 'philosophy' is our only cultural resource. To some extent this defect would be remedied by the development of a science of folklore. Gramsci gave no indication what this might consist of but, in modern terms, something like a sociology of culture seems to be indicated along the lines developed by the Institute of Contemporary Culture in Birmingham (England) or in the work of writers like Raymond Williams, Richard Hoggart and Brian Jackson in England, and of Studs Terkel, Herbert Gans, Andrew Levinson, Sennett and Cobb in the United States. For teacher education today, especially in the case of teachers of the so-called culturally deprived, Gramsci's discussion of the place of folklore in the education of teachers suggests that contextual educational theory (philosophy, sociology and history of education) should have a component in which the work of this kind of writer and cultural research institute would be subject to systematic study. By extension, the schooling of ethnic minorities and immigrants should profit from the critical study of other cultures and the attempt to distinguish in these the elements of 'philosophy' and good sense from folklore. No doubt, the native cultures of Italian or Greek children in North American schools have their own peculiar mixture of folklore (as they might be, for example, from Gramsci's Sardinia) and Western high culture. The same would be true of Pakistan and Indian immigrant children with respect to Eastern cultures.

As we have seen, the point of teachers' knowing 'a science of culture' is that they should better understand what they are up against in the classroom. But if, for Gramsci, the school represents a better culture than the deficient folkloristic culture of the home and neighbourhood, the point of understanding folklore is also the development of a sympathetic relationship between teacher and child. Adapting Marx, Gramsci insisted that 'the educator must be educated', not merely in the sense of his having academic skill and knowledge, but also in the sense of being receptive to the insights to be gained from contact with those having other conceptions of the world and of life. The teacher's education is, in part, a matter of adopting the stance of a student in relation to his own pupils: 'The relationship between teacher and pupil is active and reciprocal so that every teacher is also a pupil and every pupil a teacher' (*Notebooks*, p.350). Having a 'science' of folklore is one and a necessary thing; but seeing folklore through the eyes of those whose conception of the world it is, is not less of an educational experience for the open-minded teacher. Broccoli emphasises that

The schooling of children

although for Gramsci the sediments of folklore must be eliminated, he recognised that these exist 'for historical reasons which can be neither ignored nor violated' (1972, p.178). The child's commonsense perceptions, permeated with folklore, 'should be approached respectfully, in order not "to mortify his spontaneity" ' (ibid., p.179). (In passing, it is important to emphasise that Gramsci did not wish to stifle the imagination of the child by denying him access to 'folklore' in its other sense, embracing myths, legends, fables, etc., which are the tales transmitted from generation to generation: his own resort to folklore of this kind when communicating with his sons indicates his positive evaluation of story telling as an aid to the development of the imagination − cf. *Lettere*, nos 240, 247, 274, 301; in prison he had translated from the German some of the fables of the brothers Grimm − see *Lettere*, no. 240.) The point of teachers' learning a science of folklore − a sociology of popular culture − would be the better to connect with their students with a view to developing their understanding of both the values (the component of good sense) and the limitations (the component of superstition and folklore) in their commonsense view of the world. As Broccoli puts it, one consequence of insisting upon there being a reciprocal educational relationship between teacher and pupil (such that the teacher is also a learner) is that the teacher is not then 'an entity which is already given', but one who is developing his understanding of the contradictions and tensions implicit in the educational nexus (1972, p.165).

Nevertheless, the assumption that teachers should also be learners and, hence, still developing as human beings, in no way invalidates the requirement that they also be authorities: masters not only of pedagogical skill, but also of specialised knowledge superior to the common sense (impregnated with folklore) which the child brings with him to school. From this point of view, as authority, the teacher is a special case of the older generation whose function is to oppose the 'folklore' of childhood (e.g. Piagetian pre-operational modes of thought) with the good sense which is the accumulated wisdom of the race. Such conceptions of the adult's role are apt to be dismissed as paternalistic. No doubt this term is rightly employed, pejoratively, in reference to situations where one adult group assumes an attitude of superiority in claiming to know what is good for other adults; and, especially, where other adults or social groups (e.g. primitive peoples) are offered a diluted culture on the assumption that they have, as yet, insufficient capacity for a liberal education (see *Quaderni*, II, pp.366-8). But paternalism is an appropriate attitude in parents and, logically, in parental surrogates like teachers. Any relationship of the kind, parent-child, teacher-pupil, master-disciple is necessarily asymmetrical and authoritative, the first party to these relationships being assumed to have insight, foresight, knowledge, skill or experience which is not, at that time, available to the latter. Without this claim by one party to 'knowing better', there is no logical basis for our using any of these terms as descriptions of human relationships. And the rider that the educator must also be educated by the learner does not blunt this point. For whatever it is that learners teach to teachers, it can never be the very skill or knowledge which learners and teachers come together to learn and teach, respectively. If it were, the roles would, logically, be reversed.

However, as Gramsci acknowledged, teaching will inevitably generate opposition: conflict is 'inherent in every educational task' (*Quaderni*, I, p.115). The parent-child, teacher-pupil relationships carry within them their own dialectic. Gramsci was in no doubt that the conflict of tradition with spontaneity is necessary to development of the superior culture which the new generation will eventually articulate. If it is the new generation which must eventually bring about this cultural innovation, it cannot avoid the confrontation with tradition: 'The older generation, it seems possible to conclude, is for Gramsci the document, the history, the fountain of ideas about the world which ought to be superseded.' But to disregard this historical 'document' 'precludes having knowledge of precious elements of one's own personality; that is, renders impossible the conquest of oneself and of past history through progressively taking hold of knowledge of one's own role and of the human condition' (Broccoli, 1972, p.158).

Elsewhere, with reference to justification of the teacher's authority, I have drawn a distinction between authority conceived as a categorical imperative (which, in Kant's words,

The schooling of children

'commands a certain conduct immediately, without having as its condition any other purpose to be attained by it') and authority conceived as a hypothetical imperative (something 'not commanded absolutely, but only as a means to another purpose') (Entwistle, 1970a, pp.63-4). As this last, the justification of authority is technical rather than moral. We assess a person's claim to authority by reference to his knowledge, skill and experience, and by assessing whether these do, in fact, contribute towards the purposes of those who are asked to submit to his authority. This kind of distinction seems to be implicit in Gramsci's conception of 'technical, specialised authority' as opposed to 'arbitrary' authority (*Quaderni*, III, pp.1706-7). In these terms, the teacher's is a technical, specialised authority, vested in him by virtue of his knowledge, skill and experience. And, when seen in relationship to Gramsci's commitment to disinterested discussion, disciplined and methodological reading and research, and the simple and clear expression of one's convictions (see pp.18-20 above), such technical authority is the source of its own dissolution. As Borghi put it: for Gramsci, imposed discipline 'was the instrument of ascent towards and conquest of autonomy' (1975, p.225). It is a self-destructive authority which insists upon others acquiring the disciplinary tools which are the condition of their becoming authorities themselves. Indeed, lifelong learners are a more likely outcome of an authoritative insistence upon the acquisition of these disciplined dispositions than of the assumption that 'learning how to learn' results from leaving the learner undisciplined and untutored, with unbridled freedom to follow his own inclinations. That is to argue that the purpose of authority can be liberal, neither arbitrary nor repressive. Indeed, Gramsci did make a link between democracy and technical specialised authority (ibid.). And we turn now to examine the possibility that authority, so conceived, is a safeguard against political authoritarianism of the kind which attempts to compel by addressing the emotions, without recourse to explanation and appeal to understanding. Is there, in fact, a connection between Gramsci's suspicion of spontaneity in schooling and his hostility to Fascism and the fascist school reform of 1923?

Education and Fascism

Gramsci's insistence upon the need for didactic, authoritative teaching, as well as disciplined application to academic work by the learner, was his response to the fascist educational form introduced in 1923 by Gentile, Mussolini's first Minister of Public Instruction.[12] One important component of the reform (introduced by the former socialist, Lombardo-Radice, who became Director General of Elementary Education under Gentile) was the organisation of elementary education along progressive lines (Borghi, 1960, pp.243-4, 256). Faced with this fact, we encounter yet another paradox. For it is the conventional educational wisdom that a spontaneous, active pedagogy is liberal, appropriate to a democratic society, whilst the teacher-initiated and structured transmission of academic knowledge is dismissed as authoritarian, even fascist, in its implications for restricting freedom of thought and autonomous personal growth. Apparently, therefore, we need to account for two mistakes: Fascism's error in attempting to service an authoritarian political regime with a liberal educational reform, and Gramsci's failure to appreciate that his commitment to a critical approach towards the cultural heritage requires a pedagogy which encourages student self-activity and eschews didacticism. With reference to the possibility that the regime was mistaken, Borghi has concluded that the 'efforts to introduce progressive educational methods into the Italian elementary school were in conflict with the authoritarian tendencies of the fascist government and were condemned to sterility' (1960, p.256; cf. ibid., p.248, on a similar consequence of the reform as it affected the universities). In terms of the notion that the mistake was Gramsci's, the following discussion argues that, to the contrary, his implication that a thoroughgoing, child-centred progressivism is friendly to political authoritarianism was a prophetic insight which cannot be ignored in the current debate about the respective merits of free as against structured learning, or the relationship between political socialisation and different pedagogical styles. By the same token, if Gramsci was not mistaken, neither were the Fascists, and Mussolini could claim without self-contradiction both that his government's educational reforms 'were the most Fascist of all the Fascist reforms' and that they were progressive (Hibbert, 1975, p.62; see also Marraro, 1936, p.299; Minio-Puluello, 1946, p.123).

In the present day when memory associates it with phenomena like the Holocaust and use of the word 'Fascist' is almost always pejorative, it is difficult to imagine that Fascism could ever have been styled 'progressive' in any sense, or that it could have evoked anything but antipathy in the liberal-democratic world outside the fascist states themselves. In the modern world the ideology of Fascism is repugnant, whilst fascist political regimes attract widespread hostility. But in the 1920s and early 1930s this was not the case. Nolte argues that during the first two years of the regime, Mussolini himself had no intention of being anything other than 'the head, not the dictator, of a social democracy' (1965, p.217). His first Cabinet included men from all the political parties and contained only four Fascists (Hibbert, 1975, p.51). It was the popular revulsion at the murder in 1926 of the popular Socialist deputy, Giacomo Matteotti, which led to the withdrawal of the opposition from the Italian Parliament and made fascist totalitarianism inevitable. It was from this date that imprisonment (including Gramsci's) or exile became the fate of Fascism's opponents on the Left. But much of the rest of the world continued to take a benign view of the Italian political situation. M.M. Thompson's judgment, made with reference to the fascist educational reforms, that 'the Fascist movement is one of the most striking social, political and cultural phenomena of our time' was certainly not intended as negative criticism (1943, p.17): neither was it unique. Hibbert chronicles the sympathetic reception accorded Mussolini by all shades of opinion in the Western democracies. In Britain, statesmen from Churchill to Lloyd George and newspapers from the *Daily Mail* to the *Manchester Guardian* (which later joined the campaign for Gramsci's release from prison) rendered favourable judgments which 'were not exceptional verdicts'. Moreover 'in America the praise was as emphatic as it was in Europe,' the President of Columbia University, for example, concluding that 'Fascism is a form of government of the very first order of excellence'. Hibbert concludes that 'few men ... were not favourably impressed' (1975, pp.95-9; see also Nolte, 1968). Indeed, the critical literature of Fascism often saw it, as large numbers of the Italian people had initially perceived it, as 'merely a slight flaw which was not too great a price to pay for the return of order and security' (Nolte, 1965, p.214; cf. also Hibbert, 1975, p.46). Fascism might have faults, and no doubt its development was 'frankly antidemocratic', but 'as a matter of fact in their negative or failing aspects there is not much to choose between either the Fascist or the democratic states' (M.M. Thompson, 1934, p.42).

Especially in the United States, Gentile's educational reforms were appraised as a positive, vigorous, creative development, of widespread interest beyond the boundaries of Italy itself (see for example, Duggan, 1929; M.M. Thompson, 1934). In these contexts the word 'Fascist' is often merely descriptive, rarely pejorative, and accounts of the principles underlying the reforms do, indeed, read like summaries of progressive educational theory. Marraro concluded that (despite 'Fascist aberrations') Gentile's educational aims reflected those of the great educators in being concerned with spiritual development rather than transmission of knowledge (1936, p.4; see also Codignola, 1930). The schools before Gentile are described in terms which are reminiscent of those in which advocates of progressive education denounce conventional schools:

> The various subjects taught were divided into watertight compartments, as though no connection existed between history, literature and philosophy, between Latin and Greek grammar and the Latin and Greek classics, or between the latter and Italian literature. The boys were made to write compositions on copy book maxims, with no relation to real life or to what they could be expected to know anything about. Their learning was based on textbooks containing cut-and-dried facts, stereotyped judgments and epithets applied to periods of history, civilisation, and historical personages and tables of racial geneologies. (Villari, 1926, p.176; and cf. Marraro, 1936, p.14; M.M. Thompson, 1934, p.8).

By contrast, Gentile 'was determined to educate the minds of the pupils and teach them to study, learn and assimilate and not merely to cram their brains with disconnected facts ... with notes and facts and stock phrases in order to secure diplomas and degrees' (Villari, 1926, pp.179, 174). And again, 'The school as organised by Gentile aims to educate the whole man: the physical, the social, the aesthetic, the religious, the intellectual aspects, each in a manner appropriate to it' (Marraro, 1936, p.301; and cf. p.56). So much does this reflect the conventional, progressive educational wisdom that it raises the questions of how far, and in what sense, Gentile's educational theories and reforms can be categorised as fascist at all. On this point the reactions of his Italian contemporaries were mixed.[13] One response to what looks like a confusion of means and ends (the pursuit of political authoritarianism through educational liberalism) is to wonder how far the 1923 reform of the elementary school was effected in practice. Even if appropriate documentary evidence on this point were available,[14] it is beyond the scope of this discussion to examine that question in detail. It is sufficient to recall that a decade after the reform observers of the Italian school system were praising its attachment to both progressive education and to fascist principles. And the question is whether, even in principle, the two are compatible, as Mussolini assumed. Both Broccoli (1972, p.173) and Manacorda (1976) suggest that Gramsci's own uncertainty about how exactly the Gentile reform was being implemented in Italy led him to direct his polemic against spontaneity and activity at the founding fathers of the 'new' education, that is to question in principle its educational values.[15]

A further problem in attempting to find fascist implications in this 'new', active education, aiming to substitute pupil self-activity for the alleged didacticism and rote memorisation practised by the traditional school, is that it was not unique to Italy. As well as being at its zenith in the USA, it was practised in the USSR for a period in the 1920s, a fact which disturbed Gramsci (Edinburgh Letters, no. CIII). The 1920s also saw the evolution in Britain of the progressive primary school in the spirit of the slogan, in the Hadow report of 1931, that 'the curriculum is to be thought of in terms of activity and experience rather than of knowledge to be acquired and facts to be stored.' Gramsci based his own

The schooling of children

criticism of the new pedagogy, in part, on a review of Carleton Washburne's *New Schools in the Old World*, a comparative study of individual progressive schools in England, Belgium, Holland, Germany and Czecho-slovakia (*Quaderni*, II, pp.1183-5). Clearly, in the inter-war years throughout Europe and North America, the new, active, progressive educational ideas were in the air. But, then, so was Fascism; indeed, Nolte has argued that it was the characteristic feature of the era: 'we cannot do otherwise than call the era of the world wars an era of fascism' (1965, ch. 1). But for Gramsci — as for countless others with the passage of the inter-war years — Fascism came to appear not so much an interesting socio-political experiment (a kind of political Band-aid covering up democracy's scars) as a tyranny to be resisted in persecution and suffering. And his grappling with what he took to be Fascism's espousal of the new, active education, as he grappled also and concurrently with its political tyranny in Italy, suggests that he saw a connection between the two; that is, between political authoritarianism and the educational dogma of free pupil activity, with its denial of teaching as concerned with transmission of information which needs to be acquired by the learner as a cognitive resource necessary for critical engagement with the educated and well-informed adversary, and for the creation of a cultural and political counter-hegemony. As Borghi shows, those responsible for the fascist educational reform made a great deal of play with the notion of liberty, thus contributing to that 'mental confusion which induced many Italians into accepting Fascism as a liberation movement' (1960, p.237).

The defence of what is often pejoratively dismissed as 'information mongering' or 'educational banking' is precisely that an innovative, democratic society requires not merely 'spontaneity', but also citizens who are well informed. And being well informed means having information, storing knowledge and facts, the importance of which the rhetoric of the 'new' education denied and which modern progressive educational theory still denies. The admirers of Gentile's reforms, critics of the traditional Italian school, took it as a virtue that the new 'teaching is formative, not informative' (Marraro, 1936, p.18). And this moulding function is seen as the antithesis of an informing function: 'the Italian school of today does not limit itself to the imparting of mere information and to the furnishing of cultural instruments. Its aim is to mould and fashion souls . . .' (ibid., p.25). The mischief here is not that of concluding that education should be formative (indeed, Gramsci himself repeatedly employed the same Italian equivalent in characterising education) but in the notion that formation occurs aside from the learning of information about the universe. That is, the importance of an informed formation, which would be the condition of self-discipline (formation by one's self) and which was precisely Gramsci's position, is denied. Implicitly, when people are well informed, this gets in the way of 'fashioning their souls'. And that is precisely the point of an educational theory which denies the imperative to engage with objective knowledge, which ridicules memorisation, thus making the learner the prisoner of the present and, if the political present is a tyranny, leaving him without cognitive resources to question the propaganda that what exists is the best of all possible worlds: 'the fascist school and press are created (or tolerated) by the state. They are essentially organs of propaganda not criticism. It follows that public opinion is essentially a matter of emotion rather than of information' (Schneider and Clough, 1929, p.200). Self-styled, radical, progressive rhetoric often does, indeed, tend to elevate the emotional life above the intellectual and cognitive.

The control of information associated with Fascism is the *denial* of information, even of its own history. Nolte describes Italian Fascism as 'that movement which lacked the courage to acknowledge its real prehistory' (1965, p.243). He had in mind, particularly, the fact that for twenty years the bound volumes of the newspapers in which Mussolini had practised journalism could not be borrowed from Italian libraries. It is not too much to claim that a political system which, thus, denies access to information is well served by an educational ideology whose polemic constantly derides the acquisition of information and which elevates the experience of the immature above 'knowledge to be acquired and facts to be stored'. The political authoritarian who would form the young with an emotional disposition in favour of his own ideology does well to canvas the merit of ignorance, the value of not having a memory of the past or information about contemporary social and cultural alternatives. His ally is not the schoolmaster functioning as authority and requiring the learning of the facts of history, geography, or science, but the anonymous teacher encouraging spontaneity and 'autodidactism' which Gramsci criticised precisely because of its repudiation of the notion of cultural transmission. Indeed, his insistence upon the school's task as that of combating folklore through the teaching of philosophical and scientific 'good sense' is understandable in view of the assertion of fascist intellectuals that 'miracle and mystery', rather than reason, are what nurture societies (Karier, 1967, ch. 10). If, as Nolte argues, the style and methods of Fascism require 'the unshackling of primitive instincts, the denial of reason, the spellbinding of the senses by pageantry and parades' (1965, p.20), then it is understandable that fascist education should emphasise the value of the spontaneous, natural and untutored response of the individual to his social environment. It should not strain credulity at all to argue that democracy, above all, is dependent on the well-informed citizen and is ill-served by schooling which eschews the disciplined transmission of information in favour of the alternative of leaving children to follow their own spontaneous dispositions. It is difficult to see the point of emphasising the value of freedom of thought without also stressing the need to learn the cognitive repertoires which liberate thought, or of a concept of freedom of action without there being knowledge of the manifold alternatives which confront the human agent in a modern society. In fact, sympathetic outside observers of fascist education in Italy (like Marraro) were quite consistent in praising the denial of facts to children in school whilst accepting the fascist doctrine that the individual's real liberty consisted in his dissolution within the totalitarian nation state.

We have seen that for Gramsci, spontaneity ('the act as such, unaccompanied by any objective consciousness or self-reflection', *Notebooks*, p.372, note 66), which was not rooted in knowledge of a cultural tradition, leaves the individual a prey to the fortuitous, chaotic and arbitrary impact of the environment. Another Italian critic of Fascism also underlined its celebration of spontaneity and its ideological kinship with the rhetoric of progressive education (M.M.

Thompson, 1934, p.43, quoting Crespi):

> Fascism is just activity for activity's sake, the negation of any standard of truth beyond the capacity of being and doing all that one succeeds in being and doing at any moment. It is the apotheosis of immediacy, of passing impulse, of uncriticised and uncriticisable self-assertion considered as synonymous with unlimited freedom.

Mussolini himself underlined the political utility of immediacy as against reflection when he argued that the Italians 'should not try to understand Fascism, but to experience it' (Hibbert, 1975, p.58). And those educationists like Lombardo-Radice whom Borghi (1960, p.243) assumes were destined to fail because of their equivocation and oscillation between liberalism and authoritarian statism may, indeed, have grasped intuitively that the sort of educational rhetoric which celebrates experience and denies the place of information — about both the contemporary universe and the cultural tradition — in the classroom is an ideology which is not unfriendly towards the development of political authoritarianism.

The theme that progressive education has links with Fascism is not entirely unfamiliar in the theory of education. G.H. Bantock once argued that the late Senator Joseph McCarthy's witch-hunt against alleged 'unAmerican activities' in the 1950s was explicable 'when associated with the mental climate induced by Deweyism over the last fifty years'. But the relationship between the two is not a logically necessary connection. Progressive educationists are rarely consciously committed to Fascism. On the contrary, they are usually genuine in their belief that the schools should make a contribution towards individual freedom. The danger lies in the extremism of the progressive polemic which, being usually counter-cyclical in intention, is the vociferous expression of a half-truth, as Gramsci himself recognised (see below, pp.105-7). The difficulty about espousing freedom as an educational aim is that freedom is essentially a negative concept, signalling an absence of restraint. It is not so much something one possesses as a condition in which others do not dominate, dictate or circumscribe one's thought and action. In that sense, freedom cannot be learned in school or anywhere else.

The schooling of children

It depends upon whether and how other people exercise power in relation to oneself. When educationists speak of 'learning to be free' or of 'education for freedom', they have in mind that remaining free requires an ability to recognise threats to one's liberty and, beyond that, they are concerned that a person should acquire resources which contribute to the 'use' of freedom; that is, for organising his life in ways that are productive or creative. When there is talk of freedom as something positive (freedom 'for' or 'to' rather than 'from'), this is a recognition that being free may lead to nothing more than idleness and that people ought to be spending their time productively, perhaps creatively. But such 'positive freedom' requires an awareness of what forms of human activity are possible and of the kinds of knowledge and skill which their performance entails. Thus, both as a defence against tyranny and as an avenue towards purposive activity, 'education for freedom' requires more than the encouragement of untutored, spontaneous responses to the environment. In its positive sense of having knowledge and skill appropriate to autonomous, creative activity, freedom can only be an *outcome* of schooling, not its major resource. As one Italian Gramscian scholar puts it: 'Liberty cannot be a point of departure; it ought to be a point of arrival' (Motzo, 1969, p.251).[16]

Thus, it is arguable that to emphasise discipline, intellectual order and the authoritative transmission of 'the thought of the past' is to inoculate the learner against political authoritarianism, as well as to transmit the skills and knowledge necessary for the pursuit of radical social change (*Duemila*, I, p.47):

> The struggle against capital develops on three fronts, the economic, the political and the ideological. But in reality these fronts reduce to a single one, that is of 'knowing' which supersedes 'spontaneity' and which gives the worker the understanding of the conditions in which he struggles, of the fundamental tendencies which operate in the system of relationships, of the process of development which society undergoes to sustain within itself irreducible antagonisms etc.

The schooling of children

Politics and schooling: correspondence or contradiction?

A polemic against an active, free, spontaneous pedagogy and the justification of intellectual discipline and teacher authority by a political radical like Gramsci helps to focus the respective theoretical merits of a correspondence as against a contradictory model of the school (see Bowles and Gintis (1976) for elaboration of both models; cf. also Karabel and Halsey (1977)). Put briefly, a correspondence model sees the school as a microcosm of the larger society: its organisation and social relationships accurately reflect the economic, political and social norms of the wider society and its disciplines and pedagogical routines socialise the young towards acceptance of the economic and social *status quo*. As we have seen in discussing fascist education, the conventional educational wisdom is that there is a simple correspondence between political regimes and particular modes of school organisation. Thus, an authority-based, teacher-initiated curriculum and a didactic pedagogy are assumed to be fertile for the development and maintenance of political authoritarianism. On this assumption, no distinction is drawn between authority and authoritarianism, and the traditional school is often simply dismissed as a fascist institution. The didactic teacher is assumed to correspond to the political dictator applying censorship to the media of communication, telling people what they ought to think and employing repressive disciplinary methods to ensure that there is no expression of opinion or political activity unfriendly to the regime. Similarly, it is from a correspondence model that the passive pedagogy of the teacher who 'helps' children to learn what *they* define as educational knowledge is assumed to be the guarantee of a democratic society committed to radical social change. Here the assumption is that a liberal political regime can only be sustained by a free school where nothing is imposed, where students make up their own minds what is worth knowing and 'create' their own values.

By contrast, there is the contradictory model in which adults come to behave differently, even opposite, to the ways in which teachers taught them to behave, as though the truth about schooling is that, in the words of John Fowles, it encourages 'conditioning by antithesis'. It is, of course, a tenable hypothesis which finds some support in common everyday experience that the disciplines imposed by adults are as likely to produce reaction as conformity. Children do not purely and simply internalise the dogmas of their parents and teachers, and they not infrequently reject the values and ideologies of their mentors whilst retaining respect for them as persons, even as teachers. That rebellion or contradiction, as often as passive conformity, should be the outcome of dogmatic teaching need not strain credulity. So far as there might be a relationship between the disciplinary ethos of schools and political commitment, these are as likely to be negatively as positively correlated. It is a fact that Gramsci did rebel against the conditions of his schooling (quoted by Fiori, 1970, p.26):

> What was it that stopped me from turning into a stuffed shirt? It was an instinct of rebellion awakened by the fact that I, who had got ten out of ten in everything, could not go on studying, while the butcher's boy, the chemist's boy, all the rich men's sons were able to.

But this was rebellion against the way in which educational opportunity was distributed in an inequitable social system, not revolt against the norms and disciplines of a repressive pedagogy. The explanation of Gramsci's radicalism is that the seeds of enlightenment derived from his schooling fell on a soil of discontent. What impelled him to revolutionary political commitment was not the carry over (correspondence) of a radical education nor reaction (contradiction) against repressive schooling but indignation at his own personal and family circumstances as these reflected the impoverished conditions of the Sardinian peasantry. (In 1932 he wrote: 'I have almost always known only the most brutal aspects of life', *Lettere*, no. 299.) From the same schooling, other of his school fellows, differently circumstanced, would grow up to be conventionally bourgeois. His own younger brother, for example, who passed through the same school system when his family was in less straitened circumstances, became a Fascist. Gramsci's experience only underlines a commonplace fact — that the founders of Marxism were products of conventional school systems, whose formative political education was acquired in the context of adult life. Marx and Engels themselves, for example, were products of the traditional German *gymnasium*. And it is not only radical traditional intellectuals, but also generations of working-class intellectuals committed to radical social change, who have been the products of traditional schooling, in the latter case of the traditional elementary school. For half a century the tendency has been to disparage elementary education as, in Tawney's words, 'educational shoddy'. In the context of a protracted struggle for 'secondary education for all', this polemic against elementary education was understandable. Nevertheless, in industrial societies, generations of working-class leaders had no formal education but elementary schooling, a fact no doubt recognised by Gramsci when defending the historical Italian elementary school.

These facts point to the hypothesis that the impetus towards a person's political orientation of one kind or another owes little to the ideology of schooling. In this connection, it is interesting that Bowles and Gintis, who develop a correspondence theory of schooling in which schools are nothing more than a component of the repressive apparatus of corporate capitalism, also have resort to a contradictory model in order to explain how political radicals like themselves manage to emerge from such alienating and repressive institutions. However, their contradictory model explains this radicalism not in terms of reaction against, or contradiction of, coercive discipline or indoctrination but as a response to environmental pressures which (much as in Gramsci's case) prompt parents, students and others to express dissatisfaction with the *status quo*.

A version of the correspondence theory which Bowles and Gintis and other neo-Marxists (e.g. Hextall and Sarub) embrace is that not only do schools correspond to factories, teachers to bosses, subject specialisation to the minute division of labour, and marks, grades and diplomas to wages or salaries, but also that the knowledge which the student 'produces' in response to these 'rewards' is as much a commodity as is the product of the labour of the automobile or textile worker. Marx's notion that under capitalism the worker is alienated from what he produces is applied to what the student produces – his learning. Whatever superficial attraction the correspondence theory has (and it is obviously only an educational metaphor, not an empirically testable generalisation) becomes dubious when applied to the acquisition of knowledge and skill. With reference to the details of this version of the correspondence theory, we have seen that Gramsci took an altogether different view of the functions of grades and examinations. And whilst it is true that he conceived schooling as work and the pupil as worker, he did not commit himself to the absurd assumption that the child could be alienated from his academic work in the strong Marxian sense; that is, that the child's work – his learning – could be expropriated as though it were a commodity. No doubt people often 'forget' what they have learned in school or anywhere else (though such 'forgetting' often means that learning has become part of one's tacit knowledge, or available at the level of recognition rather than reproduction memory) but a good deal of knowledge and skill acquired in school is remembered throughout life or becomes the cognitive foundation of further learning. The commodities which a worker produces *are* given up in exchange for something else. But the pupil who got an A for learning long division still has (knows) long division, just as he continues to possess the literacy (perhaps in more than one language), the historical, geographical, scientific and other knowledge that he learned in school. The use to which he puts his knowledge and skill is another matter. In a sense he cannot help using it as he reads newspapers, magazines and books, listens to radio, watches television and travels, whether on holiday or on business. In this informal way, the knowledge we acquired at school and elsewhere is the context in which we understand the news, engage with works of imagination, become involved in conversation with workmates and friends, and make sense of daily experience without constantly having to have the lumber of encyclopedias, atlases, works of reference and dictionaries constantly at our elbows. This capital or store of knowledge is, at least, the guarantee against perpetually interrupting experiences by having constantly to go and look things up. As to the more deliberate use of our knowledge, we can, as Gramsci acknowledged, become intellectual snobs or pedants; or, like himself, we can

The schooling of children

employ our erudition in social criticism aimed at radical social change; or we can use our knowledge and skill to defend the *status quo*. As Gramsci also recognised (*Notebooks*, p.391), a knowledge of Marxism can be used to defend capitalism: 'In Russia', he argued, 'Marx's *Capital* was more the book of the bourgeoisie than of the proletariat' (*Political Writings*, p.34). But whatever it is we come to know as a result of schooling, what cannot happen is that our knowledge is expropriated in exchange for grades or diplomas, much as the factory operative yields up the cans of beans he processes in exchange for a weekly wage. No doubt there are 'hidden' consequences of the ways in which we examine, evaluate and reward academic work in educational situations. But none of these consequences can be alienation of the learner from what he learns in Marx's strong sense of that term.[17] In a weak sense, no doubt, students are often alienated from schooling in the sense of being bored, resenting the hard work it necessarily entails, or finding an imposed curriculum irrelevant — much like the student who once confided to me that he had bitterly resented, as an undergraduate reading philosophy, being made to study Kant, but who had now concluded that it was the most significant educational experience in his life.

The fact that knowledge and skill acquired in school (often unwillingly) can be put to a variety of ideological uses depending upon the imperatives of the extra-school environment suggests that the conception of a neutral or disinterested school is as cogent as those of correspondence or contradiction. Marx took the view that schools for children had to be neutral, a biased education being the province of adult education (see below p.176). This, as we shall presently show, was essentially Gramsci's standpoint. He wrote repeatedly of the need for a disinterested school. By this he seemed to have at least two things in mind. First, that the schooling of children should not be vocational in the sense of providing technical or professional training: a 'unity' school should transmit a common humanistic culture to every child without premature vocational specialisation. Thus, the school should be disinterested as to the future occupational destiny of the child. But, second, the humanistic culture of the school should enshrine the traditional academic values of objectivity, pluralism ('the fact remains that every conception has its thinkers and experts to put forward, and authority does not belong to any one side' — *Notebooks*, pp.338-9), rationality — the disinterested pursuit of knowledge. We have already noted (p.19 above) Gramsci's insistence that his club for young adolescents should foster disciplined, methodical disinterested discussion of social and moral issues. No doubt one of Gramsci's defences against the charge that his pedagogy was dogmatic or didactic would have been that there is no threat to the autonomy of the individual learner in a pedagogy which is dogmatic about liberal educational values.

Quite aside from the question of his attitude towards the problem of bias, Gramsci saw the futility of instruction in socialism outside the appropriate industrial context: commitment to revolutionary social change must grow out of industrial experience. But to believe that schools are neutral to social objectives and to emphasise that political education can only fructify in the practical experience of adults does not rob schooling of its importance. On this view school is an indispensable foundation for further education, in ensuring the necessary mastery of language and other intellectual tools and assimilation of the cultural past with which present experience must engage dialectically as the spur to social action.

The structure and organisation of the school system

Although Gramsci's prescriptions for curriculum and method are evidently conservative, he saw no contradiction in concluding that the school was supportive of bourgeois hegemony and in favouring the kind of method and content (suitably modernised) which was largely indistinguishable from his own schooling. This seeming paradox is resolved, in part, by his insistence that the hegemonic function of the school system lies in its organisation rather than in its curriculum, or in the 'hidden curriculum' implicit in teaching method (*Notebooks*, p.40):

The traditional school was oligarchic because it was

intended for the new generation of the ruling class, destined to rule in its turn: but it was not oligarchic in its mode of teaching. It is not the fact that pupils learn how to rule there, nor the fact that it tends to produce gifted men, which gives a particular school its social character. This social character is determined by the fact that each social group has its own type of school, intended to perpetuate a specific traditional function, ruling or subordinate. If one wishes to break this pattern one needs, instead of multiplying and grading different types of vocational schools, to create a single type of formative school (primary-secondary) which would take the child up to the threshold of his choice of job, forming him during this time as a person capable of thinking, studying and ruling — or controlling those who rule.

This is to argue that the school serves and maintains the existing hegemony not because of what or how it teaches, but because it denies a traditional humanistic education to children of the subaltern classes. When the young Gramsci denounced the traditional classical school as a bourgeois organism in the worse sense of the word because it represented a perverted ideal, he was clear that its perversion consisted in being a class school, available only to children of the bourgeoisie and denied to those of the working class (*Political Writings*, pp.25-6). As Urbani puts it: 'in the past the educational principle was fully implemented but through restricted social groups' (in *Formazione*, p.332). Gramsci's demand was for a school which 'does not mortgage the child's future, a school that does not force the child's will, his intelligence, and growing awareness to run along tracks to a predetermined station' (*Political Writings*, p.26).

Part of his criticism of the 1923 fascist school reform was that it intended, through the introduction of more rigorous entrance requirements, to restrict access to secondary schooling even more than had hitherto been the case, whilst increasing the number and types of alternative vocational schools (Schneider and Clough, 1929, p.104). Borghi believes that Gramsci took this widening of the gap between the traditional secondary school and vocational schools to be the most significant and most fascist characteristic of the

Gentile reform (1975, pp.230-1). It has been estimated that the restrictive nature of the fascist reform was such that a 10 per cent reduction in the number of secondary schools and a similar reduction in the number of classes in remaining schools, coupled with the imposition of a ceiling of thirty-five pupils per class, had effectively reduced the number of secondary school pupils by 20 per cent (Minio-Puluello, 1946, p.19). Even one of Gentile's successors at the Ministry of Education, the so-called 'socialistic Fascist' Bottai, complained that under the Gentile reform the secondary schools had more than ever become the preserve of the middle class. Hence, for Gramsci, the crucial school reform was not curricular, but structural in the direction of the replacement of segregated secondary schools by schools comprehensive of different social and occupational strata. Indeed, as Manacorda shows, Gramsci's proposal was to bring into a single hierarchical structure the traditional educational institutions already existing in Italy – elementary school, *gymnasium*, *lyceum*, university. Everyone was to complete the first three levels, though in a reduced period of nine or ten school years compared with the existing thirteen. Manacorda notes that Gramsci's model for this was the Soviet ten-year school which was, however, unknown to Gramsci, reduced to nine years in the period 1927-34 (Manacorda, 1976, pp.208-9; cf. *Notebooks*, p.30). What he wanted was not the destruction of the traditional humanistic secondary school, but that it should be made universally available, especially to those groups whose only education had formerly been elementary in character or who were threatened by a developing system of specialised vocational schools 'designed not merely to perpetuate social differences but to crystallise them into Chinese complexities' (*Notebooks*, p.40). Gramsci's solution was a common school 'designed to develop in each human being an as yet undifferentiated general culture', a school without *specific* vocational focus, but with an underlying curricular and methodological orientation emphasising the universal cultural imperative towards work as a means of realising what Marx called 'species-being'.

In this emphasis upon the democratisation of structure through the establishment of a comprehensive or unity school, Gramsci has much in common with Marxist (and even social democratic) proposals for school reform elsewhere in Europe. English Marxist educationists, for example, have put their energies into a campaign for structural reform of the system along comprehensive lines and have not dismissed the traditional curriculum as bourgeois and irrelevant to working-class children. Traditional Marxists have seen curriculum reform as a matter of securing a common curriculum (essentially an organisational matter) by making the traditional curriculum of the school universally available. Elsewhere in Europe wherever comprehensive schooling has been established, accompanying curriculum reform has tended to accept the traditional subject structure with marginal modifications aimed at modernisation (e.g. the replacement of classics by linguistics in Sweden and a tendency to admit social disciplines like economics, sociology, and international affairs into the curriculum). But again, except for the new radical Left (and some conservative educationalists, e.g. G.H. Bantock in Britain) there has historically been no insistence from Marxists upon replacing the traditional subject curriculum with one focused upon 'working-class culture', whatever that might be.[18]

No doubt, from a North American perspective, any educational reform merely designed to establish comprehensive secondary schools looks old-fashioned. Bowles and Gintis remind us that, more than a century ago, Horace Mann introduced into the State of Massachusetts a system of Common Schools freely providing an education without 'distinction of rich and poor, of bond and free' (1976, pp.167, 173). But any modification of the organisation of schooling which remains within the framework of a bureaucratically managed public system of schooling (as Gramsci's proposals do) cuts little ice with those radical critics of schooling who see the democratisation of schooling as necessarily requiring the establishment of non-bureaucratic alternatives.

In fact, there is some ambiguity in Gramsci's attitude towards the role of the state in education. He has recently been invoked by Frith and Corrigan as a practising Communist whose writings would be relevant if 'reworked' in the context of modern political practice. This reference to Gramsci is in the context of Frith and Corrigan's remarking the paradox that whilst the organised labour movement has been in the forefront of the struggle for state education, 'critical educational theorists of all types are agreed that state education is one of the more important (if not the most important) institutions by which the bourgeoisie establish and maintain their hegemony and reproduce the conditions of capitalist production' (1977, pp.254-6). We have already noted that a neo-Marxist version of the correspondence theory analyses schooling in terms of the production and exchange processes of corporate capitalism. Whatever the merits of this correspondence model, it has inspired a number of responses which are unfriendly to the notion of state education. One response has been the de-schooling advocacy of Illich and others. From assumptions about both student demand and teacher supply, networks or webs of private educational initiatives (perhaps with some public financial and administrative assistance) have been proposed as the solution to ever-escalating public educational budgets and to the problem of student alienation from the traditional school. Others have proposed the establishment of small free schools (the storefront schools, for example), free in the sense of being privately financed and, therefore, independent 'of the flag which flies in the corner of the classroom' (Kozol, 1972), rather than in the sense of favouring a free or open pedagogy. The young Gramsci did favour a similar approach. His early writings advanced the view that, since the state is committed to preservation of its own (the existing) hegemony, a counter-hegemonic educational initiative could not be expected from the state: 'We socialists ought to be advocates of the free school, of the school left to private and community initiatives. Freedom of the school is possible only if the school is independent of control by the State' (*Scritti*, p.85). 'Private' initiatives here refers essentially to local groups and political party and workers' associations, especially the latter: 'popular schooling should be placed under the control of the great workers' unions' (Davidson, 1977, p.77 quoting Gramsci in *Avanti*, 1916).

The difficulty with this conception of the school — as free only when it is independent of public finance — is that in a mass educational system it is not clear how universal and free education can be made available on this basis. Although

Kozol provided an Appendix to his book listing sources available to those wishing to establish free schools for the disadvantaged, there has not been any growth of the free school movement (confined to only a few urban areas in the United States) in the period since he wrote. And it seems that Gramsci's early position on this question was, like Kozol's, rhetorical rather than practical. In the *Notebooks* he had evidently come round to the view that the educational enterprise is such that private resources would be quite inadequate to the task: 'The entire function of educating and forming the new generations ceases to be private and becomes public; for only then can it involve them in their entirety, without divisions of group or caste' (*Notebooks*, p.30). Frith and Corrigan take it as axiomatic that 'education [presumably State education] does fulfill a basic function for capitalism' (1977, p.255). The question is whether it would also be a basic necessity of socialism. Gramsci evidently thought it would, as well as concluding that it is also essential to the transitional process of social transformation. For not only was public educational provision necessary in order to abolish discrimination in the provision of education, it was also imperative in view of the increased expenditure which the comprehensive school reform would involve: the reform 'transforms the budget of the national department from top to bottom, expanding it to an unheard of extent and making it more complex' (*Notebooks*, p.30). This budgetary expansion would be fuelled by several factors. The state would have to take over from families the responsibility for maintenance of children staying longer in school, requiring a costly system of family allowances. There would also be the burden of financing an unprecedented expansion in teacher employment to reduce pupil-teacher ratios as a condition of increased efficiency, together with the provision of generous library, refectory and dormitory accommodation (ibid.).

However, as a practical programme, Gramsci recognised that establishment of a publicly financed system of comprehensive schools must be subject to gradual implementation. The economic constraints (including the need for taking children into the economy at different ages in order for them to make 'a certain immediate productive contribution', *Notebooks*, p.29) were such that a fully comprehensive system of education could not be established at a single stroke. Hence the need for compromise consisting of a transitional period in which only selected individuals would be taken into the new 'unity' school: 'initially the new type of school will have to be, cannot help being, only for restricted groups, made up of young people selected through competition or recommended by similar institutions' (*Notebooks*, p.30). Manacorda notes that Gramsci also had the Soviet Union in mind when concluding that, initially, entry to the common high school would have to be restricted (1976, p.208). Despite its rationale for a selective admissions policy in terms of economic expediency, this does not look so much different from the scholarship system which opened the doors of secondary education to working-class children before the Second World War. Elsewhere — in Britain for example — the justification for a selective and segregated system of secondary schooling was frankly and explicitly psychological (though, as Simon (1971, p.210) shows, as early as 1922 the chief official of the Board of Education acknowledged that limitation of secondary schooling was mainly economic in character: 'Broadly speaking we have to set to work on the principle that *as there are not enough places to go round*, selection to fill them must be on merit and by competition', emphasis added.) Selection was on the basis of intelligence and attainment tests, in pursuit of the liberal democratic objective of equality of opportunity. And, as we noted earlier, Gramsci's notion, that without rigorous academic discipline future scholars could not be identified from amongst the mass of those who pass through the educational system, is tantamount to a commitment to meritocracy and the notion of equality of opportunity.

That conclusion is in the *Notebooks*. But the young Gramsci had also been accused of educational elitism. Much of his earlier polemic, however, is indignation at the injustice which excluded the able poor, like himself, from secondary education in favour of socially privileged students for whom education would be at best an opportunity for ostentatious display (the schooling of 'wiseacres'), at worst a casting of pearls before swine (*Scritti Giovanile*, p.59):

Culture is a privilege. Schooling is a privilege. And it ought not to be so. All young people ought to be equal before culture. The State ought not to finance out of everyone's money the school only for the mediocre and deficient sons of the well-to-do, whilst excluding the intelligent and capable children of the proletariat.

And he went further, calling for the exclusion from secondary schools of the rich but stupid (*Sotto La Mole*, pp.238-9):

Make it so that only he who has the aptitude, the intelligence and the necessary motivation goes to school, and that schooling be not a privilege for those who can afford it; free the school from the interlopers, from the future misfits, and compel these to go to work.

Yet here is another paradox. Despite the democratic rhetoric of the notion of the equality of all young people before culture, there are also what Manacorda calls 'the accents of aristocratic austerity' evident in 'an outburst which revealed his contempt for all forms of scholastic mob rule (*"oclorazia scolastica"*)' (Manacorda, 1976, p.27). For Gramsci had concluded that 'the middle and high school ought to be provided only for those who have demonstrated that they are worthy of it' (*Scritti Giovanile*, p.59), 'the intelligent wherever they are born' (ibid., p.78). Defenders of the Gentile reform which restricted access to secondary schooling through a rigorous entrance examination (including Mussolini who argued that schooling should be reserved for those who deserve it on merit – cf. M.M. Thompson, 1934, p.14) have made the point that it was intended precisely to avoid the kind of 'scholastic mob rule' which Gramsci denounced, by reducing 'the number of graduates who have been lowering the intellectual standards of the schools' (Marraro, 1936, p.104). Admission of students by examination to publicly provided secondary schools was to assure 'the privilege of an education to deserving students, and place standards of scholarship on a high plane' (ibid., p.26). No doubt the similarity of the early Gramsci's scholastic elitism and that of Gentile is explained by his early sympathy with the idealistic philosophy of Croce[19] and Gentile. But it is not surprising that, historically, the polemic against privilege should express itself as advocacy of educational arrangements which recognise the claims of merit and serious academic intention: 'in reality Gramsci's discourse is neither idealistic nor aristocratic, but a vindication of the proletariat's right to culture, and also of its cultural autonomy when confronting the bourgeoisie' (Manacorda, 1976, p.28). Some of Gramsci's earlier writings appear as a defence of the school against what we now sometimes call a student 'fun culture'. Manacorda argues that Gramsci saw in this 'the symptoms of one of those moral crises which seem to accompany political and social upheavals' (ibid., p.27). Hence Gramsci's call for a defence of the school and the seriousness of instruction and for a restoration of the discipline of study 'because the school gives something to society and the money which the State allocates to public instruction, sweat out of the workers' toil, should not be squandered' (*Scritti*, p.103). (This notion that it is the middle and upper classes, not the working class, which benefit quite disproportionately from public monies invested in education — and particularly from increased expenditure in secondary and higher education — was, of course, part of the recent rationale for deschooling society; see e.g. Illich.)

But even the mature Gramsci of the *Notebooks*, fully committed to the development of universal secondary schooling for all in the comprehensive (unity) school, recognised the dangers of educational dilution implicit in such a reform: 'Wider participation in secondary education brings with it a tendency to ease off the discipline of studies, and to ask for "relaxations" ' (*Notebooks*, p.42). This anticipates current criticism of comprehensive schooling on the grounds that it tends towards dilution of the academic curriculum in favour of other educational objectives such as emotional or moral development. He also acknowledged (a point made by conservative critics about attempts to achieve equality of educational opportunity) that the universalisation of secondary schooling through creation of the comprehensive school brings into academic schools children who lack 'the propitious environment' provided by a home strongly committed to a literary culture. He was clear that some homes offer a more favourable environment for academic schooling than others (*Notebooks*, pp.42, 31):

> Undoubtedly the child of a traditional intellectual family acquires this psycho-physical adaptation [i.e. to the notion that learning is hard work] more easily . . . . In a whole series of families, especially in the intellectual strata, the children find in their family life a preparation, a prolongation and a completion of school life; they 'breathe in', as the expression goes, a whole quantity of notions and attitudes which facilitate the educational process properly speaking.

And he continued, in a passage which anticipates Basil Bernstein's notion of an elaborated language code (characteristic of middle-class speech) which is essentially the language of education: 'They already know and develop their knowledge of the literary language, i.e., the means of expression and of knowledge, which is technically superior to the means possessed by the average member of the school population between the ages of six and twelve' (*Notebooks*, p.31). In this context it is also worth noting that Gramsci believed that from an educational point of view the Church was a much more democratic institution than the state: 'the son of a peasant or an artisan, with intelligence and ability, and sufficiently adaptable to allow himself to adapt to the ecclesiastical structure . . . can become a cardinal and pope.' But, if this happened only infrequently, he concluded that it was probably because 'aristocratic youth' acquired relevant advantages from a propitious social background: 'from their own family environment they receive a series of qualities which are of first importance for an ecclesiastical career; the tranquil assurance of their own dignity and authority and the art of dealing with and ruling others' (*Quaderni*, I, pp.495-6).

However, to this problem of the unpropitious educational environment, Gramsci's was not the solution favoured by modern conservatives, namely that Western civilisation would be safer if certain categories of children were denied access to academically oriented schools. In line with his notion that 'the environment justifies nothing' and that its unfriendly, chaotic, fortuitous impact should be mitigated, in part, through creation of appropriate human institutions, he proposed a combination of what amounts to 'head start' and boarding school or residential college: 'parallel to the common school a network of kindergartens and other institutions would develop, in which, even before the school age, children would be habituated to a certain collective discipline and acquire pre-scholastic notions and attitudes' (*Notebooks*, p.31). As for the common school itself, its proper accommodation of students from the working class and peasantry would require that it 'be organised like a college, with a collective life by day and by night, freed from the present forms of hypocritical and mechanical discipline' (ibid.). The school 'should be a college for dormitories, refectories, specialised libraries, rooms designed for seminar work etc.' (ibid., p.30). This stress upon the school as a college was precisely to underline the need for collegiality amongst teachers and students: 'studies should be carried on collectively, with the assistance of the teachers and the best pupils, even during periods of individual study etc.' (ibid., p.31).

Gramsci was obviously caught up in the seemingly intractable problem of reconciling equality and excellence, whilst perhaps displaying more optimism than is usual now that the problem is capable of solution. In this respect, from a modern perspective, he shows himself to be doubly conservative: conservative, as we have seen, with reference to curriculum and method but also, it now appears, in seeing the problem of educational equality 'as one of access, not ideology', a matter of discovering ways of bringing to the socially and economically disadvantages the benefits of the kind of education which has traditionally been reserved to the ruling class. In this respect Gramsci's position (not surprising in view of the timing of his work) exactly parallels that of the traditional European left. In the case of Britain, for example, both the traditional Marxist and democratic socialist positions on the education of the working class have been epitomised, critically, as follows:

> Even for the Marxists of the British Communist Party the problem of class in British education is for them that working-class children are denied 'what our best schools offer'. In other words, like the 'social democratic' ideology that goes back to Tawney, class injustice is seen purely in terms of unequal opportunities, and the practical problem of how you abstract out socialist 'elements'

from what have historically been created as bourgeois institutions is hardly considered. This view is optimistic about what 'good teaching' (conventionally conceived) can do, and it presents an emphasis on standards, hierarchies and established procedures as politically 'radical' in that it is seen as enhancing the opportunities of working class children to succeed (Young and Whitty, 1977, p.5; cf. Karabel and Halsey, 1977, p.43).

But the position criticised here was precisely Gramsci's position and, to the extent that criticism of it is valid, his 'error' is exactly that (emphasising access rather than ideology) for which Young and Whitty fault the traditional Left.

By contrast these educational 'radicals' now offer an approach to educational reform from the direction of sociology of knowledge and curriculum which dignifies lower-class culture (or folklore, in Gramsci's terminology) and which arises from the learner's own definition of what counts as educational knowledge. For these, the traditional democratic socialist and Marxist approaches to equality through reorganisation of the school system aimed at the problem of 'access' has been a failure. But in terms of this 'new' sociological critique it is not clear what would count as success. The 'adequacy and validity of all cultures' thesis to which adherents of the 'new' sociology of education are committed seems predicated on a hardening of class divisions not on their withering away. For example, as we noted above, Young and Whitty apparently consider it a fault of the old sociology of education, which underpinned the 'access' ideology, that it rarely treated ' "low" social class . . . as a source of desirable cultural identity'. If this means anything, it means that those of 'low' social class are to be commended for wanting to hang on to their cultural identity. Of course, putting low in quotation marks may be taken as a suggestion that those normally categorised as of 'lower' social class are not really of low class at all. That is, if class is a cultural and not merely an economic category (a point which Young and Whitty seem to be making) the culture of the lower class is as good as (perhaps even better than) that of any other class. We have seen that Gramsci would have none of this and, as I have argued elsewhere (Entwistle,

1978, ch. 3), for a Marxist the separation of cultural superstructure from economic base can make no sense at all. Such a separation does not even have the sanction of good sense. A deprived economic status affects life chances adversely, and historically (as Engels and Marx were at pains to show) it has often reduced human beings to little more than the condition of animals. If low social class were a source of desirable cultural identity, how could social revolution or even Fabian social reform be justified? It is quite unclear what social values underpin the new educational radicalism. Its social philosophy is more profoundly conservative than that of the 'failed' radicals, like Gramsci, whose cultural appeal was to the best in the tradition of Western civilisation and whose educational principle required that this should be made available in school to anyone prepared to take the pains to acquire it, along with contextual institutional reform to diminish the counter-educational influences of social environments which are not propitious for schooling. To the 'new' sociologist of education, with his insistence that 'all cultures are adequate and valid', there are, logically, no unpropitious environments for education. His is a normless concept of culture, lacking any sort of criteria (except what already exists, culturally speaking) by which the success of his proposed educational arrangements might be assessed.

If the criticism were valid that the old Left has signally failed to develop educational theory and practice which has done justice to the working class, Gramsci becomes, like them, merely a historical curiosity. But before embracing this simplistic account of the educational history of the past century, it is necessary to recognise that his insistence upon the importance of literacy and acquisition of the traditional culture followed from his conclusion that the development of a counter-hegemony would require the emergence of a corps of intellectuals organic to the working class, who could confront traditional intellectuals with equal cognitive resources.

Educational theory as counter-cyclical[20]

Manacorda has remarked the growing austerity and sobriety

in Gramsci's educational theory in both the *Notebooks* and the *Letters*, as evidenced by his emphasis upon the *work* of learning and the cultivation of intellectual discipline (Manacorda, 1976, p.17; and see, e.g. *Lettere*, no. 159). No doubt this reflected the austerity of his own circumstances in prolonged imprisonment. As we shall presently see, it also derived from his admiration for 'Americanism', the kind of discipline and self-control required of the American worker but which he felt eluded the Southern European with his disposition towards 'improvisation and dilettantism' (Broccoli, 1972, p.38). But, as Gramsci himself concedes, his emphasis upon discipline and intellectual rigour in education was also counter-cyclical, a reaction against what he took to be a misapplication of activity pedagogy in the fascist educational reform of 1923. The Genevan pedagogy on which he focused his own polemic had itself been initially a counter-cyclical attack upon the educational ideology of the Jesuits:

> It has not been taken into account that Rousseau's ideas are a violent reaction to the schooling and pedagogic methods of the Jesuits and, as such, they represent progress; but there has been formed a kind of church which has paralysed pedagogic studies and has given rise to some curious involutions (*Quaderni*, I, pp.114, 123; cf. also III, pp.1719-20).

This emphasises the importance for educational debate of a knowledge of the history of education. In Gramsci's own phrase, familiarity with 'the entire thought of the past' is as necessary to sound educational practice as it is to the practice of politics. A study of the past can show that educational theories which were coined in order to focus the need for reform of the schools often become, in the hands of subsequent generations, mere slogans which inhibit understanding of the complex of relationships that form the educational nexus. With reference to the Genevan pedagogy, what had begun as an attempt to free schooling from the constraints imposed by its institutional context of dogmatic Christianity, became itself a dogma which impoverishes schooling, through its unhealthy exaggeration of 'libertarian ideologies' (*Notebooks*, pp.32-3). As a corrective to Jesuistic pedantry, Genevan ideas represented the possibility of educational progress because, as Gramsci put it to his wife in the language of the dialectic, they 'negated a worse philosophy' (Lawner Letters, no. 42). But when applied exclusively these progressive notions are a threat to progress. It is this fact that educational theories tend to be developed counter-cyclically which emphasises the importance of the history of education. Implicitly, the history of education should be central to the education of teachers. Historical awareness is essential to their knowing that a good deal of the educational rhetoric current at any particular time is counter-cyclical, polemical exaggeration, the raising to a level of exclusive truths of what are essential but only partial components of a comprehensive educational theory.

As Gramsci argued in a different context, the progressive active school was still in its romance stage. The problem was to move towards the ' "classical", rational phase' of the activity school through discovery of a 'new connection between spontaneity and authority' (Manacorda, 1972, p.213). Here Gramsci was invoking a terminology not uncommon at the time. It recalls Whitehead's insistence upon the cyclical nature of any effective learning experience which should pass through the stages of *romance*, *precision*, and *generalisation*. The Genevan tradition emphasised the stage of romance — the setting in ferment of the mind, the mood of adventure, of liberation, the sense of perspective or relevance, which sustains the learner through the discipline, hard work and even drudgery which the precision of learning requires. A good deal of Gramsci's early writing was couched in the rhetoric of romance. But his emphasis upon the inevitability of effort, drudgery, discipline and correct standards of achievement, especially with reference to the skills of literacy, is an insistence upon the need for a stage of precision, of attention to what Whitehead called the 'grammar of the subject'. Both romance (a sense of the usefulness of knowledge) and precision (the thrust towards mastery of knowledge and skill) must be synthesised dialectically, for there to be generalisation (the putting to use of what has been learned) or *praxis*.

Unfortunately, such is the exaggeration which counter-cyclical rhetoric seems to require, and such is often the absence of a historical dimension to the educational debate

The schooling of children

that, as with Gramsci's later writing, the polemic becomes exclusive, the acknowledgment of the antithesis muted. But his polemic against spontaneity and in favour of precision and instruction was to focus attention on the fact that there are 'two moments in the educational nexus', a fact obscured by Italian idealist educationists' exclusive emphasis upon only one of them: 'Gramsci reproaches neo-idealism for wanting to ignore the moment of coercion, for exalting and elevating to an absolute category the moment of spontaneity' (Manacorda, 1972, p.134). However, in the acknowledgment that 'Switzerland has made a great contribution to modern pedagogy' (ibid.), the younger Gramsci persists also in his mature conclusion; as, indeed, the mature Gramsci was foreshadowed in an earlier affirmation that an activity could not be deemed 'cultural' unless it were capable of being disciplined (cf. his claim that in the Factory Councils ' "spontaneity" was not neglected, much less scorned: it was *educated*' – *Quaderni*, I, p.330). To this early Gramsci, 'Liberty and discipline then, are like two opposites dialectically united, of which the one cannot exist without the other' (Manacorda, 1972, p.41), though he later stressed that the fusion of discipline with freedom is 'truly difficult and arduous' (*Quaderni*, III, p.1720). Nevertheless with reference to what constitutes a complete, effective and, especially, a radical education, the insistence upon precision, discipline, order, standards and 'sobriety' in schooling is an essential component of Gramsci's socio-educational theory, of the dialectic of his philosophy of praxis. And, as a radical theory of education, it is no less relevant to modern educational radicalism than it was half a century ago.

Schooling: towards the education of adults

We have noted Gramsci's tendency to characterise different 'moments' or phases of schooling in a terminology which was common at the time, its best-known exemplar in English being A.N. Whitehead. Whitehead extended his cyclical theory to apply not only to a single learning experience (e.g. an individual lesson which should manifest all three stages of the cycle) but also to an entire educational lifetime. Learning

The schooling of children

at different ages would differ in bringing into focus more or less of romance, precision or generalisation. Thus, the romance of infancy gives way to the precision of childhood, and both fructify in the adolescent stage of generalisation which, in turn, is also a stage of romance initiating a new learning cycle. Gramsci's own description of the brief period he spent as a parent with his infant elder son suggests that he saw this pre-school period as a stage of romance when learning is a game; though he also cautioned against the danger of retarding development even at this stage, by abandoning oneself to 'aesthetic contemplation of the child', indulging in mawkish sentimentality and denying him the intellectual stimulus to which he is capable of responding (*Edinburgh Letters*, no. LI). Certainly, however, it is evident that he regarded the period of schooling — especially the first three or four years — as dominated by precision. At this stage the problem was that of 'mitigating and rendering more fertile the dogmatic approach which must inevitably characterise these first years' (*Notebooks*, p.30). The mistake often made by adults lies in postponing until the adolescent years this necessarily dogmatic, coercive stage of discipline. In a letter to his brother Carlo, he distinguished sharply between the periods before and after puberty (*Lettere*, no. 162):

> Before puberty, the child's personality is not yet formed and it is easier to guide his life and make him acquire determined habits of order, of discipline, of work: after puberty, the personality forms itself more impulsively and extraneous intervention becomes odious, tyrannical, intolerable. Now, it happens that parents come to feel responsibility for their children precisely in this second period, when it is too late: so that the stick and violence come on the scene, producing limited results. Why not concern oneself with the child in the first period instead?

Characterising Gramsci's distinction between these earlier and later phases of learning, Manacorda uses the words 'heteronomy' and 'autonomy', words which were also employed by Piaget to distinguish the child's stage of moral development from that of the adolescent (Manacorda, 1972, pp.211-12). Although modern pedagogy derived from Piaget tends to reverse the Gramscian order of priorities (arguing that is, for a liberal spontaneous approach to learning in childhood) Piaget himself was quite undogmatic (indeed, he had almost nothing to say) about the kind of pedagogy appropriate to the different stages.

However, towards the end of secondary schooling, in order to facilitate the transition to the more liberal stage of higher education, Gramsci envisaged a diminution of the dogmatic pedagogy which a stage of precision necessarily entails. In this upper stage of secondary schooling, 'one has entered the phase of intellectual maturity in which one may discover new truths. Hence in this phase the fundamental scholastic activity will be carried on in seminars, in libraries, in experimental laboratories' (*Notebooks*, p.33). In this transitional stage towards higher or adult education, 'learning takes place especially through a spontaneous and autonomous effort of the pupil, with the teacher exercising a function of friendly guide – as happens or should happen in the university' (ibid.). That is, Gramsci believed (as did Whitehead) that beyond the school learning passes into a stage of generalisation, as the cognitive 'baggage' acquired in school is employed by adults in experiences which are critical and creative. School learning is the instrument for evaluation of the existing culture and for its transformation into a new humanistic culture: 'the developing autonomy, liberalism and spontaneity of life beyond childhood can only derive from the disciplined learning of the child. For Gramsci, revolutionary spontaneity does not exclude but, on the contrary, presupposes an intellectual order' (Broccoli, 1972, p.61).

Thus, if Gramsci's insistence upon the need for precision is, in part, counter-cyclical, this apparently conservative prescription for curriculum and method during the period of childhood has also to be read in the context of the importance he attached to the education of adults. In a sense which is also anti-Rousseauan, schooling has to be seen as preparatory to educational experiences (especially in the area of political education) which can only make sense in adult life, as a worker. It would not make sense to look at any of Gramsci's educational prescriptions in isolation, apart from their contribution to a theory of education as a lifelong experience. From this comprehensive life perspective, what

The schooling of children

looks like a conservative theory of schooling is not supportive of the existing hegemony but, on the contrary, is a necessary preparation for the education of working-class intellectuals, for the creation of a new humanism and, hence, is a precondition for the exercise of working-class hegemony. As we saw, it was in denying access to the traditional curriculum of the secondary school to the children of the poor, that Gramsci judged existing educational arrangements to be supportive of the hegemonic *status quo*, and we now turn to examine his proposals for the education of adults which complement his prescriptions for the schooling of children.

Part two

The education of adults

Political education as adult education

In spite of the fact that Gramsci's pedagogical theory is conservative and his proposals for structural reform of the school system only look radical from a European perspective, and in terms of traditional Marxist educational theory, it remains a fact that he believed the achievement of working-class hegemony to be an essentially educational enterprise. He was clearly committed to the notion of education as political, not in the sense that the school's 'hidden' curriculum (its disciplinary procedures or its modes of organising learning, for example) may be claimed to 'correspond' to a particular political hegemony, but in the sense that there can be a quite explicit commitment to political enlightenment or persuasion through both formal and informal teaching. However, if education for Gramsci was political in this latter sense, it had to be adult education. Resolution of the paradox of Gramsci's pedagogical conservatism in pursuit of aims which were politically revolutionary is to be found in the fact that although his explicitly educational writings refer to the schooling of children, the key to his theory of political education lies in the education of adults, especially as workers within an occupational context. It is a mistake to look to Gramsci as authority for the view that radical social change, involving the replacement of one hegemony by another, can be engineered primarily through formal educational institutions, especially those concerned with the schooling of children. If the school had to be disinterested, especially in not prematurely foreclosing avenues into any occupation, this was not the case for adult educational institutions. As adults, now committed to a particular occupation, workers had to be educated with reference both to the technical aspects of work and to its political and cultural implications. Political activity is not a chronological outcome of political education. The two are concurrent, an engagement with theoretical knowledge whilst engaged in productive work and grappling with the political and social predicaments generated by economic activity: 'Study and culture are for us nothing but the theoretical awareness of our own immediate and supreme ends, and the way we can succeed in transforming them into action' (quoted by Davidson, 1977, p.224).

Political education in an industrial context was to be a primary objective of the Factory Councils which were established in Turin in the years following the First World War (see pp.147-8) below). And each of Gramsci's various educational initiatives — personal teaching in both formal and informal groupings, radical journalism and political education undertaken within the factories — were in service of the workers' political party; first the Italian Socialist Party, then the Communist Party. Despite the hostility which Gramsci's conception of the political party as an instrument of education drew from his colleagues, his sort of belief in the inseparability of educational and political activity is a familiar feature of working-class movements.

For Gramsci, adult political education posed what he called the ' "juridicial problem", i.e., the problem of assimilating the entire grouping to its most advanced fraction; it is a problem of education of the masses' (*Notebooks*, p.195). He believed that every adult involved actively in production was under an obligation 'to improve his or her own theoretical knowledge and professional capability' (Edinburgh Letters, no. CX). This amounts to a commitment to what we now call *éducation permanente* (Borghi, 1975, p.236). But although, as we have seen, Gramsci believed every man to be a 'philosopher', neither revolutionary political activity nor the new culture of the socialist society could be the spontaneous creation of the mass. Hence, development of working-class consciousness required the education of intellectuals organic to the working class itself. In a reciprocal educational relationship with traditional intellectuals, these would provide leadership in the counter-hegemonic movement. It is in this connection that Gramsci drew his familiar distinction between traditional and organic intellectuals. Organic intellectualism is a category of intellectual activity which is intrinsic to a particular social group defined in relation to its economic preoccupations. Thus, being a function of different kinds of economic and industrial activity, the development of organic intellectualism is contingent upon the performance of an economic role as an adult worker. In this sense, as well as being necessarily in the field of adult education, political education is intrinsic to vocational education, widely conceived (see pp.129-48 below).

In Part 2 of this study we turn to the problems posed by this conception of political education in a vocational context: the question of the education of intellectuals and their relationship with other workers; the nature and purpose of technical and vocational education.

Education and the problem of the intellectuals

A central and recurrent theme in Gramsci's thought was the problem of the intellectuals: their education and their allegiances, and the nature of their relationship with the working class. Indeed, he linked the problem of intellectuals with that of hegemony as, on some occasions, a major factor contributing to its collapse. For example, he believed one reason for the fall of medieval communes was the failure of an economic class 'which could not create its own category of intellectuals and thus exercise hegemony as well as dictatorship' (*Lettere*, no. 210).

It is not, therefore, surprising that for Gramsci a major function of schooling is the development of intellectuals: 'School is the instrument through which intellectuals of various levels are elaborated. The complexity of the intellectual function in different states can be measured objectively by the number and gradation of specialized schools' (*Notebooks*, pp.10-11). In the *Quaderni*, the notes explicitly concerned with schooling are integral to the discussion of the nature and function of intellectuals (III, pp.1513-31). But, as the second sentence in the above quotation indicates, the conception of an intellectual in Gramsci is broader than is usually associated with the word (*Notebooks*, p.97n):

> By 'intellectuals' must be understood not those strata commonly described by this term, but in general the entire social stratum which exercises an organisational function in a wider sense — whether in the field of production, or in that of culture, or in that of political administration.

In order to widen the reference of the term, Gramsci distinguished between traditional and organic intellectuals. However, this distinction is itself a source of ambiguity, an ambiguity deriving in part, from use of the words traditional and organic which themselves imply a confusion of categories. That is, whilst 'organic' should refer to place (in this case the socio-political location of an intellectual), the implication of 'traditional' should be temporal. Thus, the alternative to traditional ought to be 'new' or 'modern', while the alternative to organic should be 'detached', 'free', 'independent' or 'autonomous'. When seen as autonomous, intellectuals could be defined primarily by reference to the practice of a specific kind of intellectual activity, in the role of poet, literary critic, philosopher or historian, for example. Gramsci did, indeed, refer to traditional intellectuals in this way as 'men of letters, philosophers, artists' (*Notebooks*, p.9). But he also denied that in virtue of the exercise of these and other specific intellectual functions, intellectuals can claim autonomy, pretending to no organic relationship with a particular social class. In denying social autonomy to intellectuals, Gramsci was concerned to refute the notion which has become associated mainly with Mannheim, of the 'free floating' intellectual. In Mannheim's words, intellectuals are 'a relatively classless stratum which is not too firmly situated in the social order' (Mannheim, 1936, pp.154-5). Mannheim derived this conclusion from focusing on the class origins of intellectuals and the fact that, in this respect, they are socially heterogeneous. No doubt, some intellectuals do originate in the *rentier* class, but there are others 'whose only capital consists in their education and who may, indeed, have their social origins in the working class' (ibid.). Gramsci did not, of course, deny that some intellectuals are recruited from the subaltern classes, especially in Italy from the peasantry. But in denying that an intellectual can be 'socially unattached', he was focusing upon function rather than on social origins. He categorised intellectuals as traditional when they had functioned in the service of (and, hence, were organic to) a hegemony whose time is past, irrespective of their social origins. As Manacorda puts it (1976, p.269):

> Intellectuals are said to be traditional in this sense that they are tied to a class belonging to a former mode of production or to a class on the way to disappearing . . . the intellectual is said to be traditional, not only because he is tied to an anterior mode of production, but also in so far as he has been the organic intellectual of a departed class, since he is not organically tied to the class actually in the ascendant.

This is to claim that the logic of the words "traditional" and "organic" is not intended to denote exclusive categories: all intellectuals are organic to some hegemonic class.

Examples of traditional intellectuals who were organic to a former hegemonic class — the landed aristocracy — are (i) 'ecclesiastics, who for a long time held a monopoly of important services; religious ideology, that is, the philosophy and science of the age, together with schools, education, morality, justice, charity, good works, etc.' and (ii) what Gramsci calls the *noblesse de robe*, other categories of intellectuals which came into existence to break this ecclesiastical monopoly — 'a stratum of administrators etc., scholars and scientists, theorists, non-ecclesiastical philosophers etc.' (*Notebooks*, p.7). Examples of intellectuals tied to a class 'on the way to disappearing' are those called into service by the capitalist entrepreneur who 'creates alongside himself the industrial technician, the specialist in political economy, the organisers of a new culture, of a new legal system' (ibid., p.5). The interesting point about this second list is that it includes functionaries who do not normally consider themselves to be intellectuals — industrial technicians and, perhaps, entrepreneurs themselves. More than that, should they assume themselves to be intellectuals, they are unlikely to see themselves as 'traditional' in its implication of detachment from the socio-economic system. But 'specialists in political economy, organisers of a new culture, of a new legal system' are somewhat akin to the old *noblesse de robe* as, themselves, scholars, theorists, or administrators. And this mixture of technical and social categories in Gramsci's list of intellectuals who are organic to capitalist societies points to a further ambiguity in the notion of 'organic intellectual'.

On the one hand, as organic, intellectual activity can be technical, related primarily to the performance of a particular industrial or professional occupation. In this sense of intellectualism being organic to a technical function, the working class organic intellectual would be a product of technical education, probably exercising leadership or direction in an industrial enterprise, for example, as a foreman, supervisor or technician.[1] On the other hand, as organic, intellectual activity can be socio-political, related primarily to articulation of the economic, social and political dilemmas and interests of a particular class: in this case, where intellectualism is exercised in relation to the socio-political superstructure, a working-class organic intellectual would be the product of liberal or humanistic education, probably exercising leadership as a shop steward, union official, political organiser or propagandist.

It is clear that only the second of these categories would apply to Gramsci himself as a working-class organic intellectual and, indeed, he did distinguish between intellectuals of different types by emphasising intention or commitment rather than by reference to the type of intellectual skill or knowledge (i.e. technical or socio-political) which the intellectual possesses (*Notebooks*, p.8):

> The most widespread error of method seems to me that of having looked for this criterion of distinction in the intrinsic nature of intellectual activities, rather than in the ensemble of the system of relations in which these activities (and therefore the intellectual groups who personify them) have their place within the general complex of social relations.

Hence, existing intellectuals in Italy were categorised as

traditional by Gramsci, as distinct from organic, not by reference to their particular intellectual gifts or skills (i.e. as poets, literary critics, lawyers, economists etc.), but because they remained aloof from the lower classes, showing no interest in the development of a popular national culture.

Thus, Gramsci's conception of intellectualism indicates the exercise of an executive, managerial or leadership function, 'the capacity to direct — in a more or less indirect way — other men in the context of social life' (Urbani, 1967, p.331). It is this general, directive function which every intellectual performs within the complex of social relationships which is, for Gramsci, the necessary condition for defining an intellectual. Thus, on the question of whether Gramsci was himself a traditional or an organic intellectual, it is in terms of his own definition (i.e. relating to social function and commitment), and by reference to his roles as political organiser and journalist, that he would be categorised as a working-class organic intellectual. On the other hand, it would have to be in non-Gramscian terms (i.e. by reference to his conventional academic education in the *liceo* — a school which he condemned as oligarchic because of its selective character in serving only the bourgeoisie — and the university) that he would be categorised as a traditional intellectual; by reference, that is, to the 'intrinsic nature' of his intellectualism, the expression of his training in history, philosophy and linguistics.

One consequence of defining intellectuals by reference to commitment and social function, rather than to specific intellectual skills or interests, is that it does open the way for bringing those with a conventional academic education into the service of the working class as working-class organic intellectuals. Gramsci concluded that though an intellectual may have served the existing hegemony, the skills he has to deploy are independent of it. Ultimately, however, it was important for the working-class movement that organic intellectuals should be generated from within the working class itself, from amongst the ranks of manual workers, and not simply through the conversion of sympathetic intellectuals from other social classes. A corps of working-class organic intellectuals could hardly be said to exist if it consisted primarily of converts from other social classes. Even

Marxism itself was deficient in that 'the great intellectuals formed on the terrain of this philosophy, besides being few in number, were not linked with the people, they did not emerge from the people, but were the expression of traditional intermediary classes, to which they returned at the great "turning points" in history': initially the Reformation had also been rendered culturally sterile by the defection of intellectuals in face of persecution (*Notebooks*, p.397). Added to this possibility that in a crisis the traditional intellectual will 'return to the fold' is the fact that those who voluntarily commit themselves to the service of the working class (and Mannheim noted a tendency for intellectuals to affiliate with 'the class in need of development') are not welcomed unreservedly: at best, the working class is ambivalent towards intellectuals (Macciocchi, 1974, p.203; see also Mannheim, 1936, p.158; Boggs, 1976, p.77). Hence, the training of workers themselves, as intellectuals, was a primary need. The younger Gramsci had, indeed, written of 'the struggle against the despotism of career intellectuals' and of the need to secure 'the independence of the masses from the intellectuals' (*Scritti Giovanile*, p.301).

But here we encounter another of the several paradoxes in Gramsci's thought: for although he emphasised that the capacity for intellectuality is universal in men, we have already noted his conclusion that popular conceptions of the world – 'common sense' – are replete with superstition and folklore. Thus, on the one hand, he was optimistic about the intellectual potential of all men and insisted that 'although one can speak of intellectuals one cannot speak of non-intellectuals, because non-intellectuals do not exist' (*Notebooks*, p.9). We referred earlier to the passage (which recalls Matthew Arnold's notion that every man has the seeds of a Socrates within him) where Gramsci claims that everyone is a philosopher 'who contributes to sustain a conception of the world or to modify it, that is, to bring into being new modes of thought' (ibid.). On the other hand, we noted his conclusion that notwithstanding this universal human intellectual potential, it is also evident that philosophy finds expression in superstitions and folklore which serve to sustain the hegemonic *status quo*. Although everyone is a philosopher, 'it would not be exact to call by the name of "philosophy" every tendency of thought, every general orientation, etc., nor every "conception of the world and of life" ' (ibid., p.347). The younger Gramsci had made a similar point about culture (*Formazione*, p.98):

> For me everyone is cultured because everyone thinks and connects causes and effects. But they are cultured from the beginning, empirically, not organically. Therefore they are volatile, they indulge themselves, they become soft, or they turn violent, intolerant, quarrelsome, according to circumstances.

Evidently, the untutored intelligence of 'the folk' is in itself an inadequate basis for generating a corps of intellectuals organic to the working class and, to that end, the school's function is to wean men from their disposition to see the world in terms of folklore. Becoming an intellectual in the professional sense requires a distinctive 'apprenticeship' aimed at mastery of the intellectual's 'tools' — formal logic, the capacity to combine deduction with induction, to compare and contrast, to generalise and transfer insights from one context to another (*Quaderni*, I, p.33). 'Common sense' is itself a form of intellectualism — 'non-intellectuals do not exist' — but it is an insufficient resource of those who are to be 'career intellectuals'.

Notwithstanding his early insistence on the mass gaining independence from career intellectuals, Gramsci later returned repeatedly to the conclusion that working-class recourse to assistance from traditional intellectuals was inescapable. In the early days of the fascist regime, he emphasised the need to recreate between the working class and the intellectuals of the older generation that 'community of work' which Fascism had violently interrupted, and he underlined the positive task that intellectuals can and ought to perform in the service of the working class: by holding themselves aloof, the older generation of intellectuals would be abdicating from their obligations and their proper function (Manacorda, 1976, p.55). In fact, in the *Notebooks*, Gramsci developed his distinction between traditional and organic intellectuals in the context of demonstrating how, in the South of Italy, traditional intellectuals had failed to develop an alliance with the peasantry. As it happened (p.330), one could only have had cultural stability and an organic quality of thought if there had existed the same unity between intellectuals and the simple as there should be between theory and practice. That is, if the intellectuals had been organically the intellectuals of those masses, and if they had worked out and made coherent the principles and the problems raised by the masses in their cultural activity, thus constituting a cultural and social bloc.

This fact that subaltern classes could not rely on an alliance with traditional intellectuals was one reason why intellectuals whose origins were in those classes would have to be developed. But, pending the emergence of intellectuals originating in the lower classes, there was no alternative but to enlist the aid of sympathetic intellectuals from other social strata (*Modern Prince*, p.50):[2]

It is certainly important and useful for the proletariat that one or more intellectuals, individually, adhere to its programme and its doctrine, merge themselves with the proletariat, and become and feel themselves an integral part of it. The proletariat, as a class, is poor in organising elements, does not have and cannot form its own stratum of intellectuals except very slowly, very laboriously and only after the conquest of State power.

However, a number of problems are inherent in this notion that a corps of working-class intellectuals must be educated in alliance with traditional intellectuals. There is, first, the problem of communication. There is also the problem of elitism implicit in the notion that intellectuals are defined primarily with reference to a leadership or directive function. And, arising from the problem that intellectuals are suspect amongst the working class, there is a danger that organic intellectuals will tend to 'fly away' and become assimilated by traditional intellectuals. Gramsci addressed himself to each of those questions.

The establishment of rapport between 'the educated' and the mass requires a deliberate effort towards communication from intellectuals. To achieve this it is necessary that they *become* organic to the subaltern classes in the sense already discussed (though not, as required periodically by school reforms in some Marxist educational systems, that they necessarily have experience of manual work — see below, pp.160-5). Davidson notes that despite his early commitment to socialism, Gramsci remained unsuccessful so long as he 'only had contact with the working class as a teacher of theory' and until events drew him 'to engage in political activity of an organisational sort, which was finally to enable him to resolve the vexing role of the intellectuals and cultural propaganda in the movement' (1977, p.84); when, that is, 'he became an active part of the working class intent on changing the world for itself' (ibid., p.72). Becoming an organic working-class intellectual does not entail becoming a manual worker, but becoming actively committed to the achievement of working-class hegemony. It also requires recognition by sympathetic traditional intellectuals that the capacity for intellectualism universally latent in the human condition will only be awakened if the seminal ideas of modern (and, indeed, historical) thought are capable of translation into popular language as a condition of their assimilation within the common understanding. For his belief that what he called 'modern theory' cannot be inconsistent with 'common sense', Gramsci drew authority from philosophers themselves: 'Immanuel Kant believed it important for his philosophical theories to agree with common sense; the same position can be found in Croce' (*Notebooks*, p.199). So successful was Croce in achieving this objective that his ideas got into the newspapers and, hence, into everyday thought to an extent that there was 'a large number of Crocians who didn't know they were, and who did not even know of Croce's existence' (*Lettere*, no.262). In this connection it is interesting that a modern political theorist, Bernard Crick, who advocates the need to teach everyone fundamental political concepts, has taken the view that Rawls's lengthy, subtle elaboration of a theory of justice can be epitomised simply in the commonly understood principle of fairness.

In Gramsci's view, one of the reasons why intellectuals remain detached from the subaltern classes and fail to become organic is precisely because of their particular technical skills, their habituation, by training, towards classical rhetoric 'which is an exterior and momentary mover of feelings and passions' (*Notebooks*, p.10; cf. also Broccoli, 1972, p.176 and *Quaderni*, III, p.1901). The problem was the absence in the writings of intellectuals of any attempt to get to grips with popular reality (Manacorda, 1976, p.257): 'the typical Italian intellectual felt more tied to Annibal Caro [a translator of Latin classics] than to the peasant of Apulia or Calabria' (Pozzolini, 1970, p.114). Indeed, for this reason, Gramsci stressed that the diffusion of culture is as creative an activity as discovery and innovation (*Notebooks*, p.325):[3]

> Creating a new culture does not only mean one's own 'original' discoveries. It also, and most particularly, means the diffusion in a critical form of truths already discovered, their 'socialization', as it were, and even making them the basis of vital action, an element of co-ordination and intellectual and world order.

However, even if, as Cammett concludes, 'the language gap between the intellectuals and the masses was much greater in Italy than elsewhere' (1967, p.20), the problem of communication between intellectuals and others is universal. And Gramsci believed it to be essential in the search for common rapport that the popularisation which is necessary to 'socialise' knowledge does not degenerate into vulgarisation. He was not unaware of this danger, witness his reference to the need to defend the school against 'academic mob-rule' (Manacorda, 1976, pp.27-8; and cf. pp.98-100 above). To avoid this danger a disciplined effort towards understanding, especially through mastery of the skills of literacy, is required from everyone. Responding to a criticism that the socialist paper, *Il Grido del Popolo*, had published an article too difficult and obscure for its working-class readers, he observed that the article in question had been in response to a piece in *La Stampa* written in a precise philosophical style. *Il Grido's* response, he argued, had to be in the style of the adversary and not 'childishly puerile' (*Formazione*, p.102):

> To remain simple we should have had to impoverish the debate, to change the character of a discussion which was overflowing with concepts of the utmost importance into the most intimate and precious essence of our spirit.

To do this would not be to simplify: it would be to swindle like the vintners who sell jugs of coloured water for Barolo or Lambrusca. A concept which might be difficult in itself cannot be easily expressed without totally vulgarising it. And on the other hand, the pretence that the vulgarity is in the concept itself is the mark of base demagogues and swindlers in logic and propaganda.

Shortly afterwards, he stressed that, whenever the importance and seriousness of the topic warranted it, *L'Ordine Nuovo* would continue to publish lengthy and difficult articles demanding prolonged and attentive study from the reader (*L'Ordine Nuovo*, pp.469-70).

It is the belief that any attempt at popularisation must inevitably result in vulgarisation which leads some conservative educationists to the conclusion that talk of a common culture being enshrined in a common curriculum is a threat to civilisation itself.[4] However, this belief that culture (in Arnold's sense of 'The best that has been thought and said in the world') is beyond the reach of all but a highly intelligent and educated elite commonly fails to make a necessary distinction between the different activities of creativity (i.e. of authors, composers, scientific innovators, philosophers), interpretation (i.e. by performers, critics, teachers) and appreciation (i.e. by the lay public having greater or lesser technical knowledge of the work in question). These last are legion by comparison with those who are innovative, and Gramsci implied this distinction when calling our attention to that familiar, minimal sense of 'appreciation' represented by the ability to follow an argument without being able to reproduce it: the man of the people, he argued, 'has no concrete memory of the reasons [i.e. for accepting a conclusion] and could not reproduce them, but he knows that reasons exist, because he has heard them expounded and was convinced by them' (*Notebooks*, p.339).

However, it is evident that making the effort to understand difficult theoretical conceptions imposes upon the working class an additional burden which is not faced by the professional middle class. And this is especially true of those who will assume leadership as organic intellectuals.

For them, Gramsci insisted upon the need for a rigorous discipline aimed at mastering the standard form of the written language (see pp.25-6 above). This is an additional burden upon the working class precisely because, in contrast with other occupational groups (those whose work is, in Gramsci's phrase, 'weighted towards intellectual elaboration'), their daily working resource is not primarily the written language itself. As Hobsbawm argues, these other groups nourish their own organic intellectuals incidentally to their daily work: the bourgeoisie is able 'to generate organic intellectuals informally, by virtue of its productive functions'. Whilst Gramsci believed that all work has a cognitive core ('there is no form of human activity from which every form of intellectual participation can be excluded: *homo faber* cannot be separated from *homo sapiens*' — *Notebooks*, p.9), he also acknowledged that different occupational tasks will be weighted 'towards intellectual elaboration or towards muscular-nervous effort' and because 'the relationship between efforts of intellectual-cerebral elaboration and muscular-nervous effort is not always the same . . . there are varying degrees of specific intellectual activity' (ibid.).

It is for these kinds of reasons — because of its disposition towards folklore and the lesser cognitive content of its daily work — that the working class's own organic intellectuals will be formed only in alliance with traditional intellectuals prepared to discipline their own linguistic excesses in the interests of communication. But one of the problems inherent in the notion of traditional intellectuals providing education for working-class intellectuals is that of the danger of assimilation of the latter by the former. This danger was especially strong in the transitional stages towards socialism when, as we saw above (pp.97-8), Gramsci envisaged that compromises would have to be made in restructuring the school system. Of his notion that clever working-class children could have the type of education hitherto reserved for other classes without themselves being assimilated, Kiernan observes (1972, p.32): 'Gramsci seems to feel few misgivings about whether working class intellectuals are likely to keep their allegiance to their own class or party, or will use their new wings to fly away to other parties.' But Gramsci was not unaware of this danger. He argued that in certain conditions traditional intellectuals 'exercise such a power of attraction that in the last analysis, they end up by subjugating the intellectuals of all other social groups; they thereby create a system of solidarity between all the intellectuals, with bonds of a psychological nature (vanity, etc.)' (*Notebooks*, p.60). The conditions favouring assimilation tend to be those in which the hegemonic class is 'progressive', that is, apparently advancing the interests of the entire society. One answer to the problem of keeping intellectuals organic to the working class lies in educating them, as adults, in and through the industrial context itself: 'The initial stage in forming the new organic intellectual would be a technical and industrial education obtained directly in the shops (see below pp.144-8).

The possibility that those who have been especially educated to assume the role of an intellectual organic to the working class will become declassed is one kind of danger of elitism. But elitism of a kind is also integral to Gramsci's definition of an intellectual.[5] This entails the conception of leadership as a permanent social function: it is an essential and enduring condition of political organisation. For although Gramsci believed every man to be a philosopher, capable of intellectual activity, he also concluded that neither revolutionary political activity, nor creation of a new hegemonic culture could be the spontaneous creation of the mass of men. Untutored spontaneity is as dangerous in political organisation as it is in the 'upbringing' of children (see pp.57-8 above). Intellectuals perform a similar function in the education of the population at large to that of the adult in the schooling of children. For even if all men are capable of achieving intellectual and moral autonomy, they are not all endowed with the capacity for creativity which is necessary for significant cultural or political innovation. All men display intelligence, but all are not destined to exercise that specialised social function of being an intellectual (*Notebooks*, pp.334-5):

> Critical self-consciousness means, historically and
> politically, the creation of an *élite* of intellectuals. A
> human mass does not 'distinguish' itself, does not
> become independent in its own right without, in the
> widest sense, organising itself; and there is no organisation

> without intellectuals, that is without organisers and
> leaders, in other words, without the theoretical aspect
> of the theory-practice nexus being distinguished
> concretely by the existence of a group of people
> 'specialised' in conceptual and philosophical elaboration
> of ideas . . . innovations cannot come from the mass, at
> least at the beginning, except through the mediation of
> an *élite* for whom the conception implicit in human
> activity has already become to a certain degree a
> coherent and systematic ever-present awareness and
> a precise and decisive will.

Here Gramsci calls explicitly for the establishment of an *élite*, a word which he repeatedly uses in this context.

The notion of a specially educated elite exercising leadership in this way is usually anathema to liberal educationists and, especially, to modern educational radicals. (Indeed, it is because of the illiberal connotations of the word in everyday language that the English translators of the *Notebooks* are at pains to stress that Gramsci's usage is in a sense 'very different from that of the reactionary post-Pareto theorists of "political *élites*"'. *Notebooks*, p.334, note 18.) Educational and social elitism is to be expected from educational conservatives, but the question is how, if at all, Gramsci's elite of organic intellectuals differs from the sort of elite which is projected by conservative educational theory. Part of the answer lies in the very notion of an elite being *organic* to a particular class, articulating its predicaments, sharing its dilemmas and making 'coherent the principles and the problems raised by the masses in their political activity'. Being organic, intellectuals would not only originate in the working class, but they would also be in constant conversation with its members. Any cultural movement aiming to 'replace common sense and old conceptions of the world in general' must 'work incessantly to raise the intellectual level of ever growing strata of the populace, in other words, to give a personality to the amorphous mass element. This means working to produce *élites* of intellectuals of a new type which arise directly out of the masses, but remain in contact with them to become, as it were, the whalebone in the corset' (*Notebooks*, p.340). A reciprocal educational relationship is envisaged (ibid., p.334):

> The process of development is tied to a dialectic between the intellectuals and the masses. The intellectual stratum develops both quantitatively and qualitatively, but every leap forward towards a new breadth and complexity of the intellectual stratum is tied to an analogous movement on the part of the mass of the 'simple', who raise themselves to higher levels of culture and at the same time extend their circle of influence towards the stratum of the specialised intellectuals . . .

The notion that every teacher is always a pupil and every pupil a teacher has to be extended to every kind of social relationship especially 'between intellectual and non-intellectual sections of the population, between rulers and the ruled, élites and their followers, leaders and led' (ibid., p.350). It properly behoves any philosophical movement that 'it never forgets to remain in contact with the "simple" and indeed finds in this contact the source of the problems it sets out to study and resolve' (ibid., p.330). As we shall presently see, this dialectic between intellectuals and workers is the basis of *praxis*, the uniting of theory with practice (see pp.160-5 below).

However, modern educational conservatives not only deny that there is anything to be learned from the 'simple', but also believe that the simple mass and the intellectual minority inhabit such different cultural universes that any possibility of generally raising the cultural level in a society through the initiatives of intellectuals is out of the question. Indeed, on this view, so much are the civilised arts, sciences and philosophy the possession of a minority elite that there is no possibility of intellectuals being organic at all in Gramsci's sense, that is, organic to anything so massive as a social class. Intellectuals are organic to the clerisy, which is destined to talk only to itself. It follows that intellectuals can only be educated in segregated secondary schools and higher education, and a common culture is a possible outcome neither of a system of common schooling, nor of initiatives in the field of adult education. By contrast, Gramsci's notion of the organic relationship of an intellectual to his class does require

The education of adults

acceptance of the possibility and, indeed, the necessity of communication. He denounced the tendency of certain intellectuals to treat the workers as children rather than as men to whom it is possible to speak openly and freely (*L'Ordine Nuovo*, pp.469-70):

> If there is in the world anything which is valuable in itself,
> all are capable and deserving of enjoying it. There are
> neither two truths nor two different modes of
> discussion . . . . You want him who was a slave yesterday
> to be a man? Then begin to treat him always as a man
> and the greatest step forward will already have been made.

In Italy, some adult educational initiatives (Gramsci instanced the Popular Universities) had failed in this respect, being somewhat like pedagogical 'soup kitchens'; or like missionaries in Africa handing out 'trashy baubles' to the natives (*Scritti Giovanile*, pp.61-4, 143-5; *Formazione*, p.94). By contrast he commended the work of literary critics (De Sanctis and Renato Serra) who showed that much critical erudition is 'a vain construction of literary men', 'barbed wire fences, with watchmen shouting "Who goes there?" '. The artist, critic and teacher ought to take the willing, but diffident and humble, by the arm, seeing their function as guides rather than as watchdogs of culture (*Formazione*, pp.77-9).

Gramsci's assumption that all men are capable of enjoying anything which is intrinsically valuable was the basis of his advocacy of a common humanistic education in the unity or comprehensive school. However, the common school was necessary not only to give everyone access to the best culture, but also as a condition of there being intellectuals who, themselves products of the unity school, would have some understanding of what is involved in the dialectic engagement of theory with the practice of common everyday life. It was precisely the existence of a segregated school system which had prevented traditional intellectuals from communicating with the man in the street (Manacorda, 1976, p.313).

Gramsci's belief in the possibility of such communication was not just a theoretical assumption: accounts suggest that he was 'an intellectual to whom workers could speak without fear of revealing their own ignorance' (Davidson, 1977, pp.73,

118). His faith in the possibility of intellectuals communicating with workers was expressed in his entire life as journalist (cf. Broccoli, 1972, p.53) and active politician, and through his explicitly educational initiatives in the political clubs for young workers and in the factories of Turin. For him, political education was integral with technical education, his assumption that intellectualism is fundamental to all work being the point of departure for an approach to the education of organic intellectuals within the industrial context itself.

Technical and vocational education

Although Gramsci's conception of the intellectual is essentially political in requiring from organic intellectuals the performance of administrative or leadership roles, there is, as we saw (pp.116), a second sense in which intellectualism can be considered organic; that is, with reference to the intellectual component of a job, whether this be professional or industrial, highly skilled or (as Gramsci insists) 'unskilled'. It has to be considered how far these two senses of 'organic intellectualism' are related, particularly with reference to the problem of educating organic intellectuals. The question is whether technical education has anything to contribute towards the development of intellectualism which is necessary for the effective performance of political functions.

The two notions of technical and non-technical organic intellectualism can be brought together in the concept of vocation. Although 'vocational education' has come to refer, narrowly, to the kind of technical training which is provided in preparation for manual work (and, as in the USA, often for unskilled or semi-skilled manual work[6]), historically the word has a much broader reference. Applied especially to the traditional learned professions, the conception of a vocation implied much more than the possession of a technical competence or skill. This long-established usage recognises that the worker is involved in more than the mere production of goods and services: in this sense, 'vocational' refers to the total cultural context within which work is undertaken. As in the familiar notions of having a vocation for the church, for teaching, for practising medicine, etc., the word has moral no less than technical implications. Having a vocation meant not only wanting to practise the technical skills of preaching, teaching, healing, etc., but also being committed to the well-being of other people, essentially a moral disposition. Thus, to have a vocation is to want more than mastery of the technical skill and knowledge required to complete an industrial or professional task competently. It also entails an awareness of moral obligation, an appreciation of the political and economic implications of a job of work and, often, of the aesthetics of 'production'. And though the conception of vocation is more often applied to the practice of the 'learned' professions, the notion of there being moral, political and aesthetic dimensions of work is by no means foreign to the practice of skilled artisans. Today a sense of responsibility towards customer, client or community is as necessary for the aircraft fitter, the automobile mechanic or the bus driver as it is for the teacher, the doctor or priest. Consumers expect that work will have been carried out with a sense of responsibility which, however tacitly, requires recognition of moral obligation on the part of the 'worker' and, often, that he has aesthetic sensibility.

It follows that, as well as the learning of technical competences, vocational education implies a confrontation with ethical, political and aesthetic imperatives bearing upon an occupation. Conceived broadly in this way it gives the worker insight into the cultural context in which he practises his technical skills. Traditionally, apprenticeship involved much more than technical training: it also involved initiation by a master into the moral norms of the craft, the teaching of responsible attitudes towards the client and the brotherhood of the craft; often it was carried on within the master's family.

This broad conception of vocation and its educational correlates is essential to an understanding of Gramsci's position on technical education and the education of organic intellectuals. His notion of intellectualism which is organic to a work role is integral to his conception of work as organic to a culture. For him, work was the crux of social relationships (*Notebooks*, pp.352-3):

The education of adults

> The individual does not enter into relationships with other men just by juxtaposition, but organically, in as much, that is, as he belongs to organic entities which range from the simple to the more complex. Thus man does not enter into relations with the natural world by being himself part of the natural world, but actively, by means of work and technique. Thus the ways in which the single individual enters into relations with nature are many and complex, since by technique one should understand not only the ensemble of scientific ideas applied industrially (which is the normal meaning of the word) but also the 'mental' instruments, philosophical knowledge.

Gramsci could not conceive of culture except as an expression of man's fundamental work activity as the producer of his own civilisation: 'work is the specific mode by which man actively participates in natural life in order to transform and socialise it more and more deeply and extensively' (ibid., p.34).[7]

Hence, the idea of work as a vocation is also central to an understanding of the sense in which Gramsci believed the schooling of children to be concerned with work and, indeed, to understanding the Marxist notion of polytechnical education (see pp.151-60 below). The notion of vocational education just outlined is obviously close to the conception of vocational education which Gramsci had in mind when insisting on the school's obligation to demonstrate how an understanding of natural and social laws facilitates men's work (*Notebooks*, pp.34-5):

> The discovery that the relations between the natural and social orders are mediated by work, by man's theoretical and practical activity, creates the first elements of an intuition of the world free from all magic and superstition. It provides the basis for the subsequent development of an historical, dialectic conception of the world, which understands movement and change, which appreciates the sum of effort and sacrifice which the present has cost the past and which the future is costing the present, and which conceives the contemporary world as a synthesis of the past, of all past generations, which projects itself into the future.

The education of adults

The foundation of vocational education could be laid in schools. But for Gramsci this could be no more than cultivating a generalised disposition towards accepting the disciplines of work (hence his notion of the school *as* work, in itself a kind of technical education, as apprenticeship) and use of the curriculum to establish the cultural point of work: that is, the fact of man's creation of a civilisation out of nature through his devising of manifold tools, techniques and forms of knowledge which constitute human work. Beyond pursuit of this general polytechnical principle, Gramsci was hostile towards technical and professional biases in the schooling of children and adolescents. He viewed with disquiet what he took to be the chaotic and unprincipled development of specialised technical schools in Italy. This, he believed, had a number of unfortunate consequences.

First, it frustrated the objective of providing for everyone a humanistic education 'designed to develop in each human being an as yet undifferentiated general culture, the fundamental powers to think and ability to find one's way in life' (ibid., p.26). In his earlier writings he had put this criticism much more polemically: 'Technical schools should not be allowed to become incubators of little monsters aridly trained for a job, with no general ideas, no general culture, no intellectual stimulation, but only with an infallible eye and a firm hand' (*Political Writings*, p.27). In a different context he wrote of professional schools producing 'half men' and of the need to create schools for 'complete men' (*Scritti Giovanile*, p.146). In Italy the development of a bilateral educational structure was intensifying: alongside the complex system of technical schools there survived a rump of the traditional classical school for the dominant class and intellectuals, a leisured class, 'a tiny *élite* of ladies and gentlemen who do not have to worry about assuring themselves a future career' (*Notebooks*, p.27). It was this denial to all but a privileged few of the benefits to be derived from a general humanistic education which Gramsci criticised as oligarchic (see above, pp.93-4) (*Political Writings*, p.26):

> What the proletariat needs is an educational system that is open to all. A system in which the child is allowed to develop and mature and acquire those general features

that serve to develop character. In a word, a humanistic school, as conceived by the ancients, and more recently by men of the Renaissance. A school which does not mortgage the child's future, a school that does not force the child's will, his intelligence and growing awareness to run along the tracks to a pre-determined station.

One of Gramsci's quarrels with the Italian Socialist Party was that it had accepted what he took to be the non-socialist position that there should be specialised schools for the different social classes: 'The socialists accept the concept that the vocational school is the school of the workers. In this lies the acknowledgement that, as an hereditary fact, there ought always to be two social classes. All socialist writers have always contradicted this thesis' (*Socialismo e fascismo*, pp.523-4).

This criticism points to a second unacceptable consequence of the unplanned growth of technical schools. A child's future social role is determined prematurely by this early vocational initiation in a technical school tied closely to a particular form of economic activity. Although the justification offered for the technical schools was that they were democratic and aimed at creating 'a new type of urban intellectual', Gramsci saw them as a device destined not merely to perpetuate social differences but 'to crystallise them into Chinese complexities' (*Notebooks*, p.40). In a letter to his wife, critical of the introduction of the Dalton Plan into Soviet primary schools with 'corners' devoted to specialised interests, he commented (Edinburgh Letters, no. CIII):

> What educational end is this meant to serve? The doubt could easily arise that a policy such as this might tend to accelerate the professional aptitudes in an artificial way, and falsify their inclinations; it might lead to the teachers losing sight of the aim of the school, which is to guide children forward to a harmonious development of all their activities, until such time as the formed personality gives evidence of more deep seated and permanent inclinations — which are a more reliable guide, seeing that they emerge at a higher level of development of all the vital forces.

A year later he put to his wife the model of a modern Renaissance man, against her attempts to infer specialised interests from the activities of their sons (ibid., no. CXXXIX):

> To tell you the truth, I haven't much time for such a precocious display of tendencies, and I must admit I haven't much faith either in your capacity for ascertaining what professional aptitude they do in fact tend to reveal. I should think that in both boys, as in all other children, there are likely to be found all sorts of tendencies, towards the practical side, towards theory and towards imagination. Consequently my feeling is that it would be more proper to guide them towards a more harmonious blend of all intellectual and practical faculties, confident that specialisation in one or the other of these will inevitably take place in due time on the basis of a personality vigorously formed and totally integrated. Modern man ought to be a synthesis of the qualities which are traditionally embodied in certain national characters: the American engineer, the German philosopher, the French 'political man', thus recreating so to speak, the Italian man of the Renaissance, the modern Leonardo da Vinci becomes 'mass man' and 'collective man' without sacrificing his own strong personality and individual originality.

Commenting on both of these letters, Manacorda observes that Gramsci's warning against the risk of conditioning when the defences of the child's own personality are still weak and giving the impression that a natural spontaneous development is taking place when, in fact, these specialised inclinations are the product of a conditioned environment, is in line with his polemic against spontaneity and heredity and his conception of man as a historical-social formation, and of the individual as the product of an interaction between innate qualities and a complex social environment (Manacorda, 1976, pp. 127-8, 137).

In this connection it is interesting that Gramsci would have found within his own experience the justification for his expectation that the theoretical and practical functions of intellectualism could be fused. In a letter to his wife musing on how far his son's reported activities showed him to have a practical bent, he reproved her for implying that he himself had always been a bookworm without practical interests (*Lettere*, no. 131):

> You are mistaken if you believe that, from being small, I had tendencies as a writer of literary and philosophical works. On the contrary, I was an intrepid pioneer and never left the house without having in my pocket some seeds of corn and matches wrapped up in little pieces of waxed cloth in case I could be tossed up on a desert island and abandoned to my own resources. I was then an enthusiastic boat and cart builder and I knew perfectly all the seafaring terminology.

These practical interests had been evident in the short period he had spent with his son who 'used to believe that I could repair all broken things' (ibid.; see also Fiori, 1970, pp.18-19, for an account of Gramsci's practical interests).

One of Gramsci's requirements for the school curriculum was that it should enable students to develop the sort of disinterested stance which had been the outcome of classical studies in the traditional secondary school. Gramsci's 'new' humanism, was rooted in the old. The modern studies which were to replace the classics 'as the fulcrum of the formative school' must, in similar fashion, establish the fundamental universal values of humanism and be the means of distancing oneself from preoccupation with immediate daily concerns. Presumably this was also one reason why vocational schools were not an acceptable alternative to the traditional classical schools. In suggesting that even for the pupils themselves learning should appear disinterested, Gramsci had in mind the importance, in their own interests, of pupils having an open mind and keeping their distance from specific engagement with a particular technical bias or avocation. Indeed, one of his criticisms of the specialised vocational schools was that their products were less well equipped than the products of the traditional academic secondary schools to cope with higher professional studies. He cited the view of an Italian educationist that 'in the Polytechnics the students coming from the *ginnasio-liceo* were better prepared to cope with advanced mathematics than those from the *scuole-istituti tecnici*. This superior preparation was provided through the complex "humanistic" instruction (history, literature, philosophy)' (*Quaderni*, I, p.136).

Nevertheless, this sort of conclusion touches on a controversial point, as Gramsci himself recognised. One of the difficulties encountered in attempts to prolong and universalise schooling of the traditional humanist type is that all adolescents do not appear to welcome this extension of schooling which is disinterested in one of Gramsci's senses — that of remaining neutral in terms of orientation towards a specific occupational role. For some students, indeed, the concrete link with an occupation which a technically oriented curriculum provides may give point or relevance to conventional academic subjects like science and mathematics. To demonstrate their technical application could be the 'romance' input which motivates learners towards the 'precision' component of learning; or, in Piagetian terms, it may provide the concrete-operational basis for the learning of formal operations.[8] Gramsci was, indeed, aware of the motivational value of vocational studies and he recognised that from the point of view of 'interest', immediately relevant and practical studies probably had the advantage over the disinterestedly humanistic curriculum. He even allowed that the right combination and mode of studies could turn professional schooling into a genuinely educational experience (*Political Writings*, p.27). Clearly, modernising the curriculum whilst avoiding the dangers inherent in the clamour that schooling should have immediate relevance would be far from easy (*Notebooks*, p.40). As we have seen, Gramsci's solution was the common school without specific vocational focus, but with an underlying curricular and methodological orientation emphasising the general cultural imperative towards work. Ultimately, however, specialised technical education would be required by every worker in a modern industrial economy. The question is when exactly this ought to begin if the demand is to be satisfied that both the humanistic and the technical are necessary correlates of everyone's education. This question of the appropriate time for a shift from a general polytechnical to a specialised professional education has been a matter for continuous discussion in Marxist educational systems. At the time when Gramsci was forming his opinions on this question, taking as his model the polytechnical experiments in the USSR, opinion was divided in that country about the respective merits of fifteen or seventeen as the appropriate age for beginning specialised professional education (Nearing, 1926, p.33). Without committing himself to a particular age, Gramsci implied that the appropriate point for technical education should be at the transition from school to work. The school should bring the adolescent to the point where he is able to make a vocational choice, but specialised training should not be provided in the comprehensive secondary school: 'From a common basic education, imparting a general, humanistic, formative culture . . . via repeated experiments in vocational orientation, pupils would pass on to one of the specialised schools or to productive work' (*Notebooks*, p.27).

Gramsci's emphasis upon school as work was an affirmation of his belief that work is intrinsic to learning itself. But the idea of a pedagogy of work was also instrumental, in the sense that school ought to habituate the student towards those dispositions required by industrial work. These he epitomised in the notion of 'Americanism'. We noted earlier how he had speculated on the cultural and educational effects of Meccano which he took to be symbolic of advanced industrial civilisation (pp.55-6 above). The doubts which he at first entertained that everything in modern culture, of which Meccano was the epitome, tends towards blunting of the imagination, were soon abandoned as he came to see the inevitability of technological education (Manacorda, 1976, pp.108-11). The *Notebooks* include lengthy passages in which he attempted to come to grips with 'Americanism'. (It is interesting that Manacorda's analysis of the development of Gramsci's educational thought is subtitled 'Americanism and Conformity'; he takes it for granted that the notes on Americanism, although apparently having no direct reference to schooling, are indispensable for a proper understanding of his theory of education (cf. 1976, p.218).) Gramsci found the characteristic tendency of European intellectuals towards anti-Americanism to be 'comic'. Americans were clearly adjusting effectively to the 'Taylorisation' of work, and he doubted the ability of Europeans to get to grips with large-scale industrial mechanisation and, especially, with its implications for life outside the work situation: 'We Europeans are still too Bohemian; we think we can do a certain job and live as we please, in Bohemian fashion. Naturally mechanisation crushes us, and I'm taking mechanisation in a broad sense, to include the scientific organisation of brainwork' (Lawner Letters, no. 49). 'To put it crudely, Europe would like to have a full barrel and a drunken wife, to have all the benefits which Fordism brings to competitive power while retaining its army of parasites who, by consuming vast sums of surplus value, aggravate initial costs and reduce competitive power on the international market' (*Notebooks*, p.281). It is, of course, questionable how far these strictures on European disinclination for discipline and attachment to Bohemianism can be generalised, for example, to Northern Europe.[9] However, it is also worth noting that the most recent cycle of spontaneity and freedom in schooling was concurrent with the 'Golden Age of Leisure' rhetoric of the 1960s, with its assumption that work would become an ever more marginal concern consequent upon industrial automation.

The problem of acquiring the discipline implicit in the development of technology was a recurrent theme in Gramsci's work. In his essay on ' "Animality" and Industrialism', he posed the problem as follows (*Notebooks*, p.298):

> The history of industrialism has always been a continuing struggle (which today takes an even more marked and vigorous form) against the element of 'animality' in man. It has been an uninterrupted, often painful and bloody process of subjugating natural (i.e. animal and primitive) instincts into new, more complex and rigid norms and habits of order, exactitude and precision which can make possible the increasingly complex forms of collective life which are the necessary consequence of industrial development. This struggle is imposed from outside, and the results to date, though they have great immediate practical value, are to a large extent purely mechanical: the new habits have not yet become 'second nature'.

What he found interesting about the United States was its recognition of this problem and the attempts there to induce the puritan discipline required by the new industrialism. In this connection he pointed to the scientific management movement (Taylorism), to the interest of industrialists (like Henry Ford) in the sexual and family life of workers and to social experiments like prohibition (*Notebooks*, pp.296-7, 301-6; cf. also Clark, 1970, p.70). If these had not succeeded, the fault lay not in the fact that attempts to cultivate socio-industrial disciplines were inappropriate or misguided, but rather in the fact that they were imposed upon workers mechanically by others (*Notebooks*, p.298):

> Up to now all changes in modes of existence and modes of life have taken place through brute coercion, that is to say through the dominion of one group over all the productive forces of society. The selection or 'education' of men adapted to the new forms of civilisation and to the new forms of production and work has taken place by means of incredible acts of brutality which have cast the weak and the non-conforming into the limbo of the lumpen-classes or have eliminated them entirely.

But simply because past efforts to induce industrial discipline had been coercive and inhumane, this did not mean that the task must be abandoned. Although Gramsci did not use the term in the context, his implication is that the 'Protestant work ethic' is as necessary to Socialism as it is to Capitalism. It is true that 'the socialist state exists potentially in the institutions of social life characteristic of the exploited class'. But this potential, 'these disorderly and chaotic energies must be given a permanent form and discipline' (*Political Writings*, pp.65-6). With respect to industrial and social discipline, however, the point of a socialist society would be that industrial discipline would be self-discipline: the required discipline 'can become internalised if it is proposed by a new form of society, with appropriate and original methods' (*Notebooks*, p.303, cf. also ibid., p.34; also Broccoli, 1972, p.112). This had also been a theme of his early writings: 'To know oneself means to be oneself, to be master of oneself, to free oneself from a state of chaos, to exist as an element of order — but of one's own order and one's own discipline in striving for an ideal' (*Political Writings*, p.13). For Gramsci 'it is not the existence of discipline which compromises liberty, but the type of power which ordains it' (Manacorda, 1976, p.344). Manacorda reminds us that his Americanism was 'an americanism not of american style' and concludes: 'Gramsci was interested in americanism, it is true, and speaks of americanism; but he has socialism much more in mind, but could not speak of it in prison; and americanism is the only word possible with which to speak of it' (ibid., p.365). But Americanism was more than a euphemism for socialism; it was a necessary vehicle towards socialism. Gramsci confessed admiration for the Italian manifestations of Americanism — the Italian industrialists who were equivalents of Ford: 'They who uproot the ignorant, stubborn masses of the countryside from their quiet, lethargic somnolence and hurl them into the glowing crucible of our civilisation ... Agnelli builds factories and inevitably the workers become socialists' (*Scritti Giovanile*, pp.34-5).

As his reference to a 'new form of society' indicates, Gramsci was concerned not only with the discipline required by the worker to maintain efficient production procedures in the technical sense, when actually involved in the job of work; he also, and especially, had in mind the discipline necessary to acquire political, economic and administrative skill and knowledge necessary to develop new productive and distributive relationships and to organise steadfastly for political action. He did, indeed, consider it a cause for pride that during the workers' occupation of factories in Turin in 1920, production was often maintained at normal levels (and even increased) despite the workers' being permanently on the alert against possible attack from outside (Cammett, 1967, pp.116-17; cf. also Clark, 1977, pp.161-2, 173-4). This was the result, in large measure, of the Factory Councils giving the workers high standards of discipline and seriousness and the workers' accepting the strict discipline required by the fact that they were unable to leave the factories during the occupation: 'The use of alcoholic beverages was forbidden, and punishments for stealing were severe' (Cammett, 1967, p.115, cf. also Clark, 1977, p.159). The Turin workers had voluntarily disciplined themselves to accept the 'prohibitions' which American industrialists had attempted to impose. This example of 'Americanisation' of the Turin worker was the model for the industrial and political discipline necessary to the future Italian working class, and an emphasis on the need to acquire self-discipline

The education of adults

through membership of Factory Councils was a constant theme of *L'Ordine Nuovo* (*Political Writings*, p.67):

> Such a system of workers' democracy ... would give the masses a permanent structure and discipline. It would be a magnificent school of political and administrative experience and would involve the masses down to the last man, accustoming them to tenacity and perseverance, and to thinking of themselves as an army in the field which needs a strict cohesion if it is not to be destroyed and reduced to slavery.

It was partly in order to promote the development of discipline at work that Gramsci proposed a pedagogy where schooling was conceived *as work* (*Notebooks*, p.34; and cf. pp.53-64 above).

With reference to his fears about the possible threat to the humanist imagination implicit in the Meccano-Americanisation syndrome, Gramsci's conclusion, then, was that this offered both a challenge which Europeans could not ignore and an opportunity to develop the new culture and the new intellectualism. Serious study of the phenomenon of 'Americanism' was an example of learning from the adversary. Asking, rhetorically, 'whether the type of industry and organisation of work and production typical of Ford is rational; whether, that is, it can and should be generalised, or whether, on the other hand, we are not dealing with a malignant phenomenon which must be fought against through trade-union action and through legislation?', he concluded: 'It seems possible to reply that the Ford method is rational, that is, that it should be generalised; but that a long process is needed for this, during which a change must take place in social conditions, and in the way of life and habits of individuals' (*Notebooks*, p.312). But why should Fordism constitute an opportunity if, as Gramsci also concluded, American industrialists like Ford 'are not concerned with the humanity or the spirituality of the worker, which are immediately smashed?'

First, so far as the rationalisation of production can be carried to the extent of asking from the worker only the routine, mechanical gestures required by the conveyor belt, this frees his mind for reflection upon his condition (*Notebooks*, pp.309-10):

Once the process of adaptation has been completed, what really happens is that the brain of the worker, far from being mummified, reaches a state of complete freedom. The only thing that is completely mechanised is the physical gesture; the memory of the trade, reduced to simple gestures repeated at an intense rhythm, 'nestles' in the muscular and nervous centres and leaves the brain free and unencumbered for other occupation. One can walk without having to think about all the movements needed in order to move, in perfect synchronisation, all the parts of the body, in the specific way that is necessary for walking. The same thing happens and will go on happening in industry with the basic gestures of the trade. One walks automatically, and at the same time thinks about whatever one chooses. American industrialists have understood all too well this dialectic inherent in the new industrial methods. They have understood that 'trained gorilla' is just a phrase, that 'unfortunately' the worker remains a man and even that during his work he thinks more, or at least has greater opportunities for thinking, once he has overcome the crisis of adaptation without being eliminated: and not only does the worker think, but the fact that he gets no immediate satisfaction from his work and realises that they are trying to reduce him to a trained gorilla, can lead him into a train of thought that is far from conformist. That the industrialists are concerned about such things is made clear from a whole series of cautionary measures and 'educative' initiatives which are well brought out in Ford's books and the work of Philip.[10]

This conclusion that the body disciplined to rationalised work routines harbours a mind alive to the possibilities of revolutionary socialist action is, perhaps, optimistic. As another educationist has concluded, the mind set free by the conveyor-belt from thinking about the work the body does is more likely to escape into daydream and fantasy (Castle, 1961). The 'educative initiatives' of which Gramsci wrote have been only too successful in inducing a disposition towards escapism. However, in an early article in *L'Ordine Nuovo*, Gramsci conceded that it is a miracle 'that the worker still manages to think, even when he is reduced to operating in complete ignorance of the how or why of his practical activity. It is the miracle of the worker who takes charge each day of his own intellectual autonomy and his own freedom to handle ideas, by struggling against fatigue, against boredom and against the monotony of a job that strives to mechanise and to kill his inner life' (*Political Writings*, p.332-3). But Gramsci was clear that workers are only capable of holding on to their intellectual integrity — what he compared with Christian martyrdom — so far as they are being educated in workers' associations which generate 'the moral forces that sustain their will' (ibid.). Without this moral and educational impetus, the worker 'is intellectually lazy; he cannot and does not wish to look beyond his immediate horizon, so he lacks criteria in his choice of leaders and allows himself to be easily taken in by promises. He likes to believe he can get what he wants without making a great effort himself or thinking too much' (*Political Writings*, p.333). Again, Gramsci compared the support which the worker has from his political associations to that of a Christian community which, 'for the slave or the artisan of classical times, was the agency through which he "knew himself" and achieved his own liberation' (ibid.).

However, Gramsci seemed to see the period of intensifying mechanisation and division of labour as transitional towards the automation of production.[11] For he did see the possibility of a deepening of intellectualism through changes organic to technological development in itself; that is, through the interpenetration of work and science. His notions of a progression from 'technique-as-work' to 'technique-as-science' anticipates the modern accelerating shift from highly mechanised manual work towards automation, with the consequent diminution of the demand for manual (especially unskilled) labour and an expansion of the professions and para-professions in the middle ranges of the economy: the growth of what Macciocchi has called 'de nouvelles et très larges couches de techniciens intellectuels' (Macciocchi, 1974, p.302). Gramsci did, indeed, foresee developments which would mean that 'a part of the old working class will be pitilessly eliminated from the world of labour, and perhaps from the world *tout court*' (*Notebooks*, p.303). Whatever

The education of adults

one's sentiments about this withering of the traditional working class, it ought to bring compensations. Historically, a great deal of manual work has been degrading and soul-destroying. Moreover, the essence of the sort of freedom in work which is implied in Marx's notion of men freely moving from one occupation to another (fishing, hunting, farming, criticising at different times of day without ever becoming hunter, fisherman, shepherd or critic) is captured by an economy in which work increasingly approximates to the conditions under which the liberal professions are practised — conditions favouring a good deal of freedom about when and where work is performed and, hence, an increase in the autonomy of the worker. This also has implications for the liberalisation of professional education, especially when combined with Gramsci's notion of a merging of the two kinds of organic intellectualism already noted (p.116 above).

Alongside the intellectual whose intellectualism is organic to leadership as a socio-political function, the technological-scientific nexus of the new industrialism generates that second kind of intellectual whose intellectualism is organic to the productive process itself. But if the productive process is to serve humanistic and social ends, the new technical-scientific organic intellectual requires, above all, a component of his education to be in historical humanism. As Gramsci put it: 'from technique-as-work one proceeds to technique-as-science and to the humanistic conception of history, without which one remains "specialised" and does not become "directive" (specialised and political)' (*Notebooks*, p.10). In a passage which foreshadows the 'two cultures' debate of the early 1960s, Gramsci complained of the way in which the idealist philosophers, Croce and Gentile, had contributed towards an isolating of the natural sciences from 'thought in general' (*Quaderni*, III, pp.694-5). Such a separation of science from the cultural mainstream would make for not only the impoverishment of science, but also for the impoverishment of culture itself: 'There can be no culture without science' (Manacorda, 1972, p.357). The function of a humanistic component in technical education is to ensure that 'the specialist ... knows how to find in the innermost parts of his own specialisation that universal meaning which can become also a constituent of the industrial personality' (Urbani, 1967, p.333). In this way the specialist also becomes leader in acting 'towards other men with whom he meets or with whom he engages in concrete relationships enabling him subsequently to modify these relationships in the direction of progressive civilisation' (ibid.). Humanistic culture is only antithetical to vocational education on the assumption that work is dehumanising, the 'curse of Adam'. But on the contrary view that human culture is a product of the struggle with nature to create a civilisation — man's work — a 'humanistic concept of history' has to take account of that part of human life which is dedicated to work. In a way which points to the kind of thing Gramsci had in mind when stressing the need for a fusion of technical and humanistic education, a modern Marxist has outlined the shortcomings of those having only a technical-scientific training and, by implication, has focused the concerns which this kind of personnel ought to display with reference to the uses of science and techology (Gorz, 1977, pp.134-5):

> To a large extent, this type of technical and scientific personnel would be of little use in a society bent on meeting the more basic social and cultural needs of the masses. They would be of little use because their type of knowledge is hardly relevant to what would be needed to improve the quality of life and to help the masses to take their destiny in their own hands. For example, technical and scientific workers, though they may know a lot about the technicalities of their specialised fields, know very little nowadays about the ways to make the work process more pleasant and self-fulfilling for the workers; they know very little about what is known as 'ergonomy' — the science of saving effort and avoiding fatigue — and they are not prepared to help workers into self-organising the work process and in adjusting production technology to their physical and psychic needs. (Moreover, they are not generally capable of conveying their specialised knowledge to workers holding less or different training and of sharing it with them.) In other words, technical and scientific knowledge is not only to a large extent disconnected from the needs and

> the life of the masses; it is also culturally and semantically disconnected from general comprehensive culture and common language . . . . Hence this paradox that the main intellectual activity of advanced industrial societies should remain sterile as regards the development of comprehensive popular culture.

Technical-scientific workers who were interested, thus, in improving the quality of life (including communication with other workers) would be examples of what Gramsci had in mind by working-class organic intellectuals.

To conceive the role of intellectuals in this way is to argue that, in the sense in which we have defined it, work must become a vocation, an activity located in a broad cultural context. It was partly for this reason that Gramsci had insisted upon a prolonged period of common humanistic schooling for all children, irrespective of an individual's ultimate destination as an adult worker in a particular occupation. But in an earlier polemic against the distorting (i.e. of complete human development) effect of the professional school he had implied that a properly developed adult could profit from the right kind of professional education. (*Scritti Giovanile*, p.59). He envisaged that the impetus towards merging management with technical functions would come from both directions. For if the scientific-technical organic intellectual requires humanistic studies to provide the cultural context for his specialised technical education, the organic intellectual in the socio-political sense, whose skills and interests dispose him to be directive or political rather than technical and scientific, requires a technical component in his education. Thus, through the 'intellectualisation' of practical activity and the 'practicalisation' of theoretical activity, 'the technical and the directive functions will no longer be capable of separation' (Manacorda, 1976, pp.207, 201). Gramsci illustrated his conception of the fusing of technical and directive functions by reference to his experiences as an editor working with specialised staff on editorial committees whose collaborative efforts raised them to the status of 'cultural groups' (*Notebooks*, p.28). But he also saw the need for a marriage of technical with administrative competences as especially necessary for the political leader who 'must have that minimum of general technical culture which will permit him, if not to "create" autonomously the correct solution, at least to know how to adjudicate between the solutions put forward by the experts, and hence to choose the correct one from the "synthetic" viewpoint of political technique' (ibid.).

The vocational education which is implicit in the merging of technical and management functions aimed at humanising work and showing the different cultural and moral imperatives of a New Order, is a process which can begin in school, as Gramsci thought it must. But its fruition lies in post-school education. As with political education, to which it is obviously organically related, vocational education is adult education. This is necessarily true of its technical component. As Gramsci insisted, technical training was not to be undertaken in school as a means of premature selection for an economic role: it was, rather a continuation of education when the decision for a particular work role had already been made. In the same way, a fuller appreciation of the cultural (and, especially, political) implications of work had to be organic to a particular occupation or profession. That is to say, intellectualism organic to specific economic and social roles can only fructify within those roles. As a political and moral enterprise, vocational education can only have meaning in the experience of the worker already committed to a particular occupation.

Especially for those who would pass directly from school into productive work, two institutions would serve to contribute towards the two dimensions of vocational education, the technical and the socio-political. Trade unions would be responsible for the technical education of workers in a particular trade or industrial process (Cammett, 1967, p.85). But it was the Factory Council which was concerned with political and economic education, aimed at teaching those administrative and economic skills necessary for workers to take control of factories and administer efficiently the productive process. The councils were intended to be 'unique organs of power and supreme direction for the organisation of production and distribution, as well as for the whole complex of economic, moral, and political relations that derive from it' (Cammett, 1967, p.90 quoting Pietro Nenni;

cf. also ibid., pp.72-95; Boggs, 1976, ch. 6; Davidson, 1977, pp.113, 117; Broccoli, 1972, p.134; Clark, 1972, p.61, on Gramsci's conception of the different functions of Trade Unions and Factory Councils). This underlines Gramsci's notion that counter-hegemonic activity must be educational and not simply an attempt at forcible replacement of the capitalist class. Expropriation of the means of production without understanding of the relations of production and the administrative and fiscal skills required to organise production in complex industrial enterprises would produce what we now call lame industrial ducks, not 'the capacity to put into operation and direct the process of production of economic goods' (*Political Writings*, p.346). A knowledge of the complex of legal, bureaucratic, fiscal and distributive mechanisms which are the context of industrial technical production in any complex industrial society is as essential to worker-managers in a socialist society as it is to executives in a capitalist society. As with political democracy, industrial democracy could not flourish in a vacuum of ignorance about the economic and administrative imperatives of modern industrial enterprises or the complex national and international economies in which they function. If necessary, it was acceptable to learn industrial techniques from the adversary (Cammett, 1967, p.82; and see above pp.43-6). As Clark concludes: 'Gramsci was concerned not only with the changes in men's consciousness that were necessary for "revolution", but also with those necessary for any industrial system' (1977, p.70).

Gramsci's insistence that specialised vocational preparation — in both its technical and cultural aspects — is a function of adult education, was based upon social rather than pedagogical assumptions. His argument was that it is inequitable to predetermine social roles in childhood and early adolescence, not that it is pedagogically impracticable. The question therefore remains, is there also pedagogical efficiency in postponing specialised vocational education to a stage where it can be undertaken intrinsically to the performance of productive work in industry and the professions? This raises the perennial educational problem of the relationship between theory and practice to which we now turn.

Part three

Theory and practice in education

The philosophy of praxis

Practising teachers frequently dismiss educational theory as irrelevant to their daily endeavours in schools: what seems 'good in theory' often turns out to be practically lame on the classroom floor. Similarly, students and their parents are apt to put a discount on purely theoretical subjects which tend to be dismissed as irrelevant to life.

Although Gramsci did not directly address these problems in his educational essays, the problem of uniting theory with practice is a theme which is fundamental to his exploration of the nature of hegemony and of the counter-hegemonic education of workers towards radical political activity. Praxis is the notion he employs to point, conceptually, towards the unity of theory and practice: he refers repeatedly to 'the philosophy of praxis'. It is generally accepted by Gramscian scholars that this phrase was one of his euphemisms employed to disarm the prison censor. In Gramsci, for 'the philosophy of praxis' one should read 'Marxism' (see, for example, Hoare and Smith, 1971, pp.xi-xiii). Since Fascism also claimed to be a philosophy of praxis (*prassi*, see Minio-Puluello, 1946, p.124) this was, no doubt, a shrewd disguise. But, as with his alleged praises of traditional educational institutions in order to divert the censor from his educational radicalism, 'philosophy of praxis' is not merely used euphemistically. Gramscian scholars have made the point that substitution of the phrase for 'dialectical materialism' or 'Marxism' is more than just a prudent response to the exigencies of working in prison. It functions autonomously 'to define what he saw to be a central characteristic of the philosophy of Marxism, the inseparable link it establishes between theory and practice, thought and action' (Hoare and Smith, 1971, p.xiii; see also Prestipino, 1976, p.viii). However, Gramsci claimed that this theory-practice relationship had been inadequately formulated by Marxists.

Marx's admonition in his Eleventh Thesis on Feuerbach that 'philosophers have only interpreted the world in various ways' whilst 'the point is to change it', has often been taken as a command to abandon theory or philosophy. Richard Bernstein takes this response to be a misunderstanding of Marx's thesis, which was not an invitation to abandon philosophy, but a characterisation of what philosophy necessarily is, and an invitation to act only with understanding: 'In this thesis, Marx is characterising what he understands to be the aim of philosophy — an aim enshrined in the Cartesian tradition — but calling for the need to go "beyond" philosophy' (1971, p.6); and 'beyond', but through, philosophy is praxis. Hoffman has made a similar point in criticism of those Marxists who have drawn on the Eleventh Thesis as authority for their call to abandon philosophy (1975, p.31):

> Is Marx suggesting here that if we want to change the world, then we must *stop* interpreting it? That all theory hampers practice and must be dispensed with? Merely to formulate the question in this way demonstrates its obvious absurdity. For Marx's point is not that we must stop thinking, but that one cannot change the world by thought *alone*: revolutions are made, not in the philosopher's study, but in the real world. This means, therefore, that we do not reject every form of philosophy (i.e., cease thinking), but rather seek to formulate a *new conception of thought* which will consciously set itself the task of transforming the world and not — as philosophers have tended to do in the past — attempt to fossilise it in a reactionary manner — A concrete, practical way of thinking must supplant an abstract, metaphysical one.

Gramsci believed that Marxism had gone little of the way towards understanding how to unify theory and practice in pursuit of this task of changing the world:

> In the most recent developments of the philosophy of praxis the elaboration and refinement of the concepts of the unity of theory and practice is still only at an early stage. There still remain residues of mechanicism, since people speak about theory as a 'complement' or an 'accessory' of practice, or as the handmaid of practice.

He called for an approach towards what he called 'the full synthetic meaning of the concept', the 'correct understanding of the unity of theory and practice' in a way which put neither in a position of subservience to the other (*Notebooks*, pp.334-6).

Polytechnical education and the relationship between theory and practice

In this century, the marriage of theory and practice in education has been sought, notably, by Dewey and in those educational systems which have their roots in Marxism. In both, the theory-practice nexus has been sought in work. Dewey described the origin of what has come to be known as the project method in children's curiosity about the different properties of textiles from which their clothing was made. He concluded that a study of the various origins and manufacturing processes, as well as the different uses of different textile fibres, would encapsulate the whole of human history and, by implication, of human art and science: 'You can concentrate the history of all mankind into the evolution of the flax, cotton and wool fibres into clothing' (Dewey, 1959, p.22). If extended to cover a range of manufacturing processes, the Deweyan project would fit Gramsci's own requirement that, as the characteristic activity through which men co-operate to transform nature for their civilised purposes, work should be the focus of the curriculum (see pp.53 above).

However, it is in the practice of polytechnical education in Marxist educational systems that there have been periodic

Theory and practice in education

and systematic attempts to use work experience as the means of seeking the unity of theory and practice. Especially, children have from time to time been employed for considerable periods in productive work. But, as the periodic changes of emphasis upon work in polytechnical schools in the USSR indicate, the desired objective is elusive. In practice, work experience has often seemed educationally stultifying rather than fruitful. Evidently, the marriage of theory and practice is not achieved simple by sending children to work in neighbouring industrial enterprises. In particular, theory itself often seems to be impoverished through this device, with unfortunate consequences for practice, especially industrial practice.

The failure to achieve satisfactory unity between theory and practice stems, in part, from a confusion of motives in wanting to emphasise practical as against theoretical education. At a rudimentary level, practical work in schools is sometimes undertaken out of recognition of the difficulty of keeping children still at seatwork (usually bookwork) for long periods of time. There is some warrant for this justification of the educational value of industrial work in the passage from *Capital* where Marx himself enunciated 'the great principle' which has come to be known as 'polytechnical education' (1919, pp.528-30):

> Paltry as the education clauses of the Act[1] appear on the whole, yet they proclaim elementary education to be an indispensable condition to the employment of children. The success of those clauses proved for the first time the possibility of combining education and gymnastics with manual labour, and, consequently, of combining manual labour with education and gymnastics. The factory inspectors soon found out by questioning the schoolmasters, that the factory children, although receiving only one half the education of the regular day scholars, yet learnt quite as much and often more. 'This can be accounted for by the simple fact that, with only being at school for one half of the day, they are always fresh, and nearly always ready and willing to receive instruction. The system on which they work, half manual labour, and half school, renders each employment a rest

and a relief to the other; consequently, both are far more congenial to the child, than would be the case were he kept constantly at one. It is quite clear that a boy who has been at school all the morning, cannot (in hot weather particularly) cope with one who comes fresh and bright from his work.' Further information on this point will be found in Senior's speech at the Social Science Congress at Edinburgh in 1863. He there shows, amongst other things, how the monotonous and uselessly long school hours of the children of the upper and middle classes, uselessly add to the labour of the teacher, 'while he not only fruitlessly but absolutely injuriously, wastes the time, health, and energy of the children'. From the Factory system budded, as Robert Owen has shown us in detail, the germ of the education of the future, an education that will, in the case of every child over a given age, combine productive labour with instruction and gymnastics, not only as one of the methods of adding to the efficiency of production, but as the only method of producing fully developed human beings.

Although the young Gramsci had struggled with the idea of making schools like factories, ultimately this conception of the correlative functions of schooling and industrial work had little attraction for him and he concluded that one of the points about school itself was that it trained the scholar (and, necessarily, all children, any of whom might become scholars) for lengthy and often tedious and routine 'seat-work': 'The school if it is taken seriously does not have time for the workshop, and vice versa' (*Sotto la Mole*, p.239). Whatever the merit of Marx's view of industrial work as a refreshing rest from study (and vice versa), it evidently is not a serious insight into the problem of *uniting* theory and practice. For it is not clear *how* an experience of industrial work (especially the kind of soul-destroying work which Marx himself judged to be 'alienating' and where man, in his own phrase, is merely 'a living appendage to the machine' — 1919, pp.528-30) alongside the learning of quite unrelated theoretical knowledge in schools could constitute a uniting of theory and practice. It is interesting that those who trace the modern practice of polytechnical education to this passage in Marx are apt to quote no more than its final sentence, ignoring the remainder which, in effect, underwrites the nineteenth-century *status quo* with reference to child labour (although, as Price argues, Marx's advocacy of 'the great principle' has to be read in the context of his expectations for the human condition under conditions of Communism). Indeed, it has to be remembered that the British Labour Movement, on progressive and humanitarian grounds, spent most of the nineteenth century fighting the 'half-time' principle and seeking to extend the period of full-time compulsory education. Certainly, under the 'alienating' conditions in which industrial work is performed under capitalism, it is not clear how a working-class movement could have done otherwise. Silver analyses the evidence adduced for and against the half-time system during the prolonged debate in England during the latter half of the nineteenth century and concludes that Marx failed to report the conflicting evidence on the effects of the system, ignoring 'the criticisms and the critics'. He believes that Marx also misread the position of Owen and other radicals on the employment of children such that his polytechnical principle 'does not derive from the tradition he claimed for it' (1977, pp.154-7). Simon (1965, pp.137-42) describes something of this struggle against the half-time system and himself concludes that 'on any human grounds the system was indefensible'.

Marx himself pointed, concretely, to two benefits from the educational clauses of the Factory Act. First, he claimed that implementation of the Act gave evidence that its provisions were pedagogically practical and useful in giving refreshing rest from academic work in the form of an alternative, non-intellectual, manual activity and in bringing the child 'fresh and bright' from work to school. In fact there is little evidence that this last outcome was achieved. On the contrary, E.P. Thompson (1968b) quotes an autobiographical fragment from a victim of the half-time system, a working-class organic intellectual and political activist who was also committed to workers' adult education: 'I had worked since I was 9 years old ... working from six o'clock to 12 ... when we got to school at 2 o'clock we used to fall asleep on the desk' (see also Silver, 1977). Second, Marx saw the Act as the thin end of the wedge — 'that first and meagre concession wrung from capital' (*Capital*, p.534) – in establishing the right to education: he also claimed that the half-time principle drove the thin end of a different wedge into the romantic notion of protecting the child from the descending 'shades of the prison house' when he asserted the child's right to work, approving the 'contemporary industrial tendency to attract children and adolescents for participation in the great business of social production' (Shore, 1947, p.53, quoting Marx's instructions to the delegates to the Geneva Congress of 1866). But in approving both rights – to schooling and to work – and in asserting that the Act was successful in proving 'the possibility of combining education and gymnastics with manual labour', Marx was making, on the one hand, an ethical point and, on the other hand, the point that combining schooling with productive work is a practical possibility in organisational and economic terms. Nothing he claimed for the educational values of the Act can be construed as espistemological, that is, an account of ways in which theory and practice can be said to be related through juxtaposition of two quite different kinds of human experience. As Shore reminds us, 'Marx was not explicit in the terminology with which he described the type of education embraced in his "great principle". It was the principle itself, namely "education with production" which was important to Marx and his would-be followers' (ibid., p.65).

Nevertheless, this passage from *Capital* has been authoritative for the practice of polytechnical education in Marxist educational systems, notably those of the USSR and China. In both, the advocacy of combining schooling with manual labour (whether within schools or in neighbouring industrial or agricultural enterprises) has gone beyond the claims of Marx's own rationale. In particular, polytechnical education has been an attempt to solve the problem of the intellectuals, an intention which has only underlined the intractability of the problem of uniting theory with practice in terms of Marx's own polytechnical principle – that of simply putting manual work experience alongside schooling.

Krushchev's reforms of 1958, aimed at intensifying polytechnical education which had been a 'muted theme' since the 1930s, were proclaimed in a polemic which deplored a tendency to see schooling in terms of preparation for the learned professions and the disinclination in a growing number of families to place a properly socialist evaluation upon manual labour. Similarly the Chinese cultural revolution's actions against 'a revisionist line in education' which 'put intellectual knowledge first' was an assertion of the need for intellectuals to respect the dignity of workers and peasants (Gamberg, 1977, p.117):

> Only by having students work with those previously despised — go to factories and labour side by side with them at their machines, have them come into the schools and be the teachers, dig in their fields and live in their homes — only by those means could the new generation of students come to discover the workers' and peasants' intelligence, esteem their humanity, and learn genuinely to respect them.

The imperative to cultivate social rapport between intellectuals and workers is an essential objective of socialist education, as our examination of Gramsci's account of the problem of the intellectuals has indicated. Indeed, at first sight, Gramsci appears to be in sympathy with Marx's principle of combining study with manual work: 'Unity of manual and intellectual work . . . may be motives of inspiration for a new approach in solving the problem of the intellectuals . . .' (*Notebooks*, p.186). However, 'unity' is the key notion in this passage. For it is *unity* between theory and practice which programmes of polytechnical education have signally failed to achieve. It is evident that the academic content of those school programmes is rarely a study of the theory underlying the practice involved in the industrial work to which children are sent; nor is the manual work usually an opportunity to apply the theory learned in the classroom. In Marx's original advocacy noted above there is, of course, no claim for a fusing of work and study in this sense. But unless the polytechnical principle is conceived as an attempt to secure this kind of intimate connection between theory and practice, it is not clear that it has any contribution to make towards the task proposed in the Eleventh Thesis, of rescuing philosophy from praxical sterility by, in Hoffman's formulation, discovering 'a concrete practical way of thinking' which supplants 'an abstract metaphysical one'.

Theory and practice in education

As applied in Marxist educational systems, the merit claimed for experience of manual work is that, although it may often be physically demanding and unpleasant, it is, nevertheless, socially useful. In the literature of Chinese education, for example, a good deal of reference is made to how salutary a learning experience it is for students to be involved in collecting 'night soil'. There is never reference to what might be a relevant theoretical outgrowth of such an experience — discussion of alternative modes of sanitation. To be sure, it was claimed as a virtue of the Chinese village tea schools that the theoretical academic curriculum was organised around the study of the tea growing. This, indeed, seems the only fruitful educational pedagogical avenue towards fusing theory with practice — the attempt to theorise about what people are actually doing in productive manual work. But this sort of attempt to derive theory from practice and to improve practice by thinking about it, is usually the rock on which polytechnical education founders. Discussing Lenin's failure to transplant Marx's polytechnical principle on to Russian soil, Lilge concludes: 'its transfer from theory to practice was beset by numerous difficulties unresolved to this day' (1976, p.56). In the USSR, the tendency to mute the polytechnical emphasis from time to time is justified for various reasons. Two are of particular educational importance. First, tying theoretical studies to the practice of the particular enterprise (factory or farm, for example) where the student is sent to work violates the other principle of polytechnical education that there should be a comprehensive study of all the modes of production in a technological society, aimed at 'imparting the general principles of all processes of production', and of the culture of work. Far from experience of manual work in a particular enterprise giving the rounded perspective which Gramsci and Marxist educationists have required of the new humanistic education, work experience of this kind does, indeed, seem to be a device for crystallising the world into 'Chinese complexities' (see above pp.132-3).

But a second reason for abandoning the manual work emphasis in polytechnical education is the apparent impoverishment of intellectual education to which, in practice, it seems prone. In 1928, Krupskaya, Lenin's widow, evaluated the first Soviet cycle of polytechnical education. She concluded that 'about polytechnical education one may speak only conditionally' (quoted by Shore, 1947, p.165). Three years later she called for moderation of the polytechnical emphasis upon work experience and pointed to the problems which had become evident over the previous decade (ibid., pp.171-2):

> The successes of the country's industrialisation made possible the polytechnization of the school. But this was a new undertaking demanding of the pedagogues a very earnest preparation of which they are often short. As a result there is unskillfulness to combine theory with practice; an imperceptible slide in the direction of ignoring theory, the underestimation of the latter. It is inadmissible that labour should stand in the path of knowledge.

Krupskaya's concern about this threat to the general cultural component of the curriculum was increasingly echoed in the early 1930s and it led to the abandoning of the manual labour component of polytechnical education until a mounting post-war re-emphasis upon the polytechnical principle led to its practical reinstatement in the Kruschev reforms of the late 1950s, themselves destined to be only short-lived in this respect (see Shore, 1947. Bereday *et al.*, 1960 Price, 1974, Lilge, 1976, and Grant, 1968, on the fluctuating fortunes of polytechnical education in the USSR).

A similar fluctuation of the fortunes of work combined with study also seems likely in China. For reaction against the insistence on significant manual work experience tends to be triggered by the fear that the tendency towards anti-intellectualism which Krupskaya noted does, indeed, have adverse consequences for the development of a modern economy. The apparently unfavourable economic consequences following from a strong application of the polytechnical principle have certainly been a factor in its periodic rejection in the USSR where its 'rentability' has been questioned (Shore, 1947, p.168). Currently, it is this sort of economic imperative which has led to pressure for the restoration of the academic curriculum in China. Eckstein's study of the Chinese economy concludes by questioning the capacity of the educational system, as restructured following the Cultural Revolution, to sustain the Revolution (including replacing the revolutionary leaders with successors no less qualified and expert) in the context of economic growth. And from within China itself, especially since the death of Mao, there has been renewed questioning of the 'rentability' of linking schooling with productive work. Observers of the Chinese educational scene report criticisms of excessive focus upon moral-political objectives in combining work with study, at the expense of intellectual aims whose pursuit seems necessary for raising theory and practice to the levels required for economic development; in effect, sacrificing the long term for the short term with reference to economic growth (see Chamber, 1977, Price, 1974, Shirk, 1978). The pedagogical sequence of 'practice-theory-practice' has been replaced by 'practice-practice-practice'.

It is not difficult to understand the situations which lead to this exclusive preoccupation with practice. Intellectuals in ivory towers (attempting to solve practical problems 'with a pen, a sheet of paper and a cup of tea') and imported textbooks which refer to quite alien conditions (with reference to agriculture, for example — see Chambers, 1977) seem little help to a country interested in rapid modernisation. But, as the critics argue, if an excess of irrelevant theory is dysfunctional for economic modernisation and growth, the search for relevant theories is probably inhibited by the diminution of academic teaching and research in favour of practical work and the subjugation of academics to peasants and workers. Chambers reports criticisms of the effects of this on developments in science and engineering and cites, from his own experience, the example 'of a Chinese university's foreign language department in which teaching materials have to be scrutinised by a master worker who has no knowledge of any foreign language before they can be passed on to students'. One cannot predict that manual work experience as a component of schooling will be subject to similar fluctuations in China as it has been in the USSR. Observers of Chinese education think it unlikely to be abolished entirely, but Shirk concludes that the 'moderates' now in power will retain it mainly for its symbolic value and that, if compelled to choose between economic development and the continuing transformation of 'social-political values', 'they would prefer to sacrifice political revolution in favour of economic progress'. In any event, it is clear from the educational histories of China and the USSR that political and social exigences affecting the combination of schooling with manual work are apt to frustrate the epistemological aim of integrating work with study in the search for an understanding of how theory relates to practice.

Education and Gramsci's conception of praxis

Given his stress on the importance of schools transmitting knowledge and academic skills, and in view of his own debt to the outcomes of an academic education, it is not surprising (despite his early polemic against career intellectuals) that Gramsci did not engage in advocacy either of practical subjects in schools or part-time manual work experience for children in productive enterprises. This last would not have been consistent with his insistence upon the need to acquire the widest possible culture without premature engagement in specific work roles. It seems clear that he concluded that the manual work component of polytechnical schooling would not have made any contribution towards the development of a philosophy of praxis. Certainly he did not intend that the search for rapport between intellectuals and manual workers should result in the impoverishment of theory: if the philosophy of praxis 'affirms the need for contact between intellectuals and the simple it is not in order to restrict scientific activity' (*Notebooks*, p.332). Nor was Gramsci convinced that experience of manual work is any antidote to the snobbery of intellectuals. On the practice in the English Public (i.e. exclusively private) School at Oundle of putting upper-class boys to work at manual activities, he commented (*Quaderni*, II, p.1183):

> This example shows how necessary it is to define exactly the concept of the unitary school in which labour and theory are closely linked; the mechanical juxtaposition of the two activities can be merely snobbish. One hears tell of great intellectuals who amuse themselves working

as turners, carpenters, bookbinders, etc.; it will not be argued that in this way they exemplify the uniting of manual and intellectual work.

After all, Winston Churchill's bricklaying did not make him a socialist. And, as Voltaire concluded, cultivation of one's garden (that fundamental manual activity in which millions of middle-class suburbanites habitually engage) is likely to be the ultimate escape from social reality.

Gramsci's circumspection about the place of manual work in uniting intellectuals and manual workers is related to the meaning he attributed to 'practice'. It is clear that by practice he did not have in mind merely the application of neuro-muscular effort and skill to the utilitarian purposes of producing goods and services. In a letter to his wife he warned against having a hand-to-mouth view of practical utility (Edinburgh Letters, no. LXXIII):

> I feel that you have always given the concepts of 'utility' and 'practicality' a content which is much too mean and narrow . . . . The result is that you have had an obsessed feeling of not being 'useful' enough, and of not being 'useful' in the erroneous sense you accept as the real one.

What, then, is the 'real' sense of practicality?

It is not the practice of manual or psycho-motor skills aimed at a transformation of the physical environment which provides the non-theoretical pole of the theory-practice nexus. What Gramsci had in mind by practice was the practice of politics in the sense of 'conscious action (praxis) in pursuit of a common goal'. Hence, in this political context, what practice produces is not commodities or services but a political philosophy, a conception of the world which commits men to pursuit of social change (or, conservatively, to resist change) and, thereby, a hegemony (*Notebooks*, p.344):

> The history of philosophy as it is generally understood, that is as the history of philosopher's philosophies, is the history of attempts made and ideological initiatives undertaken by a specific class of people to change, correct or perfect the conceptions of the world that exist in any particular age and thus to change the norms of conduct

that go with them: in other words, to change practical activity as a whole.

This appears to contradict Marx's Eleventh Thesis about the nature of philosophy. But Gramsci's conception is that philosophy's normative and practice-changing prescriptions are the product of a dialectical engagement between the intellectuals' 'conceptual and philosophical elaboration of ideas' (the 'theory', if it must be separated off) and the spontaneous philosophy of common sense, an admixture of good sense and folklore. To the extent that simple, ordinary men 'educate the educators', it is not in terms of how manual work is actually done, as distinct from theoretical knowledge of technical processes, but in terms of their own conception of the world, folklore, the philosophy of 'common sense' (see pp.126-7 above for discussion of Gramsci's conception of this dialectic between intellectuals and workers).

It is clear that in the political sense, praxis (the fusion of theory and practice) is neither a matter of making scientific or technical theory relevant to specific tasks (and vice versa), nor (so to speak) a matter of rubbing intellectuals' noses in 'night soil' in order to teach them the crude facts of life. No doubt an understanding of what makes 'common sense' what it is, requires that non-manual workers should understand how folklore and superstition may reflect some of the brute imperatives of the kind of alienated manual work against which the founding fathers of Marxism inveighed. But how much and what kind of practical experience of the phenomenon is required to awaken this sort of sociological imagination is a moot point. It is interesting, in this connection, that one of Mao Tse-Tung's educational pronouncements may be taken as underlining Gramsci's implication that having intellectuals engage with manual workers is not primarily a matter of providing them with experience of onerous manual labour but, rather, of finding for them a laboratory in which to test their theorising. Mao argued (quoted by Price, 1974):

> The university has its workshops, and it is a plant of science and engineering. It won't do for its students to acquire knowledge only from books without working. However, it is not feasible to set up workshops in a college of arts,

and it is not feasible to run workshops for literature, history, economics or novels. The faculty of arts should take the whole society as its own workshop. Its students should contact the peasants and urban workers, industry and agriculture. Otherwise they are not much use on graduation.

Presumably the social utility of arts and economics graduates would lie in articulating the dilemmas of common everyday life in terms of their own intellectual skills and disciplines. That Mao had something of this kind in mind seems clear when he asked a year later in 1965: 'Isn't it possible to teach philosophy, literature, history all at grassroots level?' (ibid.). Similarly, Gramsci himself believed that the problem of the intellectuals would only be solved when they discovered a role, 'a specific task adequate to their capacities', in promoting discussion of the philosophical, religious and moral problems which 'economic and political action presupposes'. Without this specific intellectual role they would remain 'a dead weight in our movement' (*Formazione*, pp.95-6).

Praxis, then, is not for Gramsci an imperative towards the kinds of manual activity which polytechnical educational theory has usually required but, rather, the pursuit of insights which come from the cultural inter-relationship of different social groups or functionaries. The uniting of intellectual and manual work which he agreed might help to solve the problem of the intellectuals would be fruitful only so far as it brought different philosophies into dialectical juxtaposition and united, towards a common political goal, different kinds of workers skilled in the performance of different kinds of task. Nor was the educational process involved here merely in the direction of teaching intellectuals the unpleasant facts of life. As we have seen, the intellectuals' onslaught on superstition and folklore was no less necessary to forging a philosophy of praxis than was an understanding of how and why folklore is part of a social group's 'common sense'. The rhetoric of polytechnical education in Marxist educational systems often forgets that praxis is the fusing of practice *with* theory. If the educational relationship between intellectuals and workers is really to be reciprocal, then common work experience has to be as much a venue for intellectuals putting their point of view as it is for workers advancing theirs.

Given that praxis is essentially a political concept, it is understandable that Gramsci was no more than tentative about the benefits to be derived from involving intellectuals in manual work. As Davidson (1977) repeatedly shows, he was constantly canvassing the views of workers on the problems to which his journalism was addressed, such that he 'completely "proletarianised" himself' (p.118). But he did not himself go into the Turin factories as a manual worker, seeing his task rather as the political and educational one of elaborating a revolutionary theory of Factory Councils out of their functioning in the Turin automobile plants. Thus, in seeking the dialectical unification of theorists and practitioners he was insistent upon the necessary role of intellectuals in leading and organising the mass. The intellectual is skilled in 'conceptual and philosophical elaboration of ideas', that is, specialised in theorising, and it is essentially this skill which has to be enlisted in counter-hegemonic activity: 'by technique one should understand not only the *ensemble* of scientific ideas applied industrially (which is the normal meaning of the work) but also the "mental" instruments, philosophical knowledge' (*Notebooks*, p.353).

If workers and intellectuals must come together in a mutually educative relationship such that theory and practice are united through the dialectical interpenetration of different world views, this was to be achieved through the agency of political associations, especially political parties, as well as in the actual place of work (*Notebooks*, p.335; cf. also Davidson, 1977, pp.155-7):

> One should stress the importance and significance which, in the modern world, political parties have in the elaboration and diffusion of conceptions of the world, because essentially what they do is to work out the ethics and the politics corresponding to these conceptions and act as it were as their historical 'laboratory'. The parties recruit individuals out of the working mass, and the selection is made on practical and theoretical criteria at the same time. The relation between theory and practice becomes even closer the more the conception is vitally

and radically innovatory as opposed to old ways of thinking. For this reason one can say that the parties are the elaborators of new integral and totalitarian intelligentsias and the crucibles where the unification of theory and practice, understood as the real historical process, takes place.

Theory, practice and the education of teachers

It appears that the educational implications of this conception of the theory-practice relationship are twofold. First, we are again confronted with the importance of adult education. It has already been argued that both political and vocational education belong to the period when the individual has become committed to a social role as a worker. Similarly, intellectualism which is organic to one's vocational role is also an adult phenomenon. This points towards Gramsci's contribution to the first of the problems of relating theory to practice which was noted at the beginning of this discussion: the problem of the tendency of teachers to dismiss educational theory as irrelevant to their practice.

The implication is that we should be wary of approaching this problem of the unity of theory and practice in teacher education as though its solution required the substitution of practical teaching experience for theoretical studies – the search for improved technique through immersion in the routines of the job. This is usually the preferred solution to the training of teachers when educational theory seems not to 'work' in practice. But a praxically relevant teacher education would have a different priority. If, as we have seen, praxis is not essentially a matter of uniting theory with practice in relation to the techniques which aggregate in a particular industrial or professional function, but rather a matter of philosophy (in Gramsci's sense of a conception of the world), it is clear that the most obvious relevance of Gramsci's theory of praxis for teacher education lies in the philosophy of teaching. On this view, the essentially practice-relevant component of teacher education is 'contextual' as distinct from 'technical' theory. Teacher education should develop an understanding of the teacher's role which stems from a conception of the world and, within it, of the nature and function of the educational process. However romantic its ideology, this is exactly what the discredited 'Principles of Education' course in institutions of teacher training formerly attempted to do. Its concern was as much with attitudes and commitment appropriate to teaching as with a search for efficient educational method. In the same way, Gramsci's view of the teacher's role, together with his conception of the unity of theory and practice, suggests that what one should seek from educational theory is less a hand-to-mouth focus upon classroom technique, than a sense of vocational commitment (as defined above, pp.129-31), deriving from the historically familiar notion that vocation implies not simply a technical competence, but also, and especially, a complex of attitudes, beliefs and commitments which are social, moral and political (and, perhaps, religious) in character. In this connection it will be recalled that Gramsci did not look for the improvement of the teaching profession through improvement of the technical pedagogical skills of teachers; indeed, he saw virtue in the 'mediocre' practitioner committed to teaching in terms of traditional strategies. What the improvement of teaching required was not better, or different, pedagogical skills, but a deeper, or different, understanding of teaching, as a vocation. Teachers had to be made more aware of the nature and philosophical content of their task (p. 71 above). Put in terms of present-day teacher education programmes, this would intimate an emphasis upon philosophy, history and sociology of education (and, perhaps psychology of education — suitably shorn of its dominant psychometric component). But these 'contextual' components of educational theory are precisely those which come under attack as irrelevant for practice, not only from students and teachers, but also from educational administrators. It is significant that in opting for performance-based teacher training (it cannot be properly termed teacher education) some state legislatures in the United States have sought to exclude the contextual component of educational theory, an initiative which has led to the dismantling of educational foundations departments in some state colleges and universities.

Whatever limitations there may be in traditional ways of

teaching educational foundations, and whatever the case for performance-based teacher training, abolition of the one and strengthening of the other would not, in Gramsci's analysis, have served to unite theory and practice. Technical pedagogical theory has its contribution to make towards the practice of teaching (though the search for such a practically relevant theory is peculiarly elusive) but the meaning and practical implications for teachers of Gramsci's theory of praxis must be sought elsewhere — in his notion of teaching as an essentially philosophical task. Educational activity has to be conceived within the context of a philosophy or world view.

For advocates of radical social change in pluralist societies this presents the problem that there is no consensus on behalf of a particular counter-hegemonic philosophy. Amongst educational radicals there is currently discussion of what socialist teachers ought to do, on the assumption that once the nature of socialist education is defined, teachers with socialist convictions will be left to carry on in a prosyletising role. However, the problem is to justify why socialist teachers should be left alone, whilst fascist teachers, for example, should not. But this problem of whether the schools should give *carte blanche* to teachers of various political persuasions to engage in biased political education is only a symptom of a more fundamental problem in normatively pluralist societies. For education always has been praxical in Gramsci's sense and, as a value-impregnated enterprise, it could not be otherwise. His own philosophy of praxis happened to be Marxism, but any 'philosophy' — whether political or religious — which incorporates notions of the good life or the 'ideal' society is a philosophy of praxis, as is Fascism, for example. Historically, education has been essentially a religious enterprise. And as Gramsci's frequent search for relevant models (for the education of intellectuals and the task of keeping intellectuals in touch with the faithful, for example) in church and religious history indicates, he believed religious education to have been *praxical* in his own sense of the word. Indeed, it is a recurrent theme in his writings that the church has been highly successful in doing the wrong things. In unidenominational or totalitarian party political contexts, the problem of which philosophy should inspire the work of schools is not a problem. In plural societies one is driven back upon the democratic norms which justify pluralism, and it is questionable how far the consensual liberal democratic norm of 'live and let live' can constitute an adequate basis for an education which is praxical in the sense of producing a commitment towards activity in the world in order to change it. This dilemma again points to the importance of adult education in groups and parties dedicated to particular versions of the good life, as well as to conceiving schools for children in the essentially neutral role of transmitting knowledge of 'truths already discovered' (which would include, by definition, contemporary social and natural science) and those intellectual skills which are a necessary condition for recurrent adult education.

Theory, practice and the problem of relevance

Where, if anywhere, does this conclusion leave us with reference to the second educational problem of uniting theory with practice — that of making schooling relevant to everyday life? As we have already intimated, Gramsci's theory of praxis provides little authority for the search for life relevance in a curriculum where practical work experience is employed to give 'real' or everyday life orientation to the subjects of the curriculum.

Although Gramsci affirmed the need for the school to be related to life, this has to be understood in a macro-philosophical sense, rather than with reference to the micro details of everyday life. The school-life nexus has to be explored not so much in terms of the mundane imperatives of the immediate environment, as through an examination of the changing national and supra-national socio-technological structure. Indeed, an understanding of the latter with a view towards democratisation of social change is a necessary condition for lifting the socio-economic burdens which bear upon individuals and communities. As I have argued elsewhere (1978, pp.89-95), the modern advocate of community schools having a curriculum focused exclusively upon local problems ignores the fact that community problems — poverty, unemployment and inter-racial tensions, for example — almost always have their origins in institutions at the macro level: hence, their understanding and resolution (so far as schooling can make a contribution to these) requires a conception of relevance, of the relationship between school and life, which may not be immediately obvious to the learner. This is why the prescription that the learner should define 'what counts as educational knowledge' is pedagogically unsound. That Gramsci saw little possibility of immediate life relevance for the learner in his studies has to be inferred from his belief that 'all analysis made by children can only be of dead things' (*Notebooks*, p.38). To be sure, school has work relevance — school *is* work: but it is *academic* work, and the necessary discipline of academic work cannot be dressed up as play or as the product of children's spontaneous learning activity. Nor, despite Gramsci's insistence upon the orientation of the curriculum to the culture of work, can schooling assume relevance by seeming to be linked to the ongoing activities of the community. As we have seen, this sort of specific work focus of a curriculum was, for Gramsci, a denial of opportunity. If school appears adrift from children's lives outside school, it is the cultural horizons imposed by the latter which have to be widened rather than the school's culture diluted. Quite logically, if a new counter-hegemonic culture is to be forged, it cannot simply underline the existing world view of local communities.

Gramsci did affirm the need for the school to be related to life, but one has to be clear exactly why, for him, it had come adrift from life. This was not because of its emphasis upon the theoretical at the expense of the practical, but in terms of the persistence of its orientation exclusively towards a classical culture which no longer saturated Italian life as it once had as 'an essential element of national life and culture' (*Notebooks*, pp.36-7):

> The educational efficacy of the old Italian secondary school . . . was not to be sought (or rejected) in its implicit aim as an 'educative' system, but in the fact that its structure and its curriculum were the expression of a traditional mode of intellectual and moral life, of a cultural climate diffused throughout Italian society by an ancient tradition. It was the fact that this climate and way of life were in their death-throes, and that the

school had become cut off from life, which brought about this crisis in education. A criticism of the curriculum and disciplinary structure of the old system means less than nothing if one does not keep this situation in mind.

In fact, far from pointing to the need for immediate relevance in the school curriculum, Gramsci emphasised two educational requirements which are conventionally seen as the enemy of relevance. First, teaching may have to be dogmatic (especially in the earlier years); and second, the point of learning should be disinterested. Gramsci's argument for dogmatism has already been reviewed (see pp.53-64) above). His emphasis upon disinterestedness is found in his examination of the educational value of a study of classical, 'dead' languages. Anachronistic as Gramsci took the classically oriented curriculum to be, he believed that quite aside from its cultural content, it 'satisfies a whole series of pedagogic and psychological requirements' (*Notebooks*, p.38) which, by implication, would need to be met by any curriculum which might replace it. And one of the universally relevant psychological requirements instilled by the classical curriculum was the discipline required by work as a fundamental human characteristic, not only the discipline specific to a particular job of work: 'Pupils did not learn Latin and Greek in order to speak them, to become waiters, interpreters or commercial letter writers.' On the contrary, aside from the work disciplines of diligence, precision and concentration acquired through the classical curriculum, its educational outcomes were essentially disinterested: 'the real interest was the interior development of personality, the formation of character by means of the absorption and assimilation of the whole cultural past of modern European civilisation' (*Notebooks*, p.37).

But an additional virtue of the development of personality and character through this kind of assimilation of the past was that 'experience was gained unawares, without a continual self-consciousness' (*Notebooks*, p.39). Some current discussions of education and the self — in particular, their assumption that self-discovery through schooling would be something novel in educational history — ignore this obvious point that self-awareness, life-relevance, creativity, theory-practice integration are achieved as by-products of schooling conducted on conventional lines, by turning one's back upon these as immediate objectives. What Gramsci called the educational objective of general personality-formation 'must be — or appear to the pupils to be — disinterested, i.e., not have immediate or too immediate practical purposes' (*Notebooks*, p.40). He insisted that the value of classical languages in the curriculum had been that 'they educated because they gave instruction'. That is, 'these studies educated without an explicitly declared aim of doing so, with a minimal "educative" intervention on the part of the teacher' (*Notebooks*, p.39). Here, Gramsci is using 'education' in the sense of didactic moral exhortation deemed relevant to the pupil's daily-life preoccupations and needs. His schooling in ancient cultures had been life-relevant, not because obvious and deliberate linkage had been established with current social problems, but because through them 'he has plunged into history and acquired a historicising understanding of the world and of life, which becomes a second — nearly spontaneous — nature, since it is not inculcated pedantically with an openly educational intention' (ibid.). On this view, schooling that is relevant to life does not focus, exclusively, on present-day problems; it cultivates a disposition to perceive the human condition in terms of those human values, predicaments, aspirations and initiatives which are universal, that is peculiar neither to this time, nor this place. If, as Gramsci conceded, the study of ancient civilisations loses its power to illuminate the human condition in modern industrial societies, nevertheless he was clear that, in their own way, the subjects which would replace Latin and Greek must have their own universal reference and concern with the 'first' principles of humanism. The insistence that schools in the past have lacked life-relevance because they have emphasised 'classical' studies and 'received knowledge' from the arts and sciences, ignores the fact that a highly creative modern civilisation (where in many areas of human knowledge, a massively fruitful marriage of theory and practice has obviously been achieved through scientific and technological innovation) has, by definition, and as a matter of historical fact, been nurtured on traditional curricula and educational method.

Manacorda cautions that the notes on the study of Latin and Greek (altered by Gramsci in his second formulation of the problem from the present tense of the first formulation to the past tense) should be read as an epitaph to the traditional classical school rather than in its defence (1970, p.330). Nevertheless, in his references to the teaching of Latin, just as it seems clear that he wished to emphasise that its time was past, it is also evident that he was drawing our attention (using Latin as his example) to a pedagogical principle of universal validity. There is a hint of the means towards linking theory with practice in this discussion of the value of a study of classical cultures. Latin, Gramsci believed, came alive, not through a search for current relevance in the past, but through attempts to relate the concrete and the abstract. As general and abstract, theory gains relevance from its relation to the concrete: not, in the case of Latin and Greek to our contemporary present, but to the concrete present of the past. Although children can only analyse dead things, where these have once been living cultures 'in the dead object there is always present a greater living being. Thus, the language is dead, it is analysed as an inert object, as a corpse on the dissecting table, but it continually comes to life again in examples and in stories' (*Notebooks*, p.38). Indeed, for Gramsci there was pedagogical virtue in Latin precisely for being a dead language: 'The dead languages offer this paradoxical instrument of study; they are the dead still living. They can be anatomised in the living; they can be broken down into all their historic elements, without the decomposing stench of the corpse' (*Formazione*, p.92). The value of Latin was in enabling students 'to think abstractly and schematically while remaining able to plunge back from abstraction into real and immediate life, to see in each fact or datum what is general and what is particular, to distinguish the concept from the specific instance' (*Notebooks*, p.38). And, as we have already observed (pp.40-9 above), Gramsci believed this immersion in the concrete study of the past to be the essential educational experience (*Formazione*, p.93):

> It is its patient and tenacious adhesion to history which characterises the classical school. It is the historic method

carried into the study of dead languages and which ought to be carried into the study of any science whatever, because it broadens the mind and forms concrete mentalities, and not mentalities which are abstract, dogmatic and given to idle talk.

It would not be a relevant objection to this point that the traditional classical or grammar school, except at its best, signally failed to achieve this movement between the concrete and the abstract; for, as the title of the essay in which this evaluation of the classical school indicates, Gramsci was here 'In search of the educational *principle*' (emphasis added). And it is clear that the phenomenon which does often raise charges of a gap between theory and practice is a failure to relate concrete and abstract in the way indicated by Gramsci. This, rather than simply a search for 'applicable' theory in a psycho-motor sense of practice or for relevance in terms of present, everyday experience, is really the educational problem of relevance. Sometimes, no doubt, the concrete application of theory lies in practical tasks — playing the piano, growing tea, teaching children how to read, learning how to type quickly and accurately, and so on. But the concrete can also be in exemplification and particularisation for which the only medium is language itself. This is essentially true of those theoretical areas of the academic curriculum which seem to have no immediate practical or concrete exemplification in the life of the learner, certainly where there is no practical task or exercise which is intrinsically related to the theoretical study. The obvious examples of this are history and literature — both of which were academic areas of which Gramsci himself had a profound understanding, which fertilised his political theory and practice, and which would form an essential part of his school curriculum. In practice, the attempt is sometimes made to 'concretise' the study of history through practical tasks like the making of models or visiting historical sites. Whilst the latter activity can relate intrinsically to the understanding of a particular historical event, much of the craft-type activity which occurs in history lessons is no more than the kind of rest or relief from intellectual work which Marx had in mind in commenting on the benefits of combining schooling with work (see pp.151-5 above). But history is essentially an intellectual activity whose primary resource is language. Its 'practicality' is not to be sought in the performance of practical tasks, like the making of historical models, which can contribute only peripherally to historical understanding. To seek utility or practicality of this sort in the history curriculum is, in Gramsci's words, to give these notions 'a content which is much too mean and narrow'. Making history concrete usually means referring to source materials which are themselves mainly words: inventories, wills, bills of lading, Acts of Parliament, newspapers, speeches (for example, Lincoln's dedication of the cemetry at Gettysburg), letters, historical literature, biographies and autobiographies, diaries and so on. Even visits to historical remains tell us very little in the absence of verbal descriptions or documentary evidence which points, concretely, to the kind of human activity which occurred amongst sticks and stones. Without the guide's description or one's own private reading, the Colosseum is, indeed, a mere heap of stones.

It is for reasons of this kind — the fact that the concrete is to be found as often in words as in physical objects — that Gramsci's curricular and methodological proposals offer no relief from the necessary discipline of school work, especially book work, through a practically oriented curriculum. At best, such practicality would be a relief from hard intellectual work. It would contribute nothing important to the fusing of theory with practice. As we saw earlier, Gramsci took the praxical function of history, for example, to be in reminding workers of the epic struggle of humanity with 'its innumerable heroes', and in prompting their own struggle to forge a link in this chain of universal history.

This suggests the futility of seeking a unity of theory and practice in schools by juxtaposing intellectual and manual work except where theory is a necessary part of the understanding and mastery of practical or manual activities which are included in the curriculum on other grounds. To insist that there is no place for theoretical studies (of literature, history or philosophy) which do not 'pay off' in practical tasks, clearly excludes from the curriculum subjects which Gramsci knew to be essential to any schooling which claimed to be humanistic. Without contradiction and without insis-

Theory and practice in education

tence on schooling being of immediate practical relevance, he could both emphasise the importance of praxis and insist that the schools should transmit, disinterestedly, to children their cultural heritage, precisely because his stress on the need to unite theory and practice referred to the activity of adults in the political arena.

Conclusion

I have tried to show that a proper inference to be drawn from the work of Gramsci is that it is unrealistic to look to schools for a radical, counter-hegemonic education: the burden of such an enterprise lies squarely in institutions for adult education, especially in those political associations dedicated to social change and in economic associations where workers are involved in productive relationships which have their own educational imperatives. This conclusion is in sympathy with Marx's assumption that 'truths' which are partisan, dependent upon 'party prejudices', should not be taught in schools: it should be left to adults to form their own opinions on these matters 'about which instruction should be given in the lecture hall, not in the schools' (Shore, 1947, pp.84-5, quoting statement to the General Council of the International, 1869). Lenin reached a similar conclusion about the undesirability of using the schools for political indoctrination. Speculating on his reasons for drawing this conclusion, Lilge suggests that he believed 'the schools had more fundamental things to teach that could not be accomplished anywhere else' (that teaching of 'a body of received knowledge and cognitive skills'). Nor', concluded Lilge, 'can the difficulties of teaching Marxist ideology to minors have escaped him.' Gramsci also saw the school's task in this preparatory, tool-giving function: not as preparatory in socialising the individual for the passive and fatalistic performance of a particular adult role, but in providing the intellectual equipment and disposition required for continued

Conclusion

adult education.

When education is to be biased in favour of a particular political or religious ideology — when, that is, it ceases to be disinterested — it ought, in a pluralist society, to be a function of private provision. We have seen that Gramsci intended it to be within productive enterprises that trade unions and Factory Councils would provide both the technical-scientific and the managerial skills needed for workers to replace the capitalist economy. But there was also the matter of the general education of workers through what Gramsci called 'other avenues' (*altre vie*). These included, as well as formal adult educational institutions, all those which bear directly upon public opinion — the press, libraries, clubs and voluntary associations, theatres, museums, even architecture (cf. *Quaderni*, III, p.1715). But through whatever avenues, and pending the development of a fully comprehensive educational system, existing workers needed the kind of disinterested humanistic education which had been denied to all except the socially privileged. In this connection, Gramsci gave another nuance to the notion of disinterested learning. In his view, the Italian working class had been driven to improvise hurried, careless, emergency solutions to its problems: with proper cultural preparation it would approach its dilemmas 'in a disinterested manner without waiting for the stimulus of actual events' (*Formazione*, p.95). But the long-term need for adult education through avenues other than those of the formal educational system was also for the purpose of dissemination of a new, common, humanistic culture. In an early article in *Avanti*, he urged the Socialist Party to work for the creation of 'cultural associations'. He turned for models to other European nations (especially Germany and England) which he felt were well served by 'some very powerful organisations of working class and socialist culture' (ibid., p.96). He instanced the Fabian Society, at the time of its affiliation to the International, which had 'succeeded in putting into the service of this work of cultivation and spiritual liberation, a great part of the English intellectual and university world' (ibid., pp.94-6). The work of Tawney, on behalf of the Workers' Educational Association, in journeying each weekend to teach economic history to potters in Stoke and weavers in

Conclusion

Rochdale, is perhaps the best-known example of this aspect of the history of adult education.[1] Thompson (1968b) lists other influential figures and concludes that, in his own field of social history, the dialectic between teacher and adult student (what he called 'the abrasion of different worlds of experience, in which ideas are brought to the test of life') has led to the exploration of areas long neglected in university schools of history;[2] a practical example, no doubt, of Gramsci's hopes that cultural innovation would result from the conversation between professional intellectuals and other kinds of workers (see above pp.160-5; see also Simon, II, 1965, ch. ix, for a description and evaluation of this English tradition of Adult Education).

There is no doubt that in those nations where industrialism was completed much earlier than in Italy there was, in Gramsci's day, a long tradition of 'other avenues' for the pursuit of adult education, aimed at the general education of the adult population and at the development of intellectuals organic to the working class. These initiatives towards adult education were sometimes engineered from within the working class; sometimes they came from sympathetic traditional intellectuals. The question is how successful these were in promoting working-class radicalism and training intellectuals who were and remained organic to the working class, dedicated to replacing bourgeois by working-class hegemony. With reference to England, for example, Thompson's account of the making of the English working class attributed a central role to the activities of working-class autodidacts[3] and sympathetic educationists and intellectuals from other classes. And according to Thompson, the English working class was *made*, in part, through the efforts of organic intellectuals in creating class consciousness (1968a, ch. 16). Accounts of social and education history (e.g. by Simon, Silver, Hogden) that extend beyond the period covered by Thompson do suggest that working-class intellectuals have been significant and successful in the history of the working-class movement. Further research, including systematisation of existing historical data, which focuses upon Gramsci's problem of the intellectuals and their education, as well as on the development of rapport between intellectuals and the common man, should look at whether

Conclusion

and how organic intellectuals have been formed on Gramsci's model; how successful these have been in educating and transforming the political perceptions of the working class; whether organic intellectuals have been substantially educated within the Labour Movement itself (i.e. through adult education); what role traditional intellectuals played in this process; what part elementary schooling played in bringing generations of workers to a condition of readiness for adult political education; whether working-class beneficiaries of traditional secondary schooling (as in the transitional selective stage admitted by Gramsci to be economically expedient) have 'flown away' to other classes, a danger which Thompson sees as the peculiarly modern threat to 'cultural egalitarianism' (1968b).

As I have observed in several places above, modern neo-Marxist sociologists of education are apt to dismiss past efforts towards education of the working class — and, implicitly, the relevance of Gramsci and traditional socialist educational initiatives — as utterly mistaken, supportive not of a counter-hegemony but of the capitalist hegemony itself. On this view, the fights of European parties of the Left for working-class access to the best of public education have been successful only in producing workers more efficiently atuned to the industrial needs of capitalism. But, as was also observed above, necessarily lacking evidence of what the proposed 'radical' alternatives might produce, one has to conclude that, in principle, these seem utterly conservative in their implications, more likely to keep the working class in its traditional chains than to be liberating and counter-hegemonic in outcome. Gramsci had repeated resort to Romain Rolland's aphorism, 'Pessimism of the intellect, optimism of the will': implicitly, if the realisation of our social and educational blueprints is destined to elude our practical grasp, this is no reason for abandoning them for alternatives which do not even appeal to the credence of radical good sense.

Notes

Introduction

1   The term 'new sociology of education' was suggested by Gorbutt to characterise a trend in English sociology of education, especially in the work of some educationists at the University of London Institute of Education and in the Faculty of Education at the Open University. Employing Kuhn's notion of the 'paradigm shift' which characterises scientific revolutions, Gorbutt saw the intention of the new sociologists to be that of replacing what they took to be a positivist orientation in traditional sociology of Education by an alternative paradigm, through focusing attention upon the curricular implications of sociology of knowledge. Indeed, the new sociology of education is located within the sociology of knowledge: the 'management of knowledge' is its central concern. This is in contrast to the 'old' sociology of education which was allegedly located within the structural-functionalist sociological paradigm, a 'value-free' social science based on the assumption that fundamental truths about society can be derived from empirical investigation. Its reference is to an objective social world, not of man's own making, to which he must passively adjust. Hence, the school's role is concerned with socialisation in relation to given social norms. For this 'normative paradigm', the new sociologist substitutes an 'interpretative paradigm' derived mainly from Marxism and phenomenology. The innovative text for the new sociology is taken to be Young's *Knowledge and Control*, especially the essays by Young, Keddie and Esland.

  Perhaps because of its insistence on the problematic nature of all educational issues, the writing of this new school of

sociologists tends to be oblique (making considerable use of the rhetorical question, for example) rather than prescriptive. However, the following appear to be some of its implications:
  (i) What counts as 'educational knowledge' should be seen as problematic, not taken for granted as it traditionally was in schools (but was it?); in particular, the learner himself is competent to participate in defining what counts as educational knowledge.
 (ii) Such knowledge is socially determined, no group's knowledge is superior to any others'; hence all sub-cultures are adequate or valid ways of life and the curriculum should accommodate this fact; in particular, academic knowledge is in no way superior to other forms of knowledge.
(iii) The problem of equality in education is not one of access to what have been, historically, schools for the socially privileged; it lies in equality of esteem being attached to all existing modes of cultural life.

From the point of view of this study of Gramsci it is of interest that much of the new sociology reads remarkably like the subjective idealism of Gentile (1922), the Italian 'philosopher of Fascism' and Mussolini's first Minister of Public Instruction, against whose reform of education in 1923 much of Gramsci's polemic is directed.

It should be emphasised that although the new sociologists tend to share a common intellectual heritage and methodology, there is not a consensus about the precise implications of their work for schooling. Moreover, the recent writing is more circumspect, self-critical, than the original polemic (see, for example, Whitty's and Young and Whitty's contributions to (ed.) Young and Whitty (1977)). For some evaluations of the new sociology and the debate it has stimulated see, for example, Pring (1972), Lawton (1975), Bernbaum (1977), Karabel and Halsey (1977).

The Black Papers (see Cox and Dyson, (1969a and b, 1970) were a series of polemical booklets containing articles by conservative educationists in England in the late 1960s and early 1970s. Although the later publications were mainly an attack on the Labour Party's policy of replacing different kinds of secondary school with comprehensive schools (and, hence, an attack on the position taken by Gramsci on the structure of secondary schooling), the main target of the ill-assorted Black Paper authors was progressive education in the primary school and its tendency to permeate the entire educational system, including the universities. Thus, their position on curriculum and method was not unlike Gramsci's advocacy of a traditional, disciplined, structured

pedagogy, emphasising the importance of mastery of basic intellectual skills and the acquisition of 'cognitive baggage' (see above, pp.40-68).
3. See p.142 for references to texts concerned with different aspects of Gramsci's life and work.
4. Gramsci was accused of 'conspiracy, of instigation to civil war, of justifying criminal acts, and of formenting class hatred' (Fiori, 1970, p.230). He was sentenced to twenty years, four months and five days imprisonment in June 1928. See Fiori (1970), chs. 23 and 24 for an account of his arrest, early imprisonment and trial.
5. Joll concludes that 'his Marxism was a very personal one', the product of a dialogue within him between Croce and Lenin (1977, p.76).
6. Gramsci had intended to become a teacher of literature, and Davidson writes of 'his natural talent as a teacher' (1977, pp.33, 42, 71, 73). Accounts (including his own in the *Letters*) show him to have been both patient and inventive as a 'teacher' of young children (cf. *Lettere*, no. 26; Manacorda, 1976, p.77). With adults, his formal teaching (as in the *Club Vita Morale*) often appears to have been overly didactic – he lectured in 'a quiet, unemphatic, inexorable voice' (Davidson, 1977, p.70) – sometimes evoking a less than enthusiastic response. Gwyn Williams has concluded that Gramsci often sounds 'like a Marxist Head Prefect' (1975, p.252). But his socialist colleague, Tasca, claimed that 'those he instructed came out profoundly and permanently transformed, and always remained grateful to him' (quoted by Cammett (1967), p.33). Clark's conclusion is that 'he educated a party ... he was an excellent educator' (1977, p.224). See *Formazione* (pp.20-1) for Gramsci's own description of the working of one of his adult classes.

Part one The schooling of children

1. See Entwistle (1978, pp.95-108) on 'Working-class education and the politics of non-literacy', a discussion and criticism of the view that the development of electronic media of communication makes literacy unnecessary for the working class.
2. See Entwistle (1978, pp.82-5) for criticism of the view (and examination of its educational implications) that cultural deprivation is a myth and that all sub-cultures represent 'valid' and 'adequate' ways of life.
3. Davison (1977, ch. I) shows the ignorance in which the Sardinian

peasantry, amongst whom Gramsci spent his childhood, had been kept by foreign imperialists who ruled Sardinia: 'The peasant lived by a set of social norms which taught him to suffer and endure his lot on the one hand, and on the other, to react to each capricious, inexplicable mishap owed to men or nature with an equally irrational response .... Their folklore was pervaded with the idea of their own objectivity and the ineluctability of whatever happened to them.' It is not surprising that Gramsci saw their folklore as something to be destroyed through the school system, refusing to see this Sardinian peasant culture as a valid way of life. As Davidson concluded: 'Backward, ignorant, withdrawn and cruel, this society and its people presented little attraction for anyone ... [Gramsci] was no believer in the nobility of the poor or the mass; for him they were cruel and backward.' The film *Padre, Padrone* vividly evokes this Sardinian cruelty and backwardness.

4 The story of Alfred and the Cakes is told to English primary schoolchildren about a legendary incident in the life of King Alfred the Great. The story has it that when hiding incognito in the forest he was taken in by an old woman who left him to watch over a griddle of cakes on the fire whilst she went to gather fuel. Preoccupied with his problems, Alfred let the cakes burn. On her return the old woman beat and scolded him and he accepted this without demur. It is sometimes argued that myths and legends of this kind, being probably fictitious, ought not to be taught to children as history. My point is that a legend like this (or a superstition about the natural universe) may be an appropriate point of departure for the teaching of history for, even if factually untrue, the burnt cakes incident may be taken to contain a moral or psychological truth about Alfred, i.e. that he was magnanimous in his use of power (which is usually the kind of moral drawn by primary teachers from the story). Indeed, in his *History of the English Speaking People*, Winston Churchill concluded that it was his magnanimity in the use of power which earned for Alfred (alone of English kings) the title 'the Great'.

5 It is odd that Young himself should set such store by everyday, commonsense experience, as he does when rejecting the notion that 'high status', 'academic' knowledge is superior. Two of his collaborators point to the inadequacy of teachers' commonsense, everyday perceptions of children (Keddie, 1971; Esland, 1971). Esland, in particular, dismisses as 'naive and limited' the pretheoretical commonsense, 'popular view' of teachers about teaching (1971, p.83). And the inference to be drawn from Keddie's account is that some of the teachers she observes are

not only deficient is psycho-pedagogic knowledge, but also of the 'scientific' knowledge they are supposed to be teaching.

6 Popper (1972) distinguishes as 'world 2' this subjective, personalisation of knowledge and experience and rejects, as an idealist fallacy, the notion that 'world 3' (objective knowledge) cannot be distinguished from world 2.

7 I have preferred my own translation here to that of Hoare and Smith who translate *elementario* as 'primary', not elementary. Nowadays primary and elementary tend to be used interchangeably (the former in Britain, the latter in North America, for example), to refer to that *stage* of early schooling which precedes universal secondary schooling. In Gramsci's time, however, elementary was a *kind* of schooling which was terminal for most children. In its upper grades it often overlapped with secondary schooling and consisted of more than merely the teaching of the basic academic skills of literacy and numeracy. It is to this earlier elementary tradition that Gramsci was referring in defending the old elementary school. See Minio-Puluello (1946, ch. I), for an account of elementary education at the time when Gramsci was in school.

8 For an analysis of different senses of the notion of education according to nature see chapter One of C.D. Hardie's classic text, *Truth and Fallacy in Educational Theory* (1942).

9 This judgment follows from a common, if questionable, reading of Rousseau. Arguably, the apparent Rousseauan emphasis upon spontaneity and children's rights was a 'cosmetic' or motivational device, when on recalls his advice, 'Let your No be a wall of brass' and 'Never let him use a word you have not anticipated, nor do anything which you have not foreseen' — not essentially different from Gramsci's own emphasis upon the importance of authority.

10 In fact, Gentile wrote of the 'inutility of distinguishing ... education from instruction' which appears similar to Gramsci's position. However, Gentile later concluded: 'The antithesis between instruction and education is the antithesis between realistic and idealistic culture, or again, that existing between a material and a spiritual conception of life' (1922, p.190). Since his entire text is in advocacy of an idealist conception of culture and against the 'grave error' of realism, it is evident that, for him, the inutility of distinguishing instruction from education would lie (as Gramsci supposed) in giving prominence to the former as an educational function which emphasised culture as objective and real in Popper's (1972) sense. (Popper's *Objective Knowledge* is Gentile's polemic in reverse — an argument against idealism and in favour of realism.) Gramsci's point about the

importance of not separating instruction from education was the opposite of Gentile's; that is, a defence of the place of instruction in the educational process as an activity of transmitting, authoritatively, 'truths already discovered'.

11 See Entwistle (1978, ch. 2) for examination of the meanings which might be attributed to this cliché.

12 For details of the 1923 reform of the Italian educational system see Minio-Puluello (1946), Marraro (1936), Borghi (1960), Thompson, M.M. (1934). For an understanding of Gramsci's polemic, the following aspects of the reforms are of particular interest:
   (i) The intention to liberate the elementary school from a Herbartian oriented pedagogy and from syllabuses requiring the learning of facts, formulae, etc.
   (ii) The introduction of religious instruction into elementary schools and an emphasis upon nationalism.
   (iii) The rigorous selection of students for the traditional, humanistic (grammar) secondary school and the multiplication of vocational and technical schools for those not meeting the selection criteria.
   (iv) The reform of the examination system in order to assess the students's potential for judgment, 'creativity', etc., rather than his mastery of factual knowledge.

Italian students of the reform have argued that some of its provisions contradicted the intentions of other of its prescriptions. For example, the rhetorical justification of the reform was in terms of an emphasis upon liberty, but Borghi calculates that, with respect to the emphasis upon religious instruction, 'the major result of those provisions was to have banished freedom of thought from education' (1960, p.259).

13 Mussolini claimed not only that Gentile's were the most fascist of all his government's reforms, but he also expressed such confidence in them that he concluded: 'from the future fascist schools and universities the nation's new and ruling class would issue' to rule 'for at least a hundred years' (Nolte, 1965, p.211). Moreover, the first part of Mussolini's definitive statement of Fascism, *La Dottrina del Fascismo*, is usually attributed to Gentile, and from 1936 (more than ten years after Gentile's resignation as Minister of Public Instruction) this text was widely studied in most secondary schools (see Minio-Puluello, 1946, p.123; Nolte, 1965, pp.244, 259; Thompson, 1934, p.107). There appears little doubt that Mussolini himself was satisfied about the authenticity of Gentile's Fascism. Writing in the mid-1930s, Marraro, an Italian-American sympathetic to Gentile

and his educational reforms, concluded that 'Fascism amounted to little but Gentile's idealism' (1936, p.233).

On the other hand, until the mid-1930s there was continuous insistence within Italy on the need for 'Fascisization' of the school (ibid.). Bottai, appointed Minister of Education in 1935, is said to have retorted to Mussolini's claim that Gentile's School Reforms were the most fascist of all the reforms, that this was so only because there were no other educational reforms to compete with them (Minio-Puluello, 1946, p.64). Aside from Mussolini, most fascist political authorities rejected Gentile's claim that his school reform was an expression of fascist ideals, as well as his assertion (supported by official statements) that his resignation as Minister after only twenty months in office had nothing to do with criticism of his reforms generated by the 'loyal' party men who replaced him (Minio-Puluello, 1946, p.123; and cf. United States Congress, 1947, p.28). More than a decade later, with the 1923 legislation still remaining the basis of the Italian education system, critics of Gentile were still claiming that his reforms were 'conservative and reactionary and it was said that the true revolution in the schools had yet to begin' (Minio-Puluello, 1946, p.67). Bottai claimed that the system of secondary education had been completely unaffected by the 1923 reform (ibid., p.183). Under de Vecchia, appointed Minister of Education in 1935, there was 'an open challenge to the reform of 1923; its spirit and many of its provisions were quickly disappearing' (ibid., p.176).

In assessing the Fascist credentials of Gentile's reform, Minio-Puluello (ibid., p.64) makes a distinction between fascist ideology and fascist political practice and concludes that the mode of legislation was fascist but not the content of the reforms. Lombardo Radice, who became Director of Elementary Education under Gentile, claimed that the reforms were not at all politically partisan but were 'metapolitical' (Borghi, 1960, p.244). Marraro, who hailed the reforms as 'The New Education in Italy', could claim nothing more fascist in them than that: 'What is meant by the statement that the Gentile reform is Fascist is the fact that it is something in which the government has taken a great deal of pride and has therefore accepted and enforced it' (1936, p.298). In this respect, Minio-Puluello thought it possible to see Fascism as not entirely an 'ill-wind'. Both these historians of fascist education concluded that the 1923 reforms were in the 'line of normal evolution' (Minio-Puluello, 1946, pp.22, 59).

The notion that education in fascist Italy and fascist education are not identical hinges, then, on the distinction between ideology and political expediency. Although one critic cited by Marraro insisted that Croce's proposed reform when he was Minister just a few years earlier, was 'truly liberal' whilst 'Gentile's is anti-liberal and Fascist', this antithesis between the views of the two friends and collaborators is hard to sustain. Croce wrote a commendatory and uncritical Introduction to Gentile's *The Reform of Education* concluding that 'we owe it to Gentile that Italian pedagogy has attained in the present day a simplicity and a depth of concepts unknown elsewhere.' According to Marraro, Gentile 'made it clear that the reforms were not the outcome of a political movement, but the result of twenty years of discussion in educational circles' (1936, p.296). Minio-Puluello claims that had predecessors like Baccolli and Croce 'been given as free a hand as Gentile in the short spell of their administration, the schools would have been transformed in much the same way as they were in 1923-24' (1946, p.68).

14 I have in mind here that documentary evidence on classroom climates and teaching styles — as distinct from records of educational legislation, administrative structures, etc. — is comparatively rare for any educational system. Individual autobiography of teachers or former students is probably the main source of information about what actually happened on the floor of the classroom in the past.

15 It has to be acknowledged that Gentile wrote in not dissimilar terms about the fault of educationists since Rousseau in exalting liberty and denying authority. However, Gentile's advocacy of authority referred to the authority of the State against the individual and of the religious authority which, he argued, would be reinforced through introduction of the teaching of religion in schools. Gramsci, on the other hand, asserted the authority of the teacher, as instructor, in transmitting the skills and knowledge on which individual growth depended and from which personal autonomy ultimately derived (see pp.68-77).

16 I have elaborated elsewhere (1970a, ch. 2) this problem of the relationship between freedom, authority and discipline.

17 See Horton for discussion of the dilution to which the concepts of *alienation* and *anomie* tend to be subject in contemporary sociology. In the literature of education, alienation suffers from a similar weakening of its usage from that in the work of Marx himself.

18 Examples of what I have called traditional Marxist educationists would be Simon and Levitas in Britain. Simon's (1971) collection of essays provides a comprehensive account of his position.

19 Cf. Croce (1946, p.83): 'Liberty, according to one of Gladstone's

saying, is the means of promoting and creating aristocracy, not democracy. Aristocracy is truly vigorous and serious when it is not a closed but an open aristocracy, firm in rejecting the crowd, but always ready to welcome those who have raised themselves to its level.'

20 See David Riesman's essay, 'Thoughts on Teachers and Schools' (*Anchor Review*, no. 1), for the view that educational rhetoric should function counter-cyclically, a conception he derived from the model of Keynesian economic theory.

Part two The education of adults

1 On one occasion Gramsci referred to those exercising these middle-management functions as 'semi-intellectuals': 'intellectuals' were functionaries like 'engineers, office bosses, etc.' (see Davidson, 1977, pp.249-50). His notion of organic intellectuals was evidently applicable to those exercising leadership at all levels in society from creative scientists, philosophers and artists to those occupying quite humble intellectual roles (*Notebooks*, p.13).

2 Gwyn Williams reports a paucity of intellectuals in the Italian Communist Party at that time: 'At least 98 per cent of its membership was working class. The Party counted its "intellectuals" very carefully and suspiciously' (1975, p.298).

3 Part of what Gramsci had in mind here in insisting that diffusion of culture may be as creative as original discovery is that individual originality can be 'a mechanical thing', or a free and easy Bohemianism, 'a striving for novelty simply by doing the opposite of what others do' (*Quaderni*, III, p.1720).

In a different context, when considering the maxim that 'It is easier to say something new than to come to agreement about what has already been said', he concluded that 'under the pretence of originality there is much vanity and individualism, and little creative spirit etc.' (*Quaderni*, II, pp.1482-3; see also III, p.1719; cf. also Edinburgh Letters, no. CXCI).

4 For a discussion of this conservative standpoint in the works, for example, of F.R. Leavis, G.H. Bantock and Lord James, see Entwistle, 1978, ch. 5.

5 See Davidson, 1977, pp.100-7, for a discussion of the writers influencing the development of Gramsci's thought on intellectuals as elites.

6 See Lazerson and Grubb (1974) for an analysis of the concept of vocationalism and the history of vocational education in the United States.

Notes to pages 131-52

7 Lombardo Radice (1976, pp.56-7) suggests that it was an original insight of Gramsci's that man's work is his distinguishing characteristic, the basis of social relationships and the means by which he creates his civilisation. Though it echoes the well-known passage of Marx and Engels in *The German Ideology*, it is unlikely that Gramsci was familiar with this text, which had been abandoned by its authors in 1845. It was published for the first time in 1932 and not until 1968 in its first Italian edition. Marx and Engels had written:
> Man can be distinguished from the animals by conscience, by religion, by whatever you like: they themselves begin to distinguish themselves from animals as soon as they begin to produce their means of subsistence, a progression which is determined by their physical constitution. In producing their means of subsistence men indirectly produce their actual material life.

8 I have elaborated this point elsewhere (see 1970b, pp.86-9).

9 Gramsci himself made this distinction (*Political Writings*, p.371):
> In Italy the never-ending parade of 'D'Annunzios' ['D'Annunzio' is the traveller who tries to cheat on the railways, the industrialist who conceals his profits, the merchant who draws up false accounts to cheat the tax authorities], this absence on the part of the bourgeoisie of any public spirit or loyalism towards their institutions, has always held back the development of a well-ordered parliamentary state (as, for example, in England).

10 This last is a reference to André Philip, *Le Problème Ouvrier*.

11 It is necessary to distinguish from automation the large-scale mechanisation of production (and its concomitant, the minute division of labour) which characterised the first two centuries of industrialism. By contrast with mechanisation which subjugates man to the machine, automation requires the substitution of machines for men. See Entwistle (1970b) for discussion of this distinction and especially, its economic and educational implications.

Part three Theory and practice in education

1 A number of English Factory Acts (dating from 1802) had tried ineffectively to legislate for a period of schooling within the working day. This legislation was crystallised in the Act of 1844 and enforced with increasing effectiveness (see Silver, 1977).

Notes to page 178

Conclusion

1 For an account of Tawney's work in adult education see Terrill (1973, pp.36-47). This essay, suggestively titled 'He "Finds Himself" in Workers' Education', shows how much Tawney himself learned from listening to the workers in his classes.

2 Terrill suggests that Tawney himself became an economic historian as a result of his experience as a teacher in the Workers' Educational Association: certainly that his most productive period of authorship coincided with the seven year period before the First World War when he travelled the country teaching in adult classes.

3 In English social and educational history the term 'autodidact' (usually applied only to adults) generally carries positive implications; the sense, that is, of dedicated working men putting together their own studies in spite of considerable impediments. Gramsci tended to use the Italian equivalent of the word pejoratively to focus the limitations of the self-taught person. He uses the term, for example, to categorise the pupil of the progressive pedagogy, left unprotected against the arbitrary and haphazard impact of the environment, without training in the various fundamental methods and techniques. As Manacorda puts it: ' "Autodidacticism" was for him "absence of a critical and scientific discipline", "helotism" and "intellectual confusion" ' (1976, pp.170-1). It was this view of the limitations of autodidacticism which led Gramsci to insist that potential working-class organic intellectuals must acquire rigorous intellectual discipline, with the assistance of traditional intellectuals (cf. also *L'Alternativa*, pp.113-5, 115-6).

A note on sources

The main English language sources for a study of Gramsci's work are Hoare and Smith's translation of the *Prison Notebooks* (which, effectively supersedes an earlier collection, *The Modern Prince*, apart from this latter's important essay on 'The Southern Question') and two collections of the prison letters, Hamish Hamilton's translation published by the Edinburgh Review and Lyn Lawner's edition. Hoare's *Selections from Political Writings* is a recent collection of Gramsci's earlier work as a journalist, mainly from *L'Ordine Nuovo*. Wherever possible, quotations and references in the text are from these sources in English and I am especially grateful to Lawrence & Wishart for permission to quote extensively from Hoare and Smith. (Quotations from non-English sources are in my own translations.)

However, a good deal of relevant material is unpublished in English. Valentino Gerratana's critical edition of *Quaderni del Carcere* in four volumes is now the standard reference for the prison notes, as is Caprioglio and Furbini's collection of the letters, *Lettere dal Carcere*. There are several overlapping Italian collections of Gramsci's earlier writings (see Bibliography). However, most of the educationally relevant of these pieces are collected (along with extracts from the *Quaderni* and *Lettere*) in two anthologies: Manacorda's *L'Alternativa Pedagogica* and Urbani's *La Formazione dell'Uomo*. Of these, the latter is the more comprehensive, following from a more generous interpretation of what is educationally relevant.

I know of no secondary source in English which deals comprehensively with Gramsci's educational theory.* In Italian I have made extensive use of Broccoli (1972), Borghi (1969), Urbani (1967) and Manacorda (especially, 1976). This last provides an account of the development of Gramsci's thought through sequential and parallel analyses of the letters and notebooks. Borghi (1958 and 1960) provides

A note on sources

a valuable historical background on Italian education under Fascism.

There is a growing number of English language texts dealing with Gramsci's life and work. Nairn's translation of Fiori's *Life of a Revolutionary* remains the standard biography of Gramsci, whilst Pozzolini's *Antonio Gramsci* briefly examines his thought in relation to his various political and cultural interests. Davidson's (1977) is an important updating of Gramsci's biography in the light of a growing body of information on his life and work, as well as an attempt to write his 'intellectual biography' as a function of his struggle to unite theory with practice. Cammett (1967), Gwyn Williams (1975) and Clark (1977) are evaluations of Gramsci's life and work within the context of the events leading to the founding of the Italian Communist Party in 1921 and the concurrent rise of Fascism. Boggs (1976) is a short but lucid account of Gramsci's political theory, whilst Joll is a readable attempt, in the style of the 'Modern Masters Series', to combine biography with an evaluation of Gramsci's essential contribution to political thought.

* Since delivering the final typescript to the publisher I have discovered a paper by George Mardle, 'Power, tradition and change: educational implications of the thought of Antonio Gramsci' (in Gleeson D. (ed.), *Identity and Structure*, Nafferton Books). This paper also focuses the paradox of Gramsci's emphasis upon the cultural tradition whilst in pursuit of a counter-hegemony.

Bibliography

Works by Antonio Gramsci

(The words in parenthesis following each entry indicate the short title which has been used for reference in the text.)

1954 *L'Ordine Nuovo (1919-20)*, Turin, Einaudi (*L'Ordine Nuovo*).
1957 *The Modern Prince*, trans. Marks, L. New York, International Publishers (*Modern Prince*).
1958 *Scritti Giovanile (1914-18)*, Turin, Einaudi (*Scritti Giovanile*).
1960 *Sotto La Mole 1916-1920*, Turin, Einaudi (*Sotto La Mole*).
1964 *Duemila pagine di Gramsci*, ed. G. Ferrata and N. Gallo, 2 vols, Milan, Il Saggiatore (*Duemila*).
1966 *Socialismo e Fascismo. L'Ordine Nuovo (1921-22)*, Turin, Einaudi (*Socialismo e Fascismo*).
1967 *La Formazione dell'Uomo: Scritti di Pedagogia*. ed., G. Urbani, Rome, Editore Riuniti (*Formazione*).
1968 *Scritti 1915-1921*, ed., S. Caprioglio, Milan, I Quaderni de 'Il Corpo' (*Scritti*).
1971 *Selections from the Prison Notebooks*, ed. and trans. Q. Hoare and G.N. Smith, London, Lawrence & Wishart (*Notebooks*).
1971 *L'Alternativa Pedagogia*, ed., M.A. Manacorda, Florence, La Nuova Italia (*L'Alternativa*).
1974 *Letters from Prison*, trans. H. Hamilton, *New Edinburgh Review*, Special Numbers on Gramsci, nos 1 and 2 (Edinburgh Letters).
1975(a) *Letters from Prison*, trans., L. Lawner, London, Jonathan Cape (Lawner Letters).
1975(b) *Quaderni del Carcere*, ed., V. Gerratana, 4 vols, Turin, Einaudi (*Quaderni*).
1975(c) *Lettere dal Carcere*, ed., S. Caprioglio and E. Fubini, Turin,

Bibliography

Einaudi (*Lettere*).
1976 *Arte e Folclore*, ed., G. Prestipino, Rome, Newton Compton Editore (*Arte*).
1977 *Selections from Political Writings (1910-1920)*, ed., Q. Hoare, trans. J. Mathews, New York, International Publishers (*Political Writings*).

Other sources

Anderson, P.C. (1976), *Considerations on Western Marxism*, London, New Left Books.
Bantock, G.H. (1952), 'John Dewey on Education', *Cambridge Journal*, vol. V, no. 9.
Barzun, J. (1959), *The House of Intellect*, New York, Harper & Row.
Bereday, Z.F., Brickman, W.W. and Reid, G.A. (1960), *The Changing Soviet School*, Boston, Houghton Mifflin.
Bereiter, C. (1973), *Must We Educate?* Englewood Cliffs, Prentice-Hall.
Berger, P.L. and Luckman, T. (1966), *The Social Construction of Reality*, New York, Doubleday.
Berlin, I. (1976) *Vico and Herder*, London, Hogarth Press.
Bernbaum, G. (1977), *Knowledge and Ideology in the Sociology of Education*, London, Macmillan.
Bernstein, B.B. (1971-3), *Class, Codes and Control*, 3 vols, London and Boston, Routledge & Kegan Paul.
Bernstein, R. (1971), *Praxis and Action*, Philadelphia, University of Pennsylvania Press.
Blake, W.N. (1968), 'Karl Marx's Concept of Education', *Proceedings of the Philosophy of Education Society*.
Boggs, C. (1976), *Gramsci's Marxism*, London, Pluto Press.
Borghi, L. (1958), *Educazione e Scuola nell'Italia d'oggi*, Florence, La Nuova Italia.
Borghi, L. (1960), *Educazione e Autorita nell'Italia Moderna*, Florence, La Nuova Italia.
Borghi, L. (1969), 'Educazione e scuola in Gramsci' in Rossi (1969).
Bourdieu, P. (1973), 'Cultural Reproduction and Social Production', in R. Brown (ed.), *Knowledge, Education and Cultural Change*, London, Tavistock.
Bowles, S. and Gintis, H. (1976), *Schooling in Capitalist America*, New York, Basic Books.
Broccoli, A. (1972), *Antonio Gramsci e l'educazione come egemonia*, Florence, La Nuova Italia.
Cammett, J.M. (1967), *Antonio Gramsci and the Origins of Italian Communism*, Stanford University Press.

Bibliography

Castle, E.B. (1961), *Ancient Education and Today*, Harmondsworth, Penguin.
Chambers, D.I. (1977), 'The 1975-1976 Debate over Higher Education Policy in the People's Republic of China', *Comparative Education*, vol. 13, no. 1.
Clark, M. (1977), *Antonio Gramsci and the Revolution that Failed*, New Haven and London, Yale University Press.
Codignola, E. (1930), 'Italy' in I.L. Kandel (ed.), *Educational Yearbook of the International Institute of Teachers College, Columbia University 1929*. New York, Bureau of Publications, Teachers College.
Cox, C.B and Dyon, A.E. (1969a), *Fight for Education* (Black Paper), London, Critical Quarterly Society.
Cox, C.B. and Dyson, A.E. (1969b), *The Crisis in Education* (Black Paper), London, Critical Quarterly Society.
Cox, C.B. and Dyson, A.E. (1970), *Goodbye Mr Short* (Black Paper), London, Critical Quarterly Society.
Crick, B. (1975), 'Basic Concepts for Political Education', in *Teaching Politics*, September Issue.
Croce, B. (1946), *Politics and Morals*, London, Allen & Unwin.
Davidson, A. (1974), 'Gramsci and Lenin 1917-22', *Socialist Register*.
Davidson, A. (1977), *Antonio Gramsci: Towards an Intellectual Biography*, London, Merlin Press.
Davies, B. (1976), *Social Control and Education*, London, Methuen.
Dewey, J. (1959), *School and Society*, University of Chicago Press.
Duggan, S.P. (1929), 'The Fascist Conception of Education', *Historical Outlook*, vol. 20, no. 5.
Eckstein, A. (1977), *China's Economic Revolution*, Cambridge University Press.
Engels, A. (1941), *Ludwig Feuerbach*, New York, International Publishers.
Entwistle, H. (1970a), *Child-Centred Education*, London, Methuen.
Entwistle, H. (1970b), *Education, Work and Leisure*, London, Routledge & Kegan Paul.
Entwistle, H. (1971), 'The Relationship between Theory and Practice', in J.W. Tibble (ed.), *An Introduction to the Study of Education*, London, Routledge & Kegan Paul.
Entwistle, H. (1978), *Class, Culture and Education*, London, Methuen.
Esland, G.M. (1971), 'Teaching and Learning as the Organisation of Knowledge' in Young (1971).
Fiori, G. (1970), *Antonio Gramsci: Life of a Revolutionary*, trans. T. Nairn, London, New Left Books.
Flew, A. (1976), *Sociology, Equality and Education*, London, Macmillan.
Freire, P. (1971), *Pedagogy of the Oppressed*, New York, Herder & Herder.

Bibliography

Frith, S. and Corrigan, P. (1977), 'The Politics of Education' in Young and Whitty (1977).
Gamberg, R. (1977), *Red and Expert*, New York, Schocken Books.
Gentile, G. (1922), *The Reform of Education*, New York, Harcourt Brace.
Gorbutt, D. (1972), 'The New Sociology of Education', *Education for Teaching*, vol. 89, Autumn.
Gorz, A. (1977), 'Technical Intelligence and the Capitalist Division of Labour', in Young and Whitty (1977).
Grant, N. (1968), *Soviet Education*, Harmondsworth, Penguin.
Griffiths, T. (1972), *Occupations*, London, Calder & Boyars.
Hardie, C.D. (1942), *Truth and Fallacy in Educational Theory*, Cambridge University Press.
Hextal, P. and Sarup, M. (1977), 'School Knowledge, Evaluation and Alienation' in Young and Whitty (1977).
Hibbert, C. (1975), *Benito Mussolini*, Harmondsworth, Penguin.
Hoare, Q. and Smith, N.G. (1971), editors' introduction and commentary on Gramsci, *Notebooks*, 1971.
Hobsbawm, E.J. (1974), 'The Great Gramsci', *New York Review of Books*, vol. XXI, no. 5, 4 April.
Hoffman, J. (1975), *Marxism and the Theory of Praxis*, London, Lawrence & Wishart.
Holt, J. (1967), *How Children Learn*, London, Pitman.
Horton, J. (1964), 'The Dehumanisation of Anomie and Alienation: a Problem in the Ideology of Sociology', *British Journal of Sociology*, vol. 15.
Hughes, H.S. (1958), *Consciousness and Society*, New York, Random House.
Hutchins, R.M. (1952), *The Democratic Dilemma*, Uppsala, Almguist & Wicksell.
Huxley, T.H. (1893), *Collected Essays*, vol. III, London, Macmillan.
Jencks, C. (1972), *Inequality*, New York, Harper & Row.
Joll, J. (1977), *Gramsci*, London, Collins.
Karabel, J. and Halsey, A.H. (1977), 'Educational Research: A Review and an Interpretation' in J. Karabel and A.H. Halsey (eds.), *Power and Ideology in Education*, New York, Oxford University Press.
Karier, C.J. (1967), *Man, Society and Education*, Glenview, Illinois, Scott, Foresman.
Keddie, N. (1971), 'Classroom Knowledge', in Young (1971).
Keddie, N. (1973), 'Introduction' to N. Keddie (ed.), *Tinker, Tailor . . . the Myth of Cultural Deprivation*, Harmondsworth, Penguin.
Kiernan, V.G. (1972), 'Gramsci and Marxism', *Socialist Register*.
Klein, N.A. (1969), 'Cultural Hegemony and the Counter Culture' in Dell Hymes (ed.), *Reinventing Anthropology*, New York, Pantheon.

Kozol, J. (1972), *Free Schools*, London, Toronto, New York, Bantam Books.
Krushchev N. (1958), 'On Strengthening the Relationship of the School with Life and on the Further Development of the System of Public Education of the Country' in G. Counts (ed.), *Kruschev and the Central Committee Speak on Education*, University of Pittsburgh Press.
Labov, W. (1973), 'The Logic of Nonstandard English', in Keddie (1973).
Lawton, D. (1975), *Class, Culture and Curriculum*, London, Routledge & Kegan Paul.
Lazerson, M. and Grubb, W.N. (eds.) (1974), *American Education and Vocationalism; a Documentary History, 1870-1970*, New York, Teachers College Press.
Lenin, V.I. (1943a), *Selected Works*, New York, International Publishers.
Lenin, V.I. (1943b), 'What the "Friends of the People" Are', *Selected Works*, vol. I.
Lenin, V.I. (1943c), 'The Reorganisation of the Party', *Selected Works*, vol. III.
Lenin, V.I. (1943d), 'The Tasks of the Youth Leagues', *Selected Works*, vol. IX.
Lenin, V.I. (1943e), 'Proletarian Culture', *Selected Works*, vol. IX.
Lenin, V.I. (1943f), 'Pages from a Diary', *Selected Works*, vol. IX.
Lenin, V.I. (1961a), *Collected Works*, London, Lawrence & Wishart.
Lenin, V.I. (1961b), 'What is to be Done?', *Collected Works*, vol. V.
Levitas, M. (1974), *Marxist Perspectives in the Sociology of Education*, London, Routledge & Kegan Paul.
Lilge, F. (1977), 'Lenin and the Politics of Education', in Karabel and Halsey, 1977.
Lombardo Radice, L. (1976), *Educazione e Rivoluzione*, Rome, Editori Riuniti.
Macciocchi, M.A. (1974), *Pour Gramsci*, Paris, Editions du Seuil.
MacIntyre, A. (1970), *Marcuse*, London, Fontana/Collins.
MacIntyre, A. (1971), *Against the Self-Images of the Age*, London, Duckworth.
MacIntyre, A. (1975), 'The Theorist of Defeat', *New Statesman*, August 29.
Manacorda, M.A. (1966), *Marx e la Pedagogia Moderna*, Rome, Editori Riuniti.
Manacorda, M.A. (1972), Editor's Introduction and Commentary on Gramsci, *L'Alternativa*, 1972.
Manacorda, M.A. (1976), *Il Principio Educativo in Gramsci: Americanismo e Conformismo*, Rome, Armando Editore.
Mannheim, K. (1936), *Ideology and Utopia*, New York, Harcourt, Brace.

Bibliography

Marraro, H.R. (1936), *The New Education in Italy*, New York, S.F. Vanni.
Marx, K. (1941), 'Theses on Feuerbach' in Engels (1941).
Marx, K. (1919), *Capital*, vol. I, Chicago, Kerr.
McInnis, N. (1971), 'Antonio Gramsci', *Survey*, no. 43, October.
Merrington, J. (1968), 'Theory and Practice in Gramsci's Marxism', *Socialist Register*.
Minio-Puluello, L. (1946), *Education in Fascist Italy*, Oxford University Press.
Motzo Dentice di Accadia, C. (1969) response to Borghi in Rossi (1969).
Nearing, S. (1926), *Education in Soviet Russia*, New York.
Nolte, E. (1965), *Three Faces of Fascism*, London, Weidenfeld & Nicolson.
Paci, E. (1972), *The Function of the Sciences and the Meaning of Man*, Evanston, Northwestern University Press.
Peters, R.S. (1963), *Education as Initiation*, University of London Institute of Education.
Peters, R.S. (ed.) (1967), *The Concept of Education*, London, Routledge & Kegan Paul.
Popper, K.R. (1966), *The Open Society and its Enemies*, vol. I, Princeton University Press.
Popper, K.R. (1972), *Objective Knowledge*, Oxford, Clarendon Press.
Postman, N. (1971), 'Telling it like it ain't', in *Alternatives in Education*, Ontario Institute for Studies in Education.
Postman, N. (1973), 'The Politics of Reading', in Keddie (1973).
Pozzolini, A. (1970), *Antonio Gramsci: an Introduction to his Thought*, trans. A.I. Showstack, London, Pluto Press.
Prestipino, G. (1976), Introduction and Commentary on Gramsci, *Arte*, 1976.
Price, R.F. (1974), 'Labour and Education in Russia and China', *Comparative Education*, vol. 10, no. 1.
Pring, R. (1972), 'Knowledge Out of Control', *Education for Teaching*, November.
Rossi, P. (ed.) (1969), *Gramsci e la cultura contemporaneo*, Rome, Editori Riuniti.
Schneider, H.N. and Clough, S.B. (1929), *Making Fascists*, University of Chicago Press.
Shirk, S.L. (1978), 'Work Experiences in Chinese Education', *Comparative Education*, vol. 14, no. 1.
Shore, M.J. (1947), *Soviet Education*, New York, Philosophical Library.
Silver, H. (1965), *The Concept of Popular Education*, London, MacGibbon & Kee.
Silver, H. (1975), *English Education and the Radicals 1780-1850*,

Bibliography

London and Boston, Routledge & Kegan Paul.
Silver, H. (1977), 'Ideology and the Factory Child: Attitudes to Half Time Education' in McCann (ed.), *Popular Education and Socialisation in the Nineteenth Century*, London, Methuen.
Simon, B. (1960, 1965, 1974), *Studies in the History of Education*, 3 vols, London, Lawrence & Wishart.
Simon, B. (1971), *Intelligence, Psychology and Education: a Marxist Critique*, London, Lawrence & Wishart.
Smart, B. (1976), *Sociology, Phenomenology and Marxian Analysis*, London and Boston, Routledge & Kegan Paul.
Springer, U.K. (1969), *Recent Curriculum Developments in France, West Germany and Italy*, New York, Teachers College Press.
Terrill, R. (1973), *R.H. Tawney and his Times*, Cambridge, Mass., Harvard University Press.
Thompson, E.P. (1968a), *The Making of the English Working Class*, Harmondsworth, Penguin.
Thompson, E.P. (1968b), *Education and Experience*, Leeds University Press.
Thompson, M.M. (1934), *The Educational Philosophy of Giovanni Gentile*, Los Angeles, University of South California Press.
Urbani, G. (1967), Editor's Introduction and Commentary on Gramsci, *Formazione*, 1967.
United States Congress (1947), *Fascism in Action*, Washington, United States Government Printing Officer.
Villari, L. (1926), *The Fascist Experiment*, London, Faber & Gwyer.
Walter, N. (1975), 'De Profundis', *New Society*, 4 September.
Whitehead, A.N. (1932), *The Aims of Education*, London, Williams & Norgate.
Williams, G.A. (1951), 'Egomania', *Journal of History of Ideas*, vol. XXI.
Williams, G.A. (1975), *Proletarian Order*, London, Pluto Press.
Williams, R. (1973), 'Base and Superstructure in Marxist Cultural Theory', *New Left Review*, no. 83.
Williams, R. (1977), *Marxism and Literature*, Oxford University Press.
Young, M.F.D. (1971), *Knowledge and Control*, London, Collier-Macmillan.
Young, M.F.D. (1973a), 'Taking Sides against the Probable', *Educational Review*, vol. 25, no. 3.
Young, M.F.D. (1973b), 'Educational Theorising: a Radical Alternative', *Education for Teaching*, Summer Issue.
Young, M.F.D. and Whitty, G. (eds.) (1977), *Society, State and Schooling*, Ringmer, Falmar Press.

Index

action, thought and, 149-50
Agnelli, 140
Alfred the Great, 34, 183
alienation, 51, 89-91, 153-4, 162, 187
America, *see* United States
Americanism, 4, 105, 137-41; and socialism, 140
Anderson, P.C., 6
'animality', 138
apprenticeship, 130, 132
Arnold, Mathew, 44, 118, 123
assessment, 49-54
associations, political, 164-6
authoritarianism, 87; political, 3, 78-87
authorities, academic, 37-8
authority, 2, 38, 58-63, 69, 76-7, 87, 116, 187; the teacher as, 69-77, 84, 87, 187
automation, 143, 189

'back to basics', 3
banking, education as, 82
Bantock, G.H., 85, 95, 188
Barzun, J., 65
Bereiter, C., 67
Berlin, I., 66
Bernstein, B.B., 101

Bernstein, R., 45, 150
Black English, 23, 25
Black Papers, 3, 40, 59, 181
boarding school, 101
Boggs, C., 12, 192
Bohemianism, 138, 188
Bordiga, A., 15
Borghi, L., 77, 78, 82, 85, 185, 191
Bottai, 96
Bourdieu, P., 47
bourgeoisie, 11
Bowles, S., and Gintis, H., 4, 87, 89, 95
Britain, 4, 79, 81, 102, 154, 177, 184, 187, 189
Broccoli, A., 11, 19, 26, 67, 74-5, 81, 191
'bucket and pump' pedagogy, 66

Cammett, J.M., 13, 14, 122, 191
Capital, 91, 152-4, 176
capital, cultural, 46
capitalism, 91, 176; corporate, 4, 16, 89, 96
Casati Act, 21
categorical imperative, 76-7
change, social, 4, 64, 87, 91, 111, 161, 167, 168, 176

children as workers, 152-5
China, 157, 158-60; economy, 158-9; tea schools, 157
Churchill, W.S., 79, 161, 183
civil society, 2, 16
civilisation, Western, 104
Clark, M., 5, 14, 148, 191
class consciousness, 178
class, educated, 138; hegemonic, 31, 35, 36, 40; social, 36, 51; subaltern, 27, 31, 35, 40; working, 23, 37
classics, 95
Codignola, E., 23
cognitive 'baggage', 47, 53, 66, 71, 182
commodity, knowledge as a, 89-90
common sense, 21, 28-39, 73, 75, 118, 121, 162
Communism, 8, 43, 154
community schools, 168
conservative educationists, 188
contextual educational theory, 71, 74
creativity, 170-1
Crick, B., 121
critical dualism, 23
Croce, B., 44, 99, 121, 144, 182, 188
culture, 44, 48; ancient, 171; classical, 169; common, 91, 127, 177; Eastern, 74; European, 31; general, 94; high, 74; humanistic, 18, 23, 28, 91, 132, 145, 155; mainstream, 18, 28, 40, 71, 144; new, 123; new humanistic, 109; new socialist, 112; popular, 27; proletarian, 19, 43-5; of the school, 71-2, 148; science of, 73-5; socialist, 155; technical, 147; traditional, 40-1, 44, 104; of work, 158; working class, 19, 95

curriculum, 18-19, 30, 36, 38, 132, 135, 158, 168, 170-5; academic, 36; classical, 170; common, 95; hidden, 16, 92, 111; sociology of the, 2; technical, 136; traditional, 43, 95, 110, 171

daily life, 36, 43, 72
Dalton Plan, 133
Davidson, A., 121, 164, 188, 191
dead languages, 170-3
definition of educational knowledge, the, 87, 169
democracy, 3, 42, 78, 87, 167-8; industrial, 148
democratic socialist educationists, 102-31
deschooling, 96
Dewey, J., 151
dialect, 22, 23-5
dialectical materialism, 149
discipline, 53-4, 64, 70, 107, 138, 170, 187; industrial, 139; intellectual, 87, 105
duties, 23, 53, 73

Eastern culture, 74
education: active, 82; adult, 16, 18, 66-7, 91, 109-10, 111-13, 127, 147, 154, 165, 168, 176-9, 190; artificial, 60-4; as banking, 47; disinterested, 176-7; elementary, 89; fascist, 78-87, 191; for freedom, 85-86; higher 109; history of, 105-7, 178; humanistic, 93, 132-3, 136; intellectual, 157-8, 169; Jesuit, 106-7; liberal, 19, 33; lifelong, 109-10; according to Nature, 55-64; new, 81-6; 'other avenues' towards, 176-8; *permanente*, 112;

201

political, 78, 111-13, 165, 179; politics and, 3; polytechnical, 131, 136-7, 151-62, 163; as preparation, 109; principles of, 166; professional, 136, 144, 146; progressive, 3, 65, 80-6, 105-6, 181; public, 97-8; recurrent, 168; religion and, 167-8; self-discovery and, 170-1; and social change, 4; socialist, 136, 179; sociology of, 179; sociology of, new, 2-3; 30, 37, 103, 180-1; State and, the, 2, 97-103; teacher, 165-8; technical, 129, 132-48; traditional socialist, 179; and values, 67-8; vocational, 2, 53, 113, 132-48, 165; vocational and adult, 147-8; vocational in United States, 188; of the working class, 2, 40, 102

educationist. democratic socialist, 102-3; Italian idealist, 64-7; traditional Marxist, 95, 187

educator, the environment as, 59-64, 69

elites, 2, 39; educated, 123, 132

elitism, 120; educational, 98-100, 132

Engels, F., 44, 60, 89, 104, 189

England, *see* Britain

environment as educator, 59-64, 69

equality, 102; of opportunity, 54

Esland, G.M., 180, 183-4

Establishment, the, 12

ethnic minorities, 74

Europe, 18, 79, 82, 95, 177

everyday life, 39, 43, 168
examinations, 39-40, 49-52, 90, 185
excellence, 102
experience, common, 36, 43

Fabian social reform, 104
Factory Act, 134-6
Factory Councils, 112, 140, 147, 164, 177
Fascism, 2, 3, 8, 9, 20, 23; and education, 78-86
Fascist Educational Reform, the, 47, 52, 64, 77, 78-86, 93-4, 99, 105, 181, 185-7
Feuerbach, Eleventh Thesis on, 150, 162; Third Thesis on, 60-1
Fiori, G., 182, 191
Flew, A., 50-1, 59
folklore, 22, 23, 30, 32-40, 46-7, 72-5, 84, 118, 124, 162, 163
Ford, H., 139-41
Fordism, 139-42
formal operations, 136
foundations, educational, 166-7
Fowles, J., 87-8
freedom, 84-5, 107, 187; education for, 86

Gans, H., 74
generalisation, stage of, 107-8
Gentile, G., 64, 69, 80, 100, 144, 181, 184, 185-7
geography, 23
Germany, 177
good sense, 21, 30, 32-40, 45, 50, 73-4, 104, 162-3, 179
Gorbutt, D., 180
grades, 50-2, 90
grammar, 66
Griffiths, T., 8-9
gymnasium, German, 89

Index

Hadow Report, 81
half-time system, 154
Hamilton, H., 191
hegemony, 1, 2, 10-16, 25, 35, 37, 40, 71, 82, 93, 109-10, 111, 113, 148, 149, 161, 164, 167; bourgeois, 11, 13, 40, 92, 96, 178; capitalist, 16, 179; proletarian, 11, 40; working class, 109-10, 178
heritage, cultural, 46, 69, 78, 91
Hextal, P. and Sarup, M., 51
Hibbert, C , 79-80
hierarchies, academic, 51
high culture, 74
high status knowledge, 36, 183-4
history, 15, 19, 23, 41-2, 68, 70, 76, 172-4; of common sense, 38-9; of education, 105-7, 108; of philosophy, 32, 161; of thought, 37
Hoare, Q., and Smith, N.G., 7, 20, 149, 191
Hobsbawm, E.J., 10, 124
Hoggart, R., 74
Holocaust, 79
Holt, J., 50, 61-4
humanism, historical, 144; new, 20, 110, 135
Huxley, T.H., 59-60, 63-4
hypothetical imperative, 77

ideology, 32; Marxist, 176
Ideology, The German, 189
Illich, I., 96, 100
Il Grido del Popolo, 122
immigrants, 74
Institute of Contemporary Culture, 74
instruction, 53, 64-8, 70, 107, 171, 184; religious, 185, 187
intellectualism, 134-5, 165

intellectuals, 2; as autonomous, 114-15; and the bourgeoisie, 124; and capitalism, 115-16; career, 118; communication and the, 120-4, 146; and education, 113-29, as elites, 125; 'free floating', 114-15; and hegemony, 113-14, 117; Italian, 122; and the Italian Communist Party, 188; as leaders, 120, 127-30; new, 141; organic, 70, 112-13, 114-29, 144, 178, 188; problem of the, 117-29, 155-6; role of the, 162-5; as socially unattached, 114-15; traditional 37, 89, 104, 113, 114-29, 178; working class, 25-6, 55, 89, 109, 110, 112-13, 116, 154, 178

Jackson, B., 74
Jencks, C., 4

Kant, I., 76-7, 121
Karabel, J., and Halsey, A.H., 2
Keddie, N., 27, 180, 183
Kiernan, V.G., 124
Klein, N., 13
knowledge: abstract, 49, 173-5; academic, 30; as a commodity, 89-90; common-sense, 29-30; concrete, 49, 150-2; educational, 35, 36, 87, 103, 159-61; high status, 36, 183; objective, 46, 66-7, 83; school, 90-2; scientific, 36; and social interaction, 37-8; sociology of, 38, 103; store of, 90; tacit, 90
Kozol, J., 96
Krupskaya, N.K., 158-9
Krushchev, N., 155

Labour Movement, 21; British,

203

Index

154, 179
language, 21; and concrete learning, 173-4; national, 22, 24; standard forms of, 25; teaching of, 23; written, 24
languages, classical, 20, 170; 'dead', 171-3
La Stampa, 122
Latin, teaching of, 170-3
La Club di Vita Morale, 19
Lawner, L., 191
laws, natural, 22-3, 53, 131; social, 22-3, 131; State, 22, 53
learner, active 48-66
learning, abstract and concrete 172-4; active, 66; disinterested, 135-6, 170, 177; by trial and error, 60; as work, 53-5, 65-6, 105, 137
Lenin, V.I., 11, 43-5, 55, 59, 67, 157, 176, 182
Levitas, M., 187
Letters from Prison, (*Lettere dal Carcere*), 3-6, 8, 191
liberal education, 19, 33; professions, 144
liberty, 187
Lilge, F., 44, 157, 176
linguistics, 95
literacy, 2, 15, 23, 25, 55, 104, 122; politics of, 25; working class, 182
literature, 173
Lloyd George, D., 79
logic, 19, 66
Lombardo-Radice, G., 78, 85
Lombardo-Radice, L., 189
L'Ordine Nuovo, 7, 14, 25, 123, 141, 142, 191

McCarthy, J., Senator, 85
McInnes, N., 5, 14, 19
MacIntyre, A., 10

Machiavelli, N., 13
Manacorda, M.A., 5, 24, 81, 94, 98, 104-5, 108, 115, 134, 137, 139-40, 172, 191
Manchester Guardian, 79
Mannheim, K., 114, 118
manual, labour, 156-7; work, 157
Mao Tse-Tung, 159, 162-3
marks, 49-52
Marraro, H.R., 80
Marx, K., 45-6, 60, 67, 74, 89, 90-1, 94-5, 144, 150-6, 162, 173, 176, 187, 189
Marxism, 3, 19, 88-91, 118, 149-51, 162, 167, 176, 180; cultural, 3
Marxist educational systems, 120-1, 136, 157-9
Marxist-Leninism, 43
Massachesuetts, 95
mathematics, 136
Matteoti, G., 79
Meccano, 55-6, 137, 141
memorisation, 83
meritocracy, 54
middle-class values, 71
modernisation, economic, 159
Moscow, 8
Mussolini, B., 8, 10, 78, 83, 85, 99, 181, 185
myth of cultural deprivation, 27, 182

Nairn, T., 191
nationalism, 185
Nature, education according to, 55-64; as teacher, 60-4
nature, human, 62; second, 62
Naturalism, 60
natural laws, 22-3, 53, 131
neo-Marxism, 2, 3, 89
Nolte, E., 79, 82, 83
North America, 18, 95, 184
Northern Europe, 138
Notebooks, Prison, 3-6, 8, 191

204

opportunity, educational, 88
organic intellectuals, 70, 112-13, 115-29, 130-1, 178, 188
Oundle School, 160
Owen, Robert, 153-5

parties, political, 164-5
paternalism, 76
pedagogy: active, 78, 87, 105; 'bucket and pump', 66; didactic, 40, 67, 70, 87, 92; Genevan, 105
Peters, R.S., 59, 68
phenomenology, 180
philosophers, 32-4, 38-9, 45, 149; idealist, 144; professional, 28, 32
philosophy, 28-43, 74, 150; academic, 43; Cartesian, 150; history of, 32, 38-9, 161; popular, 32, 34; of praxis, 19, 41, 107; scientific, 32; spontaneous, 21, 33, 34, 35, 162; of teaching, 165-6
Piaget, J., 22, 108, 136
plural societies, 167, 177
politics and education, 2; of literacy, 25
Popper, K.R., 23, 46, 184
Popular Universities, 128
polytechnical education, 131, 136, 151-62, 163
Pozzolini, A., 26. 191
practical life, 39
practice, 146; theory and, 5, 27, 127, 134, 149-75; unity of theory and, 149-75
praxis, 5, 29, 48, 127, 149-50, 160-5; philosophy of, 19, 41, 102
precision, stage of, 38, 54, 106, 108, 136
pre-knowledge, 47
preparation, education as, 109
Price, R.G., 154

Principles of Education, 166
progress, 42
progressive education, 3, 65, 78-86, 105-6, 181
prohibition, 139
project method, 151
Protestant work ethic, 139
puberty, 108
public education, 97-8

Quaderni del Carcere, 191

radical Left, 95
radicals, educational, 103, 126, 137
Rawls, J., 121
reading, 23; teaching of, 25
Reformation, the, 41
relevance, educaton, 168-75
religion, 22, 33; and education 167, 185, 187
Renaissance, 19, 41, 133; man, 134
Revolution, Cultural, 159
Riesman, D., 187
rights, 53, 73
Rolland, Romain, 179
romance, stage of, 38, 106, 108, 136
Rousseau, 55-7, 105, 184, 187
Russia, *see* USSR

Sardinia, 7, 20, 24-5, 74, 183
'sardisms', 24
school: activity, 106; boarding, 101-2; classical, 93, 172-3; common, 136, 146; community, 168; comprehensive, 94, 97, 100, 128, 137; culture of, 71, 169; disinterested, 175; elementary, 20, 31, 53, 73, 179, 184, 185; as hegemonic, 1, 92-104; humanistic, 93-4, 132-3, 146, 174; Italian

205

elementary, 20, 22, 89; as neutral, 91, 168; professional, 146; secondary, 47; segregated secondary, 94, 98; socialist, 47; traditional, 71, 81, 92-3; traditional elementary, 89; traditional secondary, 135, 185; as work, 90, 132, 137, 169

schooling: contradiction theory of, 87-92; correspondence theory of, 87-92; as cultural transmission, 69-70; disinterested, 68, 91, 112, 176; elementary, 179; humanistic, 174; vocational, 91, 93-4, 132, 135, 185

schools, free, 87, 96; professional, 133, 146; technical, 132, 133, 135

scuola, 18

science, 23, 26-7, 37, 136; of culture, 74-5

second nature, 62-3

self-discovery, education and, 170-1

sense: common, 21, 28-39, 73, 75, 118, 121, 162-3; good, 21, 30, 32-40, 45, 50, 73-4, 104, 162-3, 179

Shirk, S.L., 159

Silver, H., 154, 178

Simon, B., 154, 178, 187

social change, 3, 4, 64, 87, 90-1, 111, 161, 167, 168, 176

social class, 36, 51

socialisation, 64; political, 78-80

socialism, 4, 40, 47, 68, 92, 139, 156, 167, 177

social laws, 22-3, 131

society, democratic, 25; socialist, 139

sociology of culture, 73-5; of the curriculum, 2; of education, new, 1, 30, 37, 103, 180-1; of knowledge, 28, 103

Southern Europe, 105

Southern Italy, 49

Soviet Union *see* USSR

specialists, 36-7, 145

spelling, 55

spontaneity, 2, 21, 33, 57-8, 70, 75, 76, 78, 81, 82, 84, 106-7

standards, 107; academic, 40; intellectual, 99

state and education, 2, 96-104

status quo, 31, 89, 110, 118

superstition, 22, 33, 34, 36, 162-3

Sweden, 95

Tawney, R.H., 89, 102, 177-8, 189

Taylorism, 26, 137-8

teacher: active, 28, 40, 58; as authority, 84, 87, 187; education of, 70-7, 165-8; and vocation, 166; Nature as, 59-64; socialist, 167

teaching: dogmatic, 88, 170; formative, 82-3; of language, 23; of Latin, 170-3; philosophy of, 165-6; profession, 70; of reading, 25

technique, 131, 164

theory, 146; contextual educational, 71, 73; and practice, 5, 27, 120, 127, 134, 149; and relevance, 168-75; and teacher education, 165-8; traditional educational, 111; traditional Marxist educational, 111; unity with practice, 149-54

Thompson, E.P., 21, 154, 178-9

Thompson, M.M., 79

thought and action, 150

Index

trade unions, 147, 176
tragedy, 10
training, technical, 91, 129
transmission, cultural, 84
trial and error, learning by, 60
Trotsky, L.D., 43
Turin, 140-64
two cultures debate, 144

United States, 4, 79-80, 97, 129, 166; vocational education in the, 188
unskilled labourer, 143
Urbani, G., 93, 191
USSR, 81, 91, 94, 98, 133, 136-7, 152, 154-60
Ustica, 20

values, 171; academic, 91-2; education and, 67-8; middle class, 71
Vico, 66
vocation, 129-30, 131; and teacher education, 166
Voltaire, 161
voluntarism, 41

Washburne, C., 82
Western civilisation, 104
Whitehead, A.N., 106, 107, 109
Whitty, G., 38
Williams, G.A., 3, 11, 13, 15, 188
Williams, R., 10-11, 13, 74
work, 131, 136, 151-2, 170, 189; culture of, 157; learning as, 53-5, 65-6, 105, 137; school as, 132, 137, 169
workers, 160; children as, 152-5
Workers' Educational Association, 189
working class, 11, 17, 23, 37, 44; culture, 19, 95; education of the, 2, 25, 40, 102, 144; English, 178; hegemony, 35, 110, 179; intellectuals, 25-6, 55, 89, 104, 110, 154, 178-9; literacy, 182; movement, 178-9; old, 143; radicalism, 178-9; speech, 23
world view, 32, 36
worthwhile activities, 68
writing, 23

Young, M.F.D., 28-30, 35-6, 39, 40, 43, 180, 183
Young, M.F.D., and Whitty, G., 103, 181

3143